Such Devoted Sisters ✻

THOSE FABULOUS GABORS

Such Devoted Sisters

Those Fabulous Gabors

❋ ❋ ❋

Peter Harry Brown

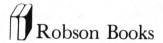

Robson Books

First published in Great Britain in 1986 by Robson Books Ltd.,
Bolsover House, 5–6 Clipstone Street, London W1P 7EB.

British Library Cataloguing in Publication Data

Brown, Peter Harry
    Such devoted sisters: those fabulous Gabors.
    1. Gabor, Eva   2. Gabor, Magda   3. Gabor,
    Zsa Zsa   4. Entertainers—United States—
    Biography
    791′.092′2   PN2285

ISBN 0-86051-361-0

Printed in Great Britain by St Edmundsbury Press, Bury St Edmunds, Suffolk

For Fran and Jerry Brown

❋ Contents

Book Five: The Wages of Fame

Book Six: Bedtime Stories

Book Seven: Survival

❊ Sources and Acknowledgments

Much credit goes to my editor, Toni Lopopolo, who asked for a book about "the three smart girls from Budapest." Thanks also go to her assistant, Andrew Charron. And a special word of thanks to Zsa Zsa for her cooperation and candor.

I'm indebted to the libraries of the Los Angeles *Times,* the London *Daily Mirror,* the New York *Post,* the Chicago *Tribune,* the New York *Daily News,* and especially to the *National Enquirer,* which, through its senior editor, Paul Levy, produced a treasure of clippings and background information on the Gabors. Another invaluable source was the Palm Springs *Desert Sun* and its society editor, Allene Arthur, who has covered the Gabor family during its long tenure at the California desert resort.

The archivists at the Academy of Motion Picture Arts and Sciences (particularly Carol Epstein) produced 2,000 clippings on Zsa Zsa and Eva, plus the confidential scrapbooks of Hollywood gossip columnists Louella Parsons and Hedda Hopper. Thanks to videotape collectors Michael Poston and Cheryl Thompson, Vidtronics of Philadelphia, Marlowe's Collector's Bookstore in Hollywood, and Barbara Messing. For the *Green Acres* information I thank producer-creator Paul Henning and cast members Tom Lester and Alvy Moore. Special thanks go to my wife Pamela, whose suggestions gave the book dimension; to Marjorie Miller, professor in the UCLA writers' program; and to Natalie Goodwin and Roger Freeman.

A note on sources: It comes as no surprise that all four Gabors (Zsa Zsa, Eva, Magda, and Jolie) have lived in a goldfish bowl since 1945. Their every move has been catalogued by gossip columnists and discussed on the talk shows. When they are in New York, for instance, newspaper, radio, and television journalists report where they eat, what they eat, who they talk to, who they dance with, and, quite often, who they take home. In more recent years, the *National Enquirer* has dogged their progress with the jet set. At various times, the *Enquirer* has even hired private detectives to follow them to secret rendezvous. (Particularly when a divorce can be smelled in the air.)

As if these sources weren't enough, the Gabors have been active on the talk shows, as can be attested by anyone with a television set. They have told their life stories again and again. Amazingly, the texts of the four Gabor autobiographies seem to have been transcribed from these appearances, so similar is the wording. And yet, all four constantly change their stories. For instance, the real story of those weeks in 1945 when Zsa Zsa was committed to a private sanitarium is lost in a maze of conflicting testimony. There are sixteen different versions —including five varying accounts by Zsa Zsa herself. The same is true about many phases of their lives. The story of Eva's first marriage differs from one account to the other.

Sources included 250 hours of videotape (Zsa Zsa herself maintains that "my life story is on the talk shows; all you have to do is play them back"), 1,000 gossip column items, 3,000 newspaper and magazine clippings, and dozens of syndicated biographies, including four versions in French and six versions in London newspapers.

This information was all condensed onto more than 3,000 file cards and then combined with more than fifty interviews. What emerges is the most plausible story of their lives. In some cases the varied stories are told so that the reader may make up his or her own mind.

❋ The Legend

Several years ago an old friend visited Jolie Gabor for the first time in almost forty years. She greeted him at the door of her Palm Springs home wearing a hostess gown with diamonds sparkling on her wrists. The man had last seen her when she was a frightened, impoverished refugee fleeing from the Nazis. The desert sun streamed through the windows and illuminated a scene of sumptuous luxury. Antique crystal, Georgian silver, and golden tableware caught the glittering light. The visitor, almost intimidated by the luxury, hesitated at the door. "Come in, come in," Jolie said warmly. While she conducted the grand tour, the visitor was mesmerized by her gallery of photos showing her with the world's rich and famous, with her many millionaire sons-in-law, and with her renowned daughters.

As Jolie settled on the sofa to pour tea, he asked her quietly, "How did all this happen?"

She smiled. "It's a long, long story. And darling, you probably wouldn't believe it anyway."

Such Devoted Sisters ✳

THOSE FABULOUS GABORS

❋ *Prologue*

The Gabor sisters are three of the
world's true celebrities . . . they are
famous for being famous.
　　　—ELSA MAXWELL, 1952

*T*he bridal bed is majestic, soaring up from the rich
carpet in great swirls of gilt and spreading out like a
vast frame around the lady who inhabits it. Pastel-colored panels of
theater velvet plunge from the four golden posts supporting the can-
opy and are gathered in folds by thick silk cords. Legend has it that
the bed once belonged to the Empress Josephine when she welcomed
not only Napoleon but a series of lovers that history has only guessed
at. And it's not at all unlike the great beds of Marie Antoinette and
the Marquise de Pompadour at the Palace of Versailles. Whatever the
grand origin of the bed, it is particularly appropriate for its present
owner, Zsa Zsa Gabor.

With the flick of a wrist, enormous curtains are drawn aside, revealing a plate-glass window under which spread Beverly Hills, Bel Air,
pockets of Hollywood, and in the distance the skyscrapers of downtown Los Angeles. At her elbow, on an exquisite table of the Louis
Quinze style, sits a bank of telephones linking her to scores of jet set
friends and, more importantly, to her mother, Jolie, and her two
sisters, Eva and Magda. It's not unusual for her to have Eva on one
line and Magda on the other—with Zsa Zsa relaying bits of brilliant
conversation back and forth. The phones serve as a lifeline linking
three hearts that have beaten in unison since the sisters were children
in Budapest.

Zsa Zsa is only a more exaggerated version of her sisters. Her

5,000-piece wardrobe is slightly more baroque than Eva's and Magda's. Her progression through high society is a bit more splashy, and her tumultuous love life (including seven husbands and twenty-two lovers) is simply a more vivid copy of her sisters' private lives. They are variations on a theme, as if three distinctly different Impressionist artists had painted the same subject.

All three seem to have taken different roads to reach the same place. Their celebrity borders on infamy; their wealth hovers near ostentation, but their hearts, for the most part, are in the right place.

When the story began, they were just three young girls from Hungary, prettier than most. Not particularly well connected, they were comfortable, ambitious, but not wealthy. Trading on charm and an uncanny ability to make each man feel like a king, they left a collapsing Europe and became three famous women of their day.

❋ BOOK ONE

Hungarian Rhapsody

*I promise that you will all be rich,
famous, and marry kings.*
                    —JOLIE, 1935

❋ Precocious Children

*E*va gasped for breath and struggled hysterically to fight the terror that gripped her whole body. She tried to scream, but when she opened her mouth it filled with water. She could sense Zsa Zsa and Magda somewhere near her. They, however, were as helpless as she, none of them having been in water over their heads before. Looming nearby but moving constantly out of reach was the roomy and safe rowboat being maneuvered by their mother.

Each time one of the little girls approached and grabbed for the side, Jolie Gabor steered the craft out of their reach. "Swim! Swim!" she cried. "Little puppies can do it. So can you! Swim! It's easy."

The Gabor sisters were still in the care of a nanny when they were tossed into that murky water. But Jolie's elaborate master plan for her daughters was already conceived. They would become, she decided, superwomen.

"I wanted them to do everything and do it all the best," Jolie remembered decades later. "I still think it was correct. It made them ultimate survivors."

Once at the circus she pointed out a fire eater to Zsa Zsa and said, "When will you be able to do that?" The question was not entirely in jest.

The master plan also left the girls anxious, insecure, and vulnerable —qualities they retain today. "It was not enough for us to be simply beautiful," Zsa Zsa said. "We had to be the *most* beautiful. It was never enough for us to be chic. We had to be the *most* fashionable. Our goals remained constantly out of reach."

But they were princesses from birth, each of them furnished with a tray of silver spoons and nurtured in the prewar flush of wealth experienced by Budapest in the late 1920s and early '30s. To begin with, however, they were unwanted by their mother (who obviously changed her mind) and tolerated by a chauvinistic father who wanted a son, an heir.

It started with a morose, unhappy marriage between a Budapest debutante, Jolie Tilleman, and Vilmos Gabor, a jaded, vain product of a Hungarian officers' club who had a military school mentality.

To make it worse, Vilmos Gabor was "at least" (Jolie's estimate) twenty-two years older than the pampered schoolgirl he took for a bride.

It could be stated fairly that this was a desperate marriage, undertaken by Jolie to get out from under her own domineering family and by Major Gabor as his last chance to father an heir. The exact date of the wedding, like most things Gabor, cannot be determined, but it must have occurred about the time of World War I.

As heiress to a Hungarian jewelry fortune, Jolie grew up amid the pomp, fantasy, and luxury of the Belle Epoch. She was closeted away with imported nannies and private tutors until age twelve, at which time she began the elaborate mating dance of the European world.

She held hands with young naval cadets near the lemonade booth at a charity bazaar, accepted chocolates from a German baron at the advanced age of nineteen, and sat through unbearable tea dances arranged by her mother and aunts.

The Hungary of Jolie's youth still had one foot in the Middle Ages. Entrance to society was open only to the landed aristocracy, leaving Jolie, with her nouveau riche background, out in the cold. Since she was barred from the real upper class, a festering wound developed inside her, causing her to vow (with the ferocity of a Scarlett O'Hara) that her daughters would crash society, no counting the cost.

Her own mother, Francesca Tilleman, dismissed Jolie's frustration. "No matter," she said. "Mark my words. You will make one of the 'great' marriages in Budapest. You have the brains and ingenuity to do anything you want." Under her breath Jolie swore an oath that hers would be one of the modern marriages. When her husband took his brandy into the library, she intended to go in with him.

"The one pain in my childhood was that I was not pretty. I had pimples which never went away, a face which wasn't just pale but rather green, and mousy brown hair [the true color of all the Gabor tresses]. With Mama being so beautiful, it was very, very hard for me to take," Jolie told Hollywood columnist Louella Parsons. "There I was—a moderately attractive girl—the daughter of a particularly stunning mother."

To cope, Jolie wrapped herself in fantasy, spinning long, complicated daydreams of fame and romance. She would be a ballerina—no, better an actress, since all actresses have the world at their feet.

She was, she solemnly told her family, "saving myself for the theater, to which I will give my heart and soul."

Mama Francesca, the aunts, and even Jolie's grandmother merely nodded and said, "Good, good," all the while steering the girl closer and closer to an Old World marriage, with its bondage and subservience to the husband.

The family was praying for a solid, stuffy baron of industry. Jolie was waiting for a prince. And he showed up at a gala party held by one of Jolie's cousins at a large villa on the outskirts of Budapest. "I was to be a bridesmaid at my cousin Elizabeth's wedding," Jolie said. "At the time, I was having a flirtation with a romantically inclined partner of my father's."

Naturally, Francesca found out about it. "This is scandalous," she said. "That man is thirty years old. You are to stop this immediately."

Jolie, acting the coquette, defied her mother. "But I love him, Mama. He's as handsome as a movie star—like Douglas Fairbanks."

At her cousin's party she teased her father's amorous partner into giving her an embrace, which ended in a tango dip. He held one arm around her waist and the other at the nape of her neck. Then he bent down gracefully and kissed her.

As Jolie came out of the dizzying embrace, she caught a glimpse of a perfectly smashing Hungarian cavalry major with sandy hair tousled in great scallops, dark eyes, and the tight black uniform then in vogue on the Continent. Gold braid and regimental stripes accented impossibly broad shoulders and well-shaped legs.

His eyes flashed at her. The heels of his polished black boots snapped together smartly. And she gasped. She saw her cousin Elizabeth and rushed over to her. "Who is *he?*" "Major Vilmos Gabor," Elizabeth whispered back with this cautious warning: "Now there, my dear, is a really older man."

"How old, do you think?" she asked Elizabeth.

"Forty, maybe a little older."

"Rich?"

"Rich, darling, and ripe for the picking."

Challenging her Victorian parents, Jolie was soon seen everywhere on the arm of the handsome cavalry officer. She thought, wrongly, that by dallying with a man twice her age, she could somehow bring about parental approval for an acting career.

Instead, she'd stepped into marital quicksand. Her parents were doing some checking on their own, learning that Major Gabor was not only rich but that he had the advantage of an ancient and fine Hungarian lineage.

Naturally there was consistent patter between the major, intent on his courting, and Jolie, who was only interested in escaping her parents.

Jolie eventually paid a terrible price for this freedom. In her giddy desire to escape filial suffocation, she failed to notice that her husband was not only much older than she; he was the product of an era that considered wives to be chattel.

So stuffy and old-fashioned was he that she had to do the proposing, or die of boredom waiting for a prescribed period of engagement to end. Finally, losing patience, she blurted out: "I have no man. And in my family this is bad."

Jolie's family was of the old school where the daughters were married in turn, starting with the eldest. It was now her turn. Even in the face of Jolie's boldness, Vilmos refused to commit himself.

But when he called the next afternoon—in full Hussar dress of boots, sword, and feathered hat—he brought the engagement ring and said he had decided on a wedding day.

Jolie took it. But not before she confessed that she really wanted a career on stage, not a life in the kitchen and nursery.

"You are very young," Vilmos told her. "You will have to work very, very hard to be a great actress. I can make you happy, Jolie. Please let me try."

Then, according to Jolie, Major Vilmos Gabor, a Victorian womanizing cavalry major, offered to voluntarily sign a six-month contract. "Be my wife for six months," he allegedly said. "Then if you still wish to be an actress, I will let you go."

In some versions of the legend, Vilmos went even further. "If I do not make you deliriously happy, we will get a divorce. I promise you this."

Jolie apparently rushed out and with her own limited funds hired an attorney to draw up the six-month legally binding pact. However, when she brought it home for her parents to witness, they all rushed away in horror—as did the rest of the family.

Therefore, two notaries, who were a bit surprised at the irregular pact, were hired as witnesses. If this is indeed true, Jolie Gabor predated modern marriage contracts by about half a century.

Jolie told Louella Parsons that life was seductive and deceivingly gay to a rich young bride with a lust for freedom, finally out on the town.

Six weeks into the marriage, Jolie ran off to Vienna in an impulsive act of a girl who didn't want to grow up. But it was not without cleverness. Before she fled from Vilmos, she wrapped her growing collection of jewels, including those given by her husband, in a napkin and left them with her mother.

The luxury of the Grand Hotel in Vienna couldn't hide the depression that had descended on her like a storm cloud before she left Budapest. The bellman who carried her luggage uncomfortably watched her collapse in racking sobs. When he closed the door, she clutched her stomach and burst into tears. She was pregnant, and she hated it. She wasn't ready for it. Children—she shuddered—would trap her as surely as if she were thrown into a dungeon. It was too soon, too soon for her spirit to be subdued by the demands of children.

Vilmos was frantic with grief and rushed to Vienna to console her, his pockets loaded with diamonds.

"I still didn't love him," Jolie wrote later in a newspaper column. "But he *was* rich, and the life his wealth supplied was good."

Eight months later Magda was born, a brilliantly red-haired baby with a temper to match. The exact date of this first birth is impossible to determine. It might have been in the early 1920s or late in that decade, with all the Gabors naturally preferring the latter choice.

Magda, a dreamy, romantic infant, was adored briefly, weaned, and then confined to the nursery. "Now, Vilmos, I will go," Jolie declared. To which he replied, "I want a son, Jolie, a son. You will stay until I have one." There was a wild, dangerous look in his eyes.

According to one version, Vilmos snatched Magda out of her cradle and held her out the window, threatening to drop her three stories onto the pavement below. "Can you really walk out on your small daughter?" he asked. "What kind of woman are you?" Jolie quickly relented.

Then came Zsa Zsa, originally called Sari, a fashionable name at that time. With her second child Jolie discovered motherhood's martyrdom. Zsa Zsa stayed as long as possible at her mother's breast. She wasn't greedy but simply demanding. She seemed to have already decided that *she* was the center of any universe she inhabited.

"Now, really, I must go," Jolie pleaded.

"Again Vilmos begged me to stay. He wanted a son so desperately. To him it was the most important thing in the world. So I stayed. And I stayed and stayed and stayed." In eighteen months Eva was born. Then, of course, it was much too late. Finally, a matronly Jolie, her daughters in school, went to Vilmos one more time. "I have done all that I promised you, and more. Now I really am going to think of my career."

These were empty words. Surely Jolie knew it. Vilmos only mocked her. "After all this time, Jolie Gabor, do you really want to leave? You cannot be an actress now." He laughed. "Now you are *too old*."

The words struck Jolie's heart. She had burned to be an actress, a dancer, a singer—anything that would have put her at the center of attention. Now it was too late.

"I looked at my beautiful young daughters and decided, for good or bad, to live through them. They would be what I had wanted to be but could not."

She sat down and in the manner of a Prussian field officer mapped out a lifetime plan for her three daughters from the nursery to the grave. They would learn about everything she had thirsted for, have experiences that she could not, marry the best husbands, live in the finest homes. "Oh, it was very serious with me," Jolie said recently.

It was so serious that she turned the Gabor mansion into a cultural prison for her high-spirited daughters. Each day had an agenda. Breakfast was at seven A.M.; school from eight A.M. to noon, followed by piano lessons. "After lunch we literally played a game of musical chairs," said Eva. "While Magda studied with the piano teacher, I practiced on the other piano. Then Zsa Zsa moved from her books to my piano, and Magda rotated to her homework." Then there were dancing lessons, an hour session with the fencing master, and drills in French, German, and English until dinner. "We could talk about nothing in four languages."

Jolie knew she was dealing with three distinct individuals from the time they were turned loose in the nursery. Zsa Zsa, for instance, was covetous of her toys, cataloguing them as if they were banknotes. Magda was the most easily pleased. While still in her crib, she laughed with joy at the beauty of spring's first jonquils or the play of the morning sunshine. And Eva was intellectually precocious, trying to read her father's morning newspapers. "They were all quite different in many ways," Jolie once told the London *Daily Mirror.* "Magda was born a lady who amused herself and spun endless daydreams. Eva was an ambitious toddler and was single-minded about becoming an actress by the time she entered her teens. Zsa Zsa was a chubby tomboy who didn't become a 'femme fatale' until she was sixteen. And then she became one overnight."

Zsa Zsa says her father told her that she shrieked when a woman approached her crib, but when a man bent over her she cooed and giggled.

Mama, needless to say, was always in the wings. She wanted her daughters to be three identical extensions of herself, the famous, brilliant lady she had wished to be.

"I admit it now," Jolie said on a 1972 talk show. "I tried to make stars of my children. I wanted them not just to skate but to skate like Sonja Henie, and I wanted them to play the piano so magnificently that a Rubinstien would be green with envy."

She tried not to play favorites. Perhaps she worked too hard at being impartial. The girls themselves easily made peace with the reality that Zsa Zsa was Jolie's favorite. "I was always drawn to her." Nothing illustrates this better than her desperate attempt to win the Miss Hungary crown for the middle sister.

In those days (the mid-1930s) beauty pageants were still in their first decade, ranking somewhat above dog shows but a bit lower than the bakeoffs at the county fair. And as for society, one simply wouldn't allow one's daughter to enter such a tawdry spectacle.

For once, Jolie's fanaticism overruled her normally flawless social sense.

All the facts are clouded by the convenient memory lapses suffered regularly by the Gabors. The contest has variously been described as occurring in 1938, 1936, and 1937. Or "even earlier," Jolie said not too long ago.

Several times both Zsa Zsa and Jolie let it slip to journalists that she was, indeed, Miss Hungary and that she came within a few votes of capturing the Miss Europe crown several months later, without bothering to notice, it seems, that there was no Miss Europe pageant at that time.

The perpetuation of this myth has been greatly aided by the effects of World War II. When the Communists captured Hungary, they destroyed all records of such capitalistic contests.

But it all began one morning at six A.M. when Zsa Zsa was about fifteen. Jolie burst into the nursery and shook her awake. "Get up, Zsa Zsa. Get up quick," Jolie said. "Something very wonderful is about to happen to you."

It seems that Zsa Zsa's Aunt Rose, involved some way or another with a pageant to choose the first Miss Hungary, had spoken to Jolie at a dinner party the night before: "Jolie, why don't you let Zsa Zsa enter the pageant. You know that whoever wins will get attention all over Europe."

Jolie thought carefully for about twenty seconds before grinning slyly. "Yes, let's see what the little monkey can do."

It didn't matter to Jolie that the semifinals had already been decided or that Zsa Zsa had no talent with which to dazzle the judges. Nor did she worry about Vilmos erupting like an emotional volcano the minute he heard about it. Zsa Zsa didn't even have a long dress.

Since the finals were set for eleven A.M. that same morning, there was precious little time to get ready. Judging from Jolie's version, about half of Budapest awakened early to help Zsa Zsa win the coveted crown.

Jolie dashed to Magda's closet, which did contain several long dresses. Rummaging through the eldest sister's collection, she found a formal gown that—with ridiculous and hurried alterations—would allow Zsa Zsa to look old enough for the finals. While Jolie and Aunt Rose began the alterations, the entire household staff of twelve was called into action, leaving Major Gabor to holler for his breakfast and for his valet, who was unceremoniously pinning up Zsa Zsa's hem in the nursery.

Vilmos raged and sent toast scattering across the breakfast table.

His face reddened and his eyes narrowed. He stormed into the kitchen and, finding it empty, rushed upstairs. He arrived just in time to catch Jolie drenching his middle daughter's brown hair with peroxide from Paris. "Stop this instant!" he screamed. "You will turn her into a little tramp. Stop it right now!"

"Vilmos darling," purred Jolie, "this will be good for her. I'm just making her look a bit like Jean Harlow. It's all the rage, darling."

The fact that work wasn't even slowed and that nobody seemed to notice the Major showed exactly who wore the pants in the Gabor household.

The nerve that it took for Jolie to force Zsa Zsa into the pageant six weeks after all entries closed was typical of the Gabor determination. Walking up to the judging committee, she barked, "I *am* going to enter my daughter Zsa Zsa. You know, ladies, you really didn't advertise the dates properly, and my poor little girl had her heart set on this contest. Why, she's been training for months. But she was out of the country attending school during the preliminaries."

"Too late," said the chairman of the judging committee. "There is no way we can allow your daughter to enter at this late date."

"No matter," Jolie said, approaching the judge menacingly, "I am going to enter my daughter in this competition."

"Oh, madame." The judge sighed. "You tried this very same thing when we had the City of Budapest pageant. You tried it with Magda. You didn't make it then, and you won't now."

"We'll just see about that," she said, dragging Zsa Zsa to the backstage area.

With only one day left in the contest, Jolie comforted her daughter as their town car drove slowly through the city's streets. "No matter, darling, no matter. They are going to take you. And you are going to win."

Zsa Zsa chewed on her nails nervously. All she wanted to do was go home and read the little romance novels she had hidden under her mattress. But the limousine didn't head home as Zsa Zsa had hoped. It stopped at the hairdresser's, where she underwent a torture of face packs, skin bleaching, and a four-hour treatment that turned her hair platinum blond.

They were up well before dawn the next morning, assaulting the gates of the Miss Hungary pageant. After they gained access to the theater as regular ticket holders, Jolie tugged Zsa Zsa (her costume covered by a heavy cloak) to seats down near the stage. As the house lights dimmed, they slipped backstage.

There, a harried man with thinning hair and an even thinner temper was trying to organize the Hungarian beauties into some presentable order. He had a little gilt baton in one hand and was keeping time as he showed the young women how he wanted them to prance across the stage. "Now one and two and three, girls," he commanded. His limp wrist and little-girl's steps caused Jolie to burst out laughing. This is a man who can be intimidated, she thought joyfully.

While the sexless dance director put numbers on all ten finalists, Jolie grabbed a blank sign and wrote an entry number on the front. The orchestra picked up the overture beat, and the dance master fluttered with excitement. Jolie grabbed Zsa Zsa by her slim shoulders and shoved her mightily between two of the finalists and then watched satisfied from the wings.

The dance master tiptoed over and was about to say something when he noticed the Gabor look in Jolie's eyes. "Okay, sure. What the heck!" he said. "What difference can it make, anyway? She's entered."

After a bit of parading, smiling, and dancing to some ghastly music, the contestants were stopped one-by-one before the judges. Then a revolving stage swept them away as the judges began voting.

Almost half an hour later an elderly lady pushed her way through the crowd and handed the man a sheet of folded paper containing the names of the three finalists.

When Zsa Zsa remained on the revolving stage after the rejects filed into the wings, Jolie's heart fluttered. "I knew that if she made it into the finals she stood a unique chance to win. She had that delicate form of beauty which leaves only a very few unruffled while bowling everybody else over."

The judges, fortunately, were in the latter group.

Before the curtain opened for the presentation of the finalists and the winner, a seamstress who had known Jolie for some time rushed over to her. "Your daughter just won. I saw it on the slips," she whispered.

Unluckily for Zsa Zsa, the director of the pageant looked a bit more closely at entry number 146 and mumbled something to the rest of the judges. Just what was said and how forcefully, is unknown. Jolie said Zsa Zsa was ruled out because she was too young. "She was just not old enough to enter. But they gave her second prize anyway."

Perhaps it was Jolie's unorthodox manner of entering the contest that automatically kept her daughter from winning. Still others, no fans of the Gabors, claim that Zsa Zsa was tossed out the back door before she could reach the stage. And some believe the entire episode was manufactured later as grist for the Gabor publicity mill.

Jolie said that when she found out the judges were withholding the crown because her frail daughter was too young, she roared down upon them like an angry lioness protecting her cub. She begged, she pleaded, she whispered intimately to some of them. And she paraded the disheveled Zsa Zsa from one end of the huge hall to the other.

Zsa Zsa never became Miss Hungary. She may not even have entered the contest. But the legend goes a long way toward explaining how all the Gabors ultimately succeeded.

2

❋ Stage Mother

*M*ama Jolie walked away from the Miss Hungary pageant, leaving it a shambles. "She should have won. She should have won," she said to herself over and over again. What she really meant was "I should have won," since she viewed Zsa Zsa as an extension of herself and a symbol of what she might have been. The loss of the pageant hit her hard. "I broke down in tears after the pageant," she said. "Once again *I* had lost a career."

She also, unwittingly, had created a scandal. Vilmos, a man who savored his morning papers, was jolted awake by photos of little Zsa Zsa and the real Miss Hungary on the front pages. He let out a roar that caused his valet to shake.

Journalists claimed that Jolie tried to bribe the judges, that she had invited all of them to a party. They also wrote that she was a horribly poor sport when the final decision was made.

There was only one consolation, as Vilmos said later. All you had to do was look at the photos to see that Zsa Zsa was by far more beautiful than the winner.

Vilmos and the rest of the family expected Jolie to calm down, to take this loss bravely and proceed with the normal rearing of her family.

But she was driven by a number of factors. First, Jolie was then about thirty-five, a time of life when some women become frantic—measuring what they are with what they dreamed they would be. More often than not, there was a chasm between what they wanted and what they got. This was certainly true for Jolie.

In addition, the roar of applause that greeted Zsa Zsa when she first stepped onstage filled Jolie's ears, swelling her ambitious head. The applause, she felt, was as much for herself and what she had created as it was for Zsa Zsa; and she wanted more of it—much more.

Another contest was entered immediately, this one sponsored by a film theater. "This is a talent contest, Madame Gabor," said the manager of the theater. "Of course, the contest is tomorrow. You have only a day. But if her talent is as great as her beauty, Zsa Zsa is sure to win."

Jolie's next task was to hammer some talent into her daughter. But how? Zsa Zsa couldn't sing. When a vocal coach worked with her, the off-key results were not pleasant. And she couldn't dance. On toe shoes she resembled a bowlegged goat. What *could* she do? As Jolie told her sister, "Zsa Zsa can just barely talk properly."

"We better concentrate on her beauty," she decided. And her loveliness was uncommon. Even at fifteen her skin had the champagne color that would make her one of the world's beauties. She was not yet a polished beauty, to be sure, but the makings were there.

Jolie sat down after midnight with a cup of strong coffee and let her mind wander through all the movies she had seen, particularly American films. She remembered quite vividly an actress who had done a charming song and dance routine dressed as a toy soldier. (Most probably it was Bessie Love in MGM's *Broadway Melody of 1929.*) This her daughter could do.

But Jolie was running out of time. It was already one in the morning, and Zsa Zsa needed a costume. It had to be a toy soldier's complete with bangles and braiding. And it had to be of tiny size. After banging on doors for hours, Jolie found one man willing to open his shop. After looking through a hundred different costumes, she finally selected the one she needed.

At home she was forced to indulge in domestic espionage. Vilmos was in a rage at her efforts and threatened, however lightly, to pack the girls off to a convent if Jolie followed her collision course with fame. With the soldier's costume in a plain box tied with string, Jolie crept into the house, walked past her husband as if she were in a daze, and headed to the servants' quarters far in the back.

Eva and Zsa Zsa were sharing confidences. "Come with me," Jolie said, grabbing Zsa Zsa. Eva was left on her own. In Zsa Zsa's bedroom with the door shut, Jolie said, "I have wonderful news for you. Tonight at the movie house they are having a talent contest, a very big talent contest. You could become a finalist and go on to the Austrian-Hungarian finals in Vienna. You could become a star."

Zsa Zsa shuddered involuntarily. "I can't do anything," she whined. "I'll just be embarrassed."

"I assure you, I know what I'm doing. We can put an act together." Jolie took out the soldier's suit, helped Zsa Zsa into it, and then choreographed a little dance for her, drawing on what she had seen in the film long ago.

"It goes like this," Jolie said, doing a stiff-armed little march and twirl that was really quite charming. Zsa Zsa thought, "If Mama can do it, we would win."

"I can't do it," Zsa Zsa said, terror-stricken. "I won't."

"Nonsense," answered her mother. "I will teach you all you need to know."

"But I'm terrified," she said, turning her face away.

"And I am *not*," Jolie said.

They had eight whole hours to turn the girl into a polished trooper —or at least into a facsimile good enough for an amateur talent contest.

They stayed in the room for hours, practicing the weak little song, dancing and marching over and over again. Finally, Jolie let her daughter nap for an hour or so. It had been a grueling day, particularly for a confused fifteen-year-old.

Just before they left, Jolie grabbed her daughter: "This is terribly important to me." Those became critical words in Zsa Zsa's life: "This is important to me." Each time Zsa Zsa faltered, she believed that she was letting her mother down, disappointing her terribly.

Despite all of Zsa Zsa's hard work and practice, Jolie feared that she wouldn't be able to pull it off. "She wasn't very good; this I knew."

And Jolie was right. Although they had a long list of prizes for different categories, Zsa Zsa won nothing but a little wooden plaque saying she had been a participant. Mama had some consolation: "The winner in Zsa Zsa's category, an illegitimate child, grew up to be a 200-pound hausfrau." (A housewife—that was the last thing *any* of the Gabors wanted to be. That was an alien world!)

As in the other contest, Jolie faulted the judges. "They had voted for the wrong girls, but they hadn't seen the last of my Zsa Zsa. Not by a long shot."

Joe Pasternak, a budding Hungarian film producer who eventually became an important force at MGM, stopped Jolie as she was leaving the theater. "Your daughter is beautiful," he said. "Nothing more."

Jolie decided right then that she would follow the contest to its finale in Vienna. Zsa Zsa would compete, compete, and compete until she bloody well won *something*. (Interestingly, it was Joe Pasternak who gave Zsa Zsa her first film job decades later, as the full-blown beauty in *Lovely to Look At*.)

"We will go to Vienna, darling." She took her daughter's hand and walked haughtily away.

But they still had to overcome that one implacable foe, Vilmos. He knew that the little shopping trips and spa visits that many upper-class Hungarian women made periodically were, more often than not, rendezvous with secret lovers; and he had always refused Jolie's requests to leave the city alone. "As pretty as my wife is," he once said, "she would more than likely never come back."

Jolie confronted him the night after the dismal talent contest: "I intend to take Zsa Zsa on a little trip to Vienna this weekend. She's not in school, so it will be fun for her."

He replied as usual, "There is absolutely no reason for you to go to Vienna. If you want to go shopping, I'll give you extra money, and you can do it right here in Budapest. You will not go to Vienna."

His wife balked. "Vilmos, I can't wait. I'm going to Vienna this weekend to enter Zsa Zsa in a talent contest." Then she pleaded: "The biggest producers and directors from all over Europe will be there, and I have a feeling something good will happen. Some important person will discover our little daughter. She has to have this chance."

Vilmos grudgingly agreed, but not until he forced Jolie to swear that she would stop all this nonsense and send Zsa Zsa back to school if nothing came of it.

Jolie had deluded herself that both earlier panels of judges had been completely wrong. "The only difference between the other contestants and Zsa Zsa is that their way was paid to Vienna. We had to pay for ourselves."

The hysteria of preparation for the two earlier contests was nothing compared with this one. In three days, Jolie had seven new dresses tailored for Zsa Zsa, selected new makeup, and polished up the toy soldier act in case it was needed.

Naturally, mother and daughter stayed at the Grand Hotel in Vienna, the city's most expensive watering hole. No scrimping for them. If they lost, they were going to lose in style. "The first night we had dinner sent up, and I made calls to check on the contest," Jolie said. She learned that the final round was scheduled for the following morning. "I ran hot water into the tub, sprinkled an extra quantity of bath oil, and told Zsa Zsa to lie back in the hot water and relax. Me? I wandered around like a wounded chicken."

Meanwhile, she was trying to give the performance of her matriarchal career. To Zsa Zsa, she pretended it was all just a lark, that they would have a good time first and think of the contest second.

This contest, however, was no better than the other two. Zsa Zsa came in twelfth—second from last. They handed her a piece of paper and told her to trot along home and marry the right man. This time Zsa Zsa cried so mournfully that it broke Jolie's heart. Later she said, "I wonder if Zsa Zsa could sense that I loved her the most, that she was my shining light. Since I'd begun to spoil her in the nursery, her every sense became attuned to mine. She felt she had let me down in Vienna."

Tears or not, Jolie decided to try one last time. There was to be an official reception for the talent *winners* that evening, and somehow she wangled an invitation.

In a couple of hours, she turned Zsa Zsa into Cinderella. She went down to the hotel manager and asked him to find her the most beautiful horse-drawn carriage in the city. It was a lush, gilded coach with polished leather and tulips in crystal vases. All eyes were on them as they drove up to the open-air party. "Hold your chin up," Jolie whispered to Zsa Zsa. "Pretend you are the most important person here." (It was advice she took to heart for an entire lifetime.)

Suddenly, however, both she and her mother were star struck. "There was somebody important at every table," Jolie said. "We couldn't turn our heads fast enough."

They eased into a corner booth and waited. Then, during a lull in the awards ceremony, Jolie became the *ultimate* stage mother, the sort one reads about in accounts of early Hollywood, the sort who push their daughters through agents' doors, who make them twirl the baton or sing on Hollywood Boulevard.

Jolie, with intimidating power, forced her daughter onto an empty table and hissed, "Start singing and dancing. Quick!" Zsa Zsa's eyes turned as big as saucers. She was mortified, and her cheeks reddened.

But she slowly began singing—terribly off key. She was frightened and felt as if her arms and legs were made of lead. Her voice came out in a squeak as she sang her toy soldier's song. When Jolie realized that Zsa Zsa's voice couldn't carry over the loud conversation at the dinner, she opened her mouth wide and joined in. "Actually, I was doing most of the singing for her. I had a good voice and loved to sing. Besides, I had to face the fact that while my child, the star, looked like an angel she sounded like a crippled wren. A hush finally came over the cafe, and everyone was watching her. I was far too excited to be embarrassed. . . . For the first time I saw a new side to Zsa Zsa. As all eyes focused on her, Zsa Zsa's fear dissolved. A look of triumph was written on her face, and she whirled on the table."

Surprisingly, this gutsy, outrageous little trick worked. The opera singer Richard Tauber and Franz Lehár, composer of *The Merry Widow,* got up and headed toward the blond vision atop the table. Jolie had a startling pang of shame. She wondered if this hadn't all been just too much—the action of an aging, driven woman.

Then Tauber stood right next to the table where Zsa Zsa, by now calm, was performing. "My God, Franz, this is the girl we have been looking for. This is our Violetta."

Tauber and Lehár were soon joined by a bustling producer, Hubert Mariska. He looked knowingly at Tauber, who nodded silently. Mariska bowed to Jolie. "I am preparing an operetta called *The Singing*

Dream, and Tauber will play the lead. We have been searching for weeks to find the right girl to play the ingenue. And the part's an important one. The girl is the sixteen-year-old daughter of an American millionaire who comes to Europe just in time to complicate the plot. Your daughter is just what we have been looking for."

For the first time in her very verbal life, Jolie was speechless.

"Madame Gabor, please bring your daughter to the Theater an der Wien tomorrow morning at eleven, and let's see what happens."

Jolie cried during the carriage ride back to the hotel—both in happiness for Zsa Zsa and in memory of her own faded dreams. "The memory of a girl who had seen a play at the age of twelve came back to me. The memory of a girl who had vowed that one day she too would be up on that stage," Jolie said.

Next morning, after a few minutes of coaching by a dancing master and a practice singing session, Zsa Zsa walked onto the stage of the darkened theater and sang a number from the operetta. "I never wanted to come down," she wrote her sister Eva, who was languishing back home. "I wanted to be up there playing a part always. I never really went backwards. Life became my stage."

She got the part.

Jolie immediately called Vilmos. He was horrified, ashamed. The immodesty of one of his daughters becoming an actress was humiliating for a man of his class, for in those days actors were still considered to be Bohemians at best and gypsies or carnival tramps at worst.

"Bring her directly home," he fumed. "Wasn't the beauty contest enough? Now the stage. Listen to me, Jolie, she'll be nothing but a showgirl, little better than a tart."

His wife hung up on him and then refused to answer his calls to the hotel. When she called back several hours later it was to issue a declaration: "She's got the part, and she is going to keep it."

Vilmos sputtered with indignation for a few seconds and then went silent. Like a man of the old European school, he seems to have cut Zsa Zsa loose from the time she took the part. But he was far from ready to let Jolie drift into the dangers of international society along with her daughter. Power was on his side; he had Magda and Eva as emotional hostages.

"Find her a place to stay, get her a companion, and come right back home," he said in a menacing tone. "You have two daughters here who need you." Vilmos apparently dedicated himself to keeping his impatient wife home as long as he could. He had seen hundreds of little signs that she would break free as soon as her daughters had moved on to lives of their own. And Vilmos, on the verge of becoming an old man, was pitiable in his hysteria. Jolie was all he had.

Jolie found a sort of high class boardinghouse for Zsa Zsa and summoned one of her faithful retainers, Cuki, to chaperone her daughter in the wicked city. Reluctantly, she took the train home.

Two weeks after Jolie arrived home, Zsa Zsa called, sobbing and choking on her own words. "They fired me," she said. The producers had decided that winsome little Zsa Zsa looked and acted too young. Jolie took the next train to Vienna. When she arrived she found her little star crumpled up in a theater seat woefully watching the other actors. "They have another girl to replace me," she told her mother, pouting. The petite ingenue was jerked out of the seat and, packed off to her hotel to be made more presentable by Mama.

The producers had agreed to let Zsa Zsa test one more time, this time along with the replacement. Jolie knew she had her work cut out for her. "I even gave a poor beggar woman five schillings for good luck. I bribed everyone. I thought my whole life depended on this."

During one of Jolie's ten-hour practice sessions with her daughter, producer Mariska passed the door. He roared approval, took Jolie's hand, and said, "Madame, if only you were fifteen years younger." Jolie knew *exactly* what he meant.

Finally, Zsa Zsa got the part simply because she messed up her entrance. As she pranced across the stage, she stumbled and dipped down on one knee. The leading lady of the piece clapped her hands. "This is adorable. It is so cute."

The part was Zsa Zsa's.

But before Zsa Zsa tripped and secured the part, Jolie had harangued the producer for five days. "We have a three-year contract. I needn't remind you that this is binding," she threatened Mariska. He informed Jolie in an angry tone that her daughter couldn't sing, couldn't dance, and "certainly couldn't act."

That got Jolie's back up. "Mr. Mariska, you didn't hire her for those attributes. You hired her because she was gorgeous."

The producer rubbed a hand over his weary head. "Madame, we will make her an understudy at the same salary. Does that satisfy you?"

Zsa Zsa began crying. "Even if they take me back, I can't do the role."

Mama bore down on her daughter: "You damn well will do it."

Luckily for Zsa Zsa and Jolie another woman entered the plot. She was the beautiful Viennese actress Lily Kartzog, wife of the producer. "This is a girl who is unbelievably beautiful," she said. "She takes your breath away."

Mariska shrugged. "Well, she can't sing or dance, but she can keep that pretty face of hers faced toward the audience." Something Zsa Zsa has been doing ever since.

"Besides," Lily interjected, "Violetta is a millionaire's daughter, and Zsa Zsa looks the part."

Jolie also played up to Fritz Steiner, the show's star. Said Jolie: "He knew Zsa Zsa was a virgin and left her alone. But he propositioned me. 'If you go to bed with me, I promise to help your daughter.' Her scream of rejection could be heard out on the sidewalks in front of the theater. "But I did give him a two-carat diamond for his pinky, and he was not so overcome with his passion for me that he didn't take it."

Once again Jolie dashed home.

The Singing Dream played for three months in Vienna, making Zsa Zsa the toast of the town. Her picture was on billboards, in the fashion magazines, and even in a filmed ad for apples.

It was during this stay in Vienna that Zsa Zsa experienced her first romantic encounter. She claims to have made her first conquest in a hit-and-run affair with a German composer, Willi Schmidt-Kentner, who may have helped end Zsa Zsa's tenure as a virgin.

In her 1975 autobiography, *Jolie,* Jolie describes an amusing anecdote about her middle's daughter's virginity. One night when Zsa Zsa had been in Vienna for two months, Vilmos awoke screaming. Jolie grabbed him. "What's the matter?"

He looked at her wildly. "I know that suddenly, this very night, Zsa Zsa has lost her virginity."

His wife shrugged and pointed out that Zsa Zsa was well chaperoned.

"Never mind," he said. "She is no longer a virgin."

Jolie turned over and went back to sleep, hiding from Vilmos the fact that Zsa Zsa, as of late, had taken to drugging Cuki's nightly cocoa with a sleeping potion.

Better he should not know, she thought.

So what did it matter anyway? Virgin or not, Zsa Zsa was back home three months later.

Heavens, Jolie thought, will I ever be free of my family?

3

✳ Out of the Nest

*W*ith the same determination that caused her to toss the sisters into the lake, Jolie drove them into the marriage market with a vengeance.

She dreamed of all three walking down the aisle on the arms of millionaires, prime ministers, and maybe even a prince. Therefore it must have been a let-down when all three spread their gilded little wings and catapulted into dismal marriages.

As soon as Eva, Zsa Zsa, and Magda were old enough to go unchaperoned to debutante parties, they grabbed for husbands the first men who were willing and available.

Eighteen-year-old Magda married an impoverished aristocrat whose countdom (what there was of it) was soon confiscated by the Nazis; Zsa Zsa hooked a foul-tempered Turkish diplomat twice her age; and Eva wed a still-in-training Swedish osteopath whose main assets were his gorgeous blond hair and blue eyes. And it all happened within the span of about eighteen months.

The exact dates of the marriages, the ages of the brides, and the backgrounds of the grooms are lost, now sealed off within the Communist borders of postwar Hungary.

"It wasn't hard for me to find them husbands," Jolie remembered. "Just like my mother, who gave dowries fast so she could be free, I gave my blessings just as fast for the same reason."

Supposedly it was love at first sight for Magda and the Polish Count Jan de Bichovsky. An English schoolmate of the eldest daughter took her home for a vacation in London. The count showed up one afternoon for tea, took one look at Magda, and was smitten. He was a tall, austere man, devoted to hunting and to his Polish Cavalry regiment.

When Magda came back home to Budapest, Count Bichovsky was

on her arm. "He was nice-looking. He was an aristocrat. And she liked him, so okay," Jolie wrote in her autobiography.

However wonderful Jan looked in his regimentals and however glowing was the bride, the ceremony was a dreary little affair at the Budapest city hall, with an intimate reception held after gossip reached Hungary concerning the count. His pedigree, it seems, stretched back to the days when the Vikings were overrunning the country, but he was flat broke, and the ancestral castle was empty. To compensate, Jolie bought an entire household of furniture for the couple. And her eldest daughter, as pretty as a Renoir painting, was carted off to the forests of Poland—along with the furniture.

Her brief life as the Countess of Warsaw is shrouded in mystery. Information on her husband is even scantier. Jolie visited her ennobled daughter only once, but that was enough to convince her that the nouveau aristocratic Magda had become very grand indeed.

Jolie boarded a rather battered airplane dressed in mink, a new traveling costume, and an enormous veiled hat. She was, she thought to herself, the very picture of Greta Garbo. But a Polish storm was brewing and had reached hurricane proportions by the time she disembarked. The hat was carried off toward the forests of Russia, the hairdo destroyed, and her mink looked matted and dull.

Her grace Magda groaned. "Mama," she whispered, "pull yourself together."

"Oh, but my daughter has taken on airs," Jolie reported to friends back in Budapest. "She has not a cent of money, and they have trouble paying the grocer. But she is very, very grand."

The hauteur melted quickly some years later when the Nazis marched into Poland. Magda and Jan barely escaped with their lives, fleeing to the safety of London at the last minute.

"She'll be right back home, too," Jolie complained to one of her sisters. "Then we'll start all over again."

Meanwhile, Zsa Zsa was home and creating a furor over a small Scottie dog that Vilmos barred from the house. "Very well," Zsa Zsa declared. "I'll just find a husband—a husband who won't make me go back to school, one who will let me keep the dog." So her first marriage was an expedient one as were many others to follow.

Vilmos had never quite got over the rage he experienced when his middle daughter defied him and became an actress. Sternly, he ordered Zsa Zsa back to school. "Madame Subilia's [the Swiss boarding school attended by Magda and Zsa Zsa] was like a prison to me," Zsa Zsa recalled. "My nature was wild and romantic, and after the gaiety and freedom of Vienna I couldn't bear two more years behind the walls of a finishing school."

About a week before she was to entrain for Switzerland she ran into a somewhat drab but nonetheless sexy diplomat and decided he was a likely target. She had been modeling jewelry at the shop Jolie had recently opened in downtown Budapest. As she turned coyly to display a bracelet glittering on her wrist, she felt two dark eyes staring at her. The man, who introduced himself as a high-ranking Turkish official, began flirting with the teenage Zsa Zsa. A couple of dates, and he's mine, she thought. That would show them. That would show them all. They'd be sorry when she was hidden away behind the walls of a Turkish harem.

She became Mrs. Burhan Belge several weeks later. The bridegroom, as it turned out, was the ranking foreign affairs minister in his country, a man always addressed as "his excellency." Amusingly, Zsa Zsa immediately insisted that she be spoken to as "her excellency," even by her sisters.

Now the family boasted one deluded "countess," a teenage "excellency," and one forlorn single girl, Eva.

Panicked at being the only one left behind, Eva rushed to the altar as hastily and impetuously as her sisters. There are two different versions of the romantic scenario.

First, there's Eva's, told on dozens of talk shows and, partially, in her autobiography, *Orchids and Salami*. She says she was swept into her lover's arms by a harmless girlhood prank. One summer evening Magda, home from Poland for a visit, gave a party for Budapest's young set. And this was a party to which predeb Eva was distinctly not invited. Instead, she says, she was carted off to her grandmother's for cookies, milk, and an early bedtime.

"Supposedly, I was safe there from the menace of frivolity and champagne." Grandmother didn't seem to notice that Eva was dressed a bit formally for a playpen evening. She had chosen a dress of white shantung and was draped with jewels from her mother's cache. Grandma, always susceptible to Eva's charm, thought little of it when she stood up and announced that she was going home early. Tired, don't you know. And there was the piano to practice.

"I was determined to crash Magda's party. Once there, I saw *him* immediately—sitting dejectedly in the corner. His name was Eric Drimmer, an osteopath still in training. He was in Budapest for a brief visit before leaving for California to finish school and set up practice."

There was one thing all accounts of the romance agreed upon: Eric Drimmer was quite handsome. Eva claimed, with her usual élan, that he asked her to marry him several days after their fated meeting. "He said it directly," said Eva. "And I said 'yes' just as quickly. You can see I was the thoughtful type."

According to Jolie, the great love affair began in an entirely different manner. She says that Zsa Zsa (already Mrs. Burhan Belge of

Ankara, Turkey) flew in with a Turkish contingent to attend a gay party. "Nuci [her pet name for Jolie], I have just found the most ravishing man for Eva. He looks like a Swedish prince. Tell Eva to get up, and bring her down here right now before this guy gets away."

A suspicious Jolie demanded, "Is he for a husband or for a date?"

"Don't worry, Nuci," Zsa Zsa laughed. "He won't marry Eva, because he's just a Swedish doctor from Hollywood."

Jolie said she jerked her youngest daughter out of bed, dressed her, applied makeup, and then rushed her to the party.

This version depicts Eva and Eric as falling into each other's arms. Zsa Zsa said later that she was shocked. "This became a big, big love right away." Jolie told the London *Daily Mirror* that "the marriage was all arranged by Zsa Zsa. She was determined they would get married."

Eva claimed that Jolie hated the very idea of her first marriage. So irate was she, Eva said, that "I was summarily packed off to the Swiss Alps, then to the French Riviera, and finally to Monaco." Staying with friends, she must have been quite poor company, since she swooned over memories of Eric wherever she went. "I saw his face in the Alps and heard his voice in the ocean."

One warm afternoon Eric supposedly showed up at the front door of the villa in Monaco, where he and Eva spent a few idyllic days.

Again (in Eva's version) Jolie appeared and packed her youngest daughter off to school. "Then came my master stroke," Eva remembered. "I went off to London with Zsa Zsa, where I was spared the mental strain of trying to forget. Eric had cabled me that he was already on his way."

It may have all been a daydream, but the bride described Eric as a "Norse god with muscles of steel and a mind to match." But Jolie once said that Drimmer was "an altogether poor mate for my high-strung daughter."

Then came the wedding—about which the versions veer even further apart. Jolie claimed she gave her baby a new car, a bright red German Steyr, which set her back 5,000 pengös.

Not so, said Eva. It was Eric who gave her a compact red car—a Jaguar (his honeymoon offering).

According to Jolie, the wedding was a cozy family event with a party of sixteen at the Budapest city registry. "But, oh me, it wasn't legal," Jolie wailed. "Eric's papers were not in order."

Eva said the wedding occurred in a London public office where a lowly clerk in His Majesty's service married them. "Thus we had the blessings of the King." Mama covered herself by saying that a problem with Eric's Mexican divorce had invalidated the ceremony in Budapest. "So the poor dear ones had to remarry in London."

"Oh, it was such a tragedy when Eva found out she wasn't legally married. She was crying . . . and not just a little crying. She was bitter crying. But we had the reception anyway."

And, by the way, Jolie added, "Eva lost her virginity that night—legal or not."

Whatever the circumstances, Eva's wedding finally emptied the nest. Magda was a Polish chatelaine temporarily in Britain; Zsa Zsa was the toast of Ankara; and Eva was on the high seas headed for Hollywood.

This was the start of a glorious autumn in Jolie's life. She enjoyed the luxury of privacy, the once forbidden pleasures of lovers and long evenings in Budapest's gay nightclubs. But these days were already numbered. Hitler's shadow had fallen across Europe.

In London, Magda told Jan of her ties with the recently formed Hungarian underground and her fear of both the Nazis and the Russians. (Hungary was already allied with Nazi Germany, and Russian troops were near the country's eastern border.) The Count shared a secret of his own—he was a member of the Polish free forces in exile in England.

At the start of Europe's saddest hour, the Gabor sisters were on the verge of fame.

BOOK TWO

Three Smart Girls

Pompadour, Du Barry, Marie Antoinette—
what had they on us?
                    —ZSA ZSA, 1940

4

✳ Turkish Delight

*T*he Simplon Express was definitely not the Orient
Express. For one thing, there were no goats on the
Orient, while the Simplon in its economy class had goats aplenty. A
few wild-eyed Turks cooked shish kebab on open braziers. The Simplon resembled nothing so much as a creaking enclosed bazaar
flavored with clouds of incense, smelling of unwashed bodies, and
endowed with a symphony of Muslim chants, shrieking children, and
the incessant clacking of ill-maintained train tracks.

On the first night of her honeymoon the teen-aged Zsa Zsa stepped
out of the secure arms of her mother and into an alien world. She gave
her hand to the squat, somber Turk who was her husband and fought
back the tears burning in her eyes. Her Scottie dog, a snappish little
monster, was bundled under one arm, whimpering.

There were clouds of thick steam as the Simplon geared up to pull
out of Budapest's bustling station. Traveling luxury class, the newlyweds bypassed the goats, the braziers, and the filthy prayer rugs. The
train, a microcosm of Turkey, reflected the entire range of the country's medieval society. The just married Burhan Belges were of the
elite, and therefore were installed in a sumptuous suite complete with
twin beds. When Zsa Zsa saw one of the beds already turned down,
she flushed with embarrassment. Her psyche rebelled at the thought
of leaving everything she knew.

Burhan gallantly switched off most of the compartment's lights as
his trembling bride reluctantly prepared for bed. Then she had an
inspiration. When Burhan finally moved toward her, Zsa Zsa scooped
up her little dog and bundled it into bed next to her. Burhan stopped
in his tracks, grumbled something about not sleeping with a filthy
animal, and climbed into the other bed. Saved! Zsa Zsa breathed easy
—for *that* night. ("I knew no Muslim will lie where a dog has lain,"

she confided later.) As she drifted off to sleep, she shuddered at the thought of Ankara looming ahead and the real marriage bed that awaited her.

The complete stranger in the compartment with her would certainly become more demanding, and next time she might not be able to bluff her way out of her wifely duties. The Zsa Zsa who headed for Turkey was vastly different from the jet set beauty of later decades. Madame Burhan Belge was slightly pudgy, with rather undisciplined dishwater-blond hair and curves still hidden by baby fat. Her flashing eyes and giddy charm, however, made her easily the center of attention. For instance, when she and Burhan interrupted their honeymoon journey to visit King Zog of Albania, the lusty monarch invited Zsa Zsa to ride with him and made an open pass at her. For the first time, Zsa Zsa figured prominently in Europe's gossip columns. Under one photo of her, printed in Austria, the caption read, "A Cinderella for King Zog." The King whispered to her that she was wasted on the sour Turk, and not just a few people agreed with him.

Why did Zsa Zsa marry this melancholy Turk twice her age? To do so, she had cast aside an array of young and eligible suitors in Budapest. The answer has varied over the decades. In the 1950s, Zsa Zsa claimed she married Burhan in order to keep her Scottie dog—exiled from the house by her father. But Jolie once told the London *Daily Mirror* that her daughter married to escape from Vilmos' overprotective tyranny.

Zsa Zsa's mother also described her son-in-law as "disagreeable, ugly, but very important. . . . But a Turk! And an infidel! A diplomat could be a good match. But a Turk? . . . Zsa Zsa was certainly not in love with him, but she knew that if she could get away from Vilmos, she would be allowed more in life."

Neither story makes much sense. Zsa Zsa had already been "out on her own" in Vienna and willingly returned home. Plus, she already owned the little Scottie. The marriage may have been expedient. Probably Jolie wanted a safe diplomatic passport to protect Zsa Zsa from the fast approaching holocaust. Marriage to Burhan not only insured the passport, it got her daughter out of Hungary.

In the London *Daily Mirror* interviews, Jolie reportedly said to Zsa Zsa, "Look, my darling, if you want to marry Burhan it does not have to be forever. You can always come back home to me if you don't like him." Somehow, though, Jolie sensed that her daughter had embarked on a great adventure and that she would never come home again.

Zsa Zsa maintained that she herself had proposed to a surprised Burhan while they were walking in a Budapest park. "Excellency, will you marry me?'' she asked. Burhan was choked with surprise and pulled Zsa Zsa into a bar, where he ordered a double scotch. She took his hand slyly and said, ''There is just one condition. Will you let me keep my little Scottie?''

''Let me think about it,'' Burhan supposedly said. (According to her own legend, Zsa Zsa proposed to all of her husbands.)

During the forty-eight hours that elapsed while Burhan made his decision, Eva helped her sister look both sexier and older. Zsa Zsa wore a black dress to go dancing with the skittish bridegroom at a downtown hotel. While there, she showed her prospective husband sensual photos taken of her in Vienna. That did it! He gave in. ''Why not?'' he announced. ''We'll be married.'' ''And Mishka, my dog?'' ''Of course.'' Burhan nodded with distaste. ''If you must.''

Before she could fully accept the fact that she was married to an important political figure, a strong man whose father once had a harem, she was at his side on the Simplon Express, roaring eastward through the darkness toward Turkey. Arriving, Zsa Zsa saw screaming headlines at a newsstand: ''Barcelona Bombed!'' For the first time in her life, she was mortally frightened. The war, it's finally coming, she thought to herself. She also grasped the fact that she had quickly moved into a totally alien world. The sounds and poverty of the city, the strange smells, only made her homesick. ''What the hell am I doing here?''

A fleet of private cars collected the honeymoon couple and swept them off to the Belge family villa.

It boggles the mind! Zsa Zsa lolling back on brocade cushions, eating sweetmeats, and wearing a veil in preparation for her dark-eyed Turkish lover to enter the harem. Imagine, Zsa Zsa Gabor obedient in all things to a lord and master. As hard as it is to accept, the adolescent Gabor *was* subject to many implacable Turkish mores. It was the late 1930s in the rest of the world, but beneath the minarets of the East it was 1700. Women were chattel, and social life was heavy-handed. There was conversation and late-night drinking for the men, and needlework for the women. This was the world she had voluntarily entered. As if that weren't bad enough, her mother-in-law was a holy terror. She glided into the room to meet the new bride sporting real rubies on her vest and thick black kohl encircling her eyes. Her breath smelled of garlic and her voice was icy. She squatted cross-legged on a cushion, looked at Zsa Zsa, and shook her Old World head in horror.

''We must get her a proper trousseau,'' she said to Burhan's eldest sister. Then the matriarch clapped her hands three times. Servants appeared from the shadows to strip off Zsa Zsa's fashionable clothes and replace them with thick robes. Her hair was combed and oiled lightly with almond essence. Embroidered slippers were eased onto her feet.

The honeymoon bed, a stunning combination of red velvet, ebony, and silver filigree, loomed ominously. Zsa Zsa could avoid it no longer. The bridal ritual had not changed since the great days of the Ottoman Empire—a glittering candlelight ceremony as beautiful as it was barbaric. Zsa Zsa was washed, rubbed down with perfume, and then led through clouds of incense to that part of the Belge mansion that had once been a harem. Fawning maids wrapped her in a silken robe of unbelievable beauty, a garment that would be worn only once. She was finally settled onto the bridal cushions.

The mother-in-law saw that she was installed and leaned down to whisper, "His first two marriages were not agreeable to him. There-fore, we have very high hopes for you. You must learn to know when he is displeased. He will never, ever tell you his feelings, but instead will just walk away. You *must* learn to make him happy."

Piles of pastel-colored candies were deposited around the bed, in the ancient belief that the confections manufactured by priests in special mosques increased the fertility of the bridal bed (not to men-tion the bride).

The Belge clan could have spared themselves the trouble. Zsa Zsa said the marriage was never consummated. She has never said why, only that "in regard for my tender age some things were tolerated." In actuality, almost *everything* was tolerated by the long-suffering Bur-han.

The world will never know exactly what happened to Zsa Zsa in Turkey. But her two years behind the Muslim curtain transformed her from a giddy teenager into a sultry, worldly woman and a great beauty. Her own version depicts her as a great social success. She was such a success, in fact, that Turkey's dictator, Kemal Ataturk, founder of the Turkish Republic, was apparently her first important interna-tional conquest of the heart.

She claimed in her 1961 autobiography (*My Story,* co-written by Gerold Frank) that she set her cap for Ataturk and took to riding in the vicinity of his rambling pink palace in hopes of attracting his attention. That ploy failed. But several months later, according to Zsa Zsa, Ataturk entered a state ball in his honor and was drawn to her. She looked up through her long lashes and locked glances with the dictator, an ascetic gray-eyed man wearing impeccable black-tie din-ner clothes. He continued to look at her. The blood rushed to her face, and he sent a functionary to bring Burhan and Madame Belge to the dictatorial table.

There was appropriate romantic music, a waltz with the great one, and Ataturk was hers for the taking.

Ataturk was fifty-seven at the time and in the last year of his life. He had abolished the sultanate of Turkey in 1922 and soon became virtual dictator. He dropped his real name (Mustafa Kemal) in 1934 in favor of Ataturk, which means "father of the Turks." It was no wonder that the cloistered Zsa Zsa spun fantasies about this top Turk. Besides, she was a most unhappy bride. "Burhan left me home with the cook," she recalled. "I found myself trembling at the sound of his key in the door. His moody glances took all of the joy out of me."

She learned to brew thick Turkish coffee and to sit quietly by on the harem cushions.

Legend has it that Ataturk rescued the teenage goddess from languishing to death by summoning her to a private hideaway in Ankara's Old Town where he reclined with a huge water pipe and absorbed Zsa Zsa's charm. She always said that her liaison with the great man lasted for several months, almost up to the day of his unexpected death from a stroke. Told in her autobiography, in a score of newspaper interviews, and on the talk-show circuit, this version has become accepted as fact. In all versions, a shady merchant acted as an intermediary.

It supposedly began one terribly hot afternoon when sensible citizens of Ankara were napping. Zsa Zsa, draped in afternoon chiffon, was dawdling in a shop when a sales clerk appeared and slipped a golden key into her hand. "Someone very important wants to see you," he whispered. An address was given, and Zsa Zsa dashed out the door. Not that week, but several weeks later, she finally took the gold key and kept her appointment with fate.

The door the key opened was discreetly obscure. Inside, in a sumptuous apartment, Zsa Zsa found Ataturk waiting. All her admirer wanted was to be allowed to gaze on her beauty and bathe in her charm and witty conversation.

Though this liaison with Ataturk is impossible to confirm (or deny), Zsa Zsa made one amazing conquest that was well recorded. The quarry this time was a most adroit diplomat—Sir Percy Loren, British ambassador to Turkey. On horseback, Zsa Zsa was out one morning near the Ankara Club. Sir Percy, who looked much like today's James Bond, Roger Moore, reined in his horse and gazed hungrily at the blond Hungarian teenager. Sir Percy was dashing in a khaki riding uniform, with his blond hair tossed by the wind. At first, all he could see of Zsa Zsa was a splash of turquoise velvet and a spill of golden hair. Her head seemed in the clouds, her face a dreamy mask. He thought she was the most gorgeous woman he'd ever seen. She was bowled over as well. "Sometimes, looking at Sir Percy, I blushed to the roots," she remembered. "His face was aflame with desire."

Loren may not have physically consummated the affair, but he willingly became influential in launching Zsa Zsa on the road to international fame. The occasion was Eva's wedding to Eric Drimmer. It was to be honored at a glittering London reception and necessitated a trip across Europe to a city that was faced with imminent war.

Burhan balked at making the trip and refused to let his wife go alone. A few words from Zsa Zsa to Sir Percy, and Burhan received an official invitation from Anthony Eden, the secretary of state of Great Britain. In London, Eden was seemingly as impressed with Zsa Zsa as his friend Sir Percy. He hosted a reception for her that resulted in a social headline the next day, stating that "Mrs. Burhan Belge is the toast of the town."

"For several days, Zsa Zsa literally took over the newspapers," Jolie remembered. "All of this crept into Zsa Zsa's head, and it wasn't long before she had a very grand notion of her own importance and the importance publicity could play in her life."

The macho Burhan was not amused. He couldn't stand the competition and wasn't ready for an emancipated wife. But back in Ankara, Zsa Zsa found a way to occupy her husband, allowing her time (and freedom) to engineer her own escape from his possessive clutches.

Burhan had his heart set on leading a special Turkish mission to Egypt. But he was too far down the Turkish pecking order to be selected. Zsa Zsa, according to all her versions, let a few casual hints drop on one of the lazy afternoons with Ataturk. It was done.

This first nip at power unwittingly created a thirst that drives her today—an aching need to constantly test her own influence, to bring about impossible dreams. "She was never quite the same after," Jolie said.

It was also at this time that Zsa Zsa began displaying her high-strung temperament. Jolie experienced this firsthand when she sent her daughter a Budapest maid whom she, Jolie, had employed for years. "Now, Katie's only twenty-four years old; you *must* treat her very gently." Six months later Katie flew back to Jolie's kindly bosom. "I couldn't even recognize her," Jolie said. "She was pale, skinny, and a nervous wreck. This is a girl who a few months earlier was robust and full of laughter."

Katie burst into tears at the first sight of Jolie. Questioned carefully, she poured out a domestic horror story. She was cracked on the head for slight mistakes and then forced to stay up late to help undress Zsa Zsa and put away her clothes.

"People were right," Jolie mused. "My daughters were growing up to be too difficult—even for me."

Shortly after, Zsa Zsa flew to Budapest for a weekend, and Jolie could tell immediately that something was wrong. Over tea, Zsa Zsa toyed with a smidgen of caviar and said cattily, "Are you not of the opinion that it is *I* who is the actress in the family and *not* Eva? It just does not seem right for my younger sister, who is not an actress, to outshine me."

Jolie's mouth opened in amazement. "You're not going back to Burhan, are you?"

"No, Nuci, this is just a jumping-off place. Ankara is not for me any longer. My first move was to get away from Burhan. So I told him I needed to come back here to nurse you back from an illness. Now I'm going to America."

Zsa Zsa already had an elaborate game plan. Burhan? She would divorce him in America. Money? She had slipped off with a windfall from her husband, plus thousands of dollars' worth of diamonds and rubies.

"How will you get there?" Jolie asked in disbelief.

She answered by gaily waving her diplomatic passport.

With the blackest of misgivings, Jolie saw her daughter off at the train station. She silently wondered if she would ever see her again.

The world, by this time, was at war. Zsa Zsa's journey—by rail, carriage, ship, and at one point in India by pack train—took her four harrowing months. But she was truly frightened only once: when the Simplon Express stopped for an hour layover in Ankara. Had Burhan been tracking her? Would she at any moment be pulled off the train? It was a great relief when the train slowly pulled out into the night. Never again would Zsa Zsa look backward.

"My ambition worried me at night, followed me by day, and spoke to me in an insistent small voice which was never still," said Eva in 1945.

In 1939, Eva looked at her reflection in the mirror of her Hollywood hotel room and, all things considered, liked what she saw. Her hair was platinum blond and piled on top her head like meringue on a pie; her cheekbones were high and rouged; a chic afternoon suit clung to her generous curves. Could this be the next Garbo or Dietrich? Perhaps, Eva thought to herself. Why not?

The summer was a particularly hot one in Southern California, but she chose to ignore it and tossed a ridiculously long mink coat over her suit. Eva had seen an old Joan Crawford film in which the star went to a screen test in a mink coat and became an overnight sensation. What was good enough for Crawford was certainly good enough for a little upstart from Hungary.

Luckily, she already had the mink, a leftover luxury from her Budapest prosperity. The expensive dress, hat, and hairstyle had been wangled on credit. "I was that rare character—a pauper in mink," she later said.

It was in this superfluous finery that Eva headed to Paramount Studios, a screen test, and, she dared hope, certain fame. She was confused about only one thing—the speed at which it was all happening. On Monday she was Mrs. Eric Drimmer, a nobody. On Wednesday she had an agent, a studio, and a career.

She was discovered in typical Hollywood fashion by her own dentist. There she sat with cotton jammed in her cheek, a drill in her molar, and pain exploding in her head. As the drill was finally pulled out, the dentist said, "How would you like to become an actress, my dear?"

She may have been drowsy on Novocain, but her wits were intact. "Yes," she answered with not a trace of reticence.

"Fine," said the dentist. "There's an agent I want you to see."

The next day she stood before one of Hollywood's top flesh peddlers. "He was the original man with the X-ray eyes," Eva said. "I waited patiently for him to tell me what I had eaten for breakfast."

Her wariness, however, was soon overcome when the agent said the honeyed words: "You're going to be a short blond Garbo, a big, big star."

When she reported to a guard at the Paramount Studio gates, the word apparently hadn't worked its way down. "Miss Eva Who?" He blinked at her. "Gabor," Eva said, before beginning to spell it out: "G-a—"

"Okay, lady. You're on Soundstage Five, just up that street and to the right."

Eva had just turned seventeen and, to her horror, looked it. "It was a terrible predicament for an actress." She silently wished for four or five more years—one of the last times a Gabor would ever wish to be older.

In a soundstage office she carelessly draped her mink over a chair, crossed her legs, and feigned boredom. The director of her test escorted her onto the black and empty stage, pointed her generally in the direction of the camera, and then barked commands at her.

Somebody shoved a tattered dress box into her arms. "Now run into the lights, pull out the dress, and show your admiration."

The cameras were turning. Eva stepped across the stage in her tiny heels and waved the dress before her face. "Ooh," she said, followed by an "ah" and an inaudible "how wonderful."

No hint of emotion showed on the director's face. "Slip on the gown, dear," he said impassively.

It was done with a few more "ahs" and a punctuated "oh."

"Now I want you to cry bitterly," the director told her. "A few seconds later, please laugh hysterically."

The crying was easy enough, since Eva was terrified. The laughs came harder and caught in her throat. Finally she managed several isolated cackles.

"I drove out to Paramount prepared to elbow Marlene Dietrich out of the way," Eva recalled. "I came home wondering if I was qualified to be an extra." She waited uneasily by the telephone

"You got a contract, kiddo," the agent told her several days later. "Seventy-five dollars a week and dramatic coaching. You're a lucky girl."

If Eva had known of the pessimistic attitude toward her at Paramount she might have dashed right home to Budapest. When her slapdash screen test was played to a roomful of executives, there was a period of awkward silence as the film unreeled. "Well," said one of them, "she does have a certain personality." "Needs to lose weight," said another. "Let's take her on," said the highest-ranking official. "Sign her up at the lowest level, of course. We can always scrap her in eight months."

So Eva danced through the studio gates ten pounds lighter, $75 richer, and displaying a buoyant courage she didn't feel.

"Don't worry, you'll do fine in your second test," soothed Paramount's drama coach Florence Enright.

"Second test?" Eva groaned. "But I thought—"

Florence interjected, "Honey, it may take half a dozen tests before they really do anything with you. Let's just take things one day at a time."

The next eight months were lonely and austere for the spoiled Eva, full of personal heartbreak and artistic frustration. Her entire world revolved around a tawdry second-rate hotel room and an icy husband who was indifferent to her personal needs and who regarded her career as "blatant foolishness."

"Life had always been something that someone else arranged for me," Eva recalled. "Now for the very first time I was about to meet up with a new type of bill—one that I had to pay for myself."

Her isolation was also fueled by her inadequate command of English. Virtually no one could understand her puzzling but amusing blend of Hungarian Magyar and aristocratic British. One afternoon Eva dashed into a Hollywood drugstore to buy some stamps and ended up being served an ice cream soda. "I don't have any idea how I did it," she told Zsa Zsa. "I thought I said, 'Please give me stamps.' How did that get translated into 'Give me an ice cream soda'?"

The Hollywood that Eva experienced in 1939 was at the very peak of its golden years—never before (or since) equaled in glamour, riches, or in the quality and quantity of its art. For instance, more than 1,200 major films were made in a fourteen-month period, compared to less than 200 today. The average contract actress earned $900 a week, with stars like Marlene Dietrich taking home a $5,000 weekly paycheck. Few other places in America (much less Europe) had a standard of living so high, with more than 75 percent of the film colony earning more than $10,000 a year.

Eva felt like a kid permanently looking in the candy-store window, and the distance between herself and truly successful Europeans such as the German-born Dietrich, Austrian Luise Rainer, and fellow Hungarian Ilona Massey seemed like a yawning chasm.

To break the ice, Eva tossed a gay little dinner party for several expatriates. A package of Budapest delicacies sent by Jolie provided the inspiration. There were truffles and Russian caviar, preserved fruits and tinned salami. The hostess set up the table, arranged a bouquet of flowers, and them soaked luxuriantly in a perfumed bath. Eric, typically, decided to show up late and refused to dress formally. Looking like a million dollars in a new flowing dress, Eva glided into the kitchen. "I opened the first tin—it was rotten. Then the second —it was moldy. It was the same with all twenty cans."

Her slapdash menu that night was bacon and eggs, the staple of many another American housewife in culinary trouble. "But at least I suddenly felt less Hungarian and more American."

The next day she embarked on a crash program to improve her English. Every free afternoon and on all weekends Eva bought a ticket to one of Hollywood's movie palaces and sat through double features again and again to absorb the language. One evening she came home speaking like Norma Shearer, the next like John Wayne. But it worked. By the time of her second screen test, she could speak flat Kansan or chambermaid British with the best of them. So Americanized was her speech that later, when cast as a Hungarian or Austrian, she had to fake the accent.

In her second test she was reading for a real part, that of the ingenue in a Ronald Colman film, *My Life with Caroline.* Rumors spread about this test. If it went well, gossip had it, Eva Gabor would be granted an expensive contract and groomed for stardom.

Eva sensed the excitement the minute she reported to the set. Hairdressers and makeup men fussed over her. The director was solicitous and chatty. British character actor Reginald Gardiner, already set for *My Life with Caroline,* would himself appear opposite her in the test (an enormous concession), and Colman watched from the shadows.

An elaborate staircase set had been erected and carefully lighted with spots to outline Eva's delicate blond beauty. She was told to drift down it joyously and greet Gardiner, who was playing her husband returning from the wars.

"Eva, he'll tell you that he wants to leave," said the director. "It will be completely devastating to you. You fall apart."

He walked off but called over his shoulder, "We'd like to see real tears, Eva."

She looked at him shyly, shot a glance toward Ronald Colman's serious face, and then started down the stairs. Reginald Gardiner spoke his several lines. Eva looked stricken and then panicked. Real tears flooded down her cheeks. "Smashing, darling, smashing," Reginald whispered. From the director she got a dazzling smile.

Late that night in the Paramount processing laboratory the test film rolled slowly up into the range of a viewer. "Christ, who's this?" said one of the editors. "She's an amazing beauty." And the image was extraordinary. Eva was one of those rare translucent beauties whose face reflected its own glow, much in the manner of Lana Turner. At first it seemed as if the studio had a new star on its hands.

Eva drove home with her head in the clouds, intoxicated by her first taste of Hollywood success. She was to be, they all told her, as important to the 1940s as Greta Garbo was to the '30s. Two days later, Paramount generally and Ronald Colman specifically were shocked when Eva's test was shown on the big screen. Her performance was strong, her voice flawless, but she photographed far too young. From some angles she looked sixteen.

Knowing what the studio had planned for her, Eva was bitter and remained so for more than a decade. "If I hadn't photographed too young I would have become a big star. They had the contract already written," she said years later.

As it was, the studio agreed to renew her old contract, nothing more. But a sympathetic director consoled her with a part in a forgettable Mary Martin picture, *New York Town.* Dressed as an exquisite nurse by Edith Head, Eva dashed out onto the set to give a performance just short of Florence Nightingale's. "What are *you* doing here?" bellowed the assistant director in charge of the scene. "You look too young to be a nurse."

He turned to the casting agent. "Replace her." This in turn caused Eva to cry as only a Gabor can cry. Her voice came out in gasping wails. If he had horse-whipped her, he couldn't have created a more pitiful scene. "Please, darling," the assistant director pleaded. "If you quit crying, I promise we'll find you another part."

The sobs dwindled into a pout.

A little vignette involving horseshoes was written into *New York Town,* mainly as a gesture to the ambitious Eva. She was to flirt shyly with Robert Preston and then make a toss at the ring. "Eva," said the director, "I'd like you to miss the ring in a demure and ladylike manner."

She nodded, sober with concentration. Then she wound up and pitched a ringer.

"Cut," yelled the director. "Eva, darling, did you understand what I said?"

"Yes, I'm sorry. I'll miss this time, I promise." She leaned back against Robert Preston, fumbled a second with her horseshoe, and tossed another ringer. The director, with the production crew working at about $500 a minute, was about to explode when he had an inspiration. "This time, Eva dear, aim *directly* at the stake and we'll see what happens."

This time she missed by a mile. "That was quite good, honey," the director said.

New York Town was quickly followed by another grade B picture, *Forced Landing,* after which the actress was dropped by Paramount.

After this, Eva entered that Hollywood twilight zone known so affectionately as "between pictures," meaning that she couldn't get a job, not so much as a walk-on.

In addition, her marriage to Eric was on the rocks, partially because of their precarious financial situation. They were barely making it week to week. Eva was totally broke for the first time in her life, and she bitterly sold her small and rusting car, legalized her separation, and bought a train ticket for New York.

Arriving there to greet the just-arrived Zsa Zsa, Eva ironically found a fistful of telegrams asking her back to the film capital. One informed her that supermogul David O. Selznick, flush from his *Gone With the Wind* success, was obsessed with testing her.

She rushed back, only to find that Selznick "wasn't in" to her calls. Twentieth Century–Fox, however, offered her another screen test, liked what they saw, and sent her off to the studio drama school. Then they let her sit—taking charm lessons and rehearsing classic dramatic scenes—for about four months before offering her anything. Finally she was cast as a lady-in-waiting to Tallulah Bankhead's Catherine the Great in *A Royal Scandal.* And though Eva had only a few lines, Tallullah, at least, was impressed.

The star walked over to the film's director, Ernst Lubitsch, one afternoon. "You watch the girl. She's going to be a big star. I should think you could find more to do with her in this picture." The director nodded silently and took an immediate interest in Eva. He even tried, unsuccessfully, to build up her part. "Forget it," the studio told him. "All she's good for is window dressing." The juicy ingenue part in the same film went to Anne Baxter.

A much-annoyed Tallulah invited Eva to her dressing room for cocktails. "Darling, you belong on stage. Get out of this dump and head for Broadway. In New York they know what to do with talent."

But Eva was stuck with a year-long contract with the indifferent Twentieth Century–Fox, so she sat waiting for a casting call. It was seven months before it came, and again she was relegated to a pot-boiler, *The Wife of Monte Cristo,* followed by the equally undistinguished *Song of Surrender.* "All these roles got me halfway to nowhere. I just couldn't get a real part," Eva remembered. "And the waiting drove me nuts."

She finally began taking stage roles in some ramshackle productions staged in Hollywood. And one fated week she was part of a troupe that presented *The Affairs of Anatol* for the Hollywood USO. (The war was well under way by this time.) It was there, over coffee and doughnuts, that she later met the man who would raise her from poverty and give her the security that would eventually steer her toward stardom.

Her marriage to Eric was finally ending. According to Jolie it was Eva's ambition that killed the marriage. But in her divorce action, Eva claimed she wanted to settle down and have children, while Eric insisted that she continue working as an actress.

Dressed in an outlandish hat and veil that topped a high-fashion suit, Eva pleaded her case in divorce court. "He literally drove me into the life of a film actress," she said, clenching a lace handkerchief and dabbing at her eyes. She gave her finest performance to date. "Your honor, I wanted to raise a family, to have babies. But my husband didn't agree with me. He even objected to my having friends on my own. I had to have something to do—some kind of work. That's the only reason why I became an actress in films."

"What does your husband do?" Judge Gee Clark asked.

"He's a doctor," she replied. "And, believe me, he always treated me like one of his cases."

Judge Clark was most impressed and granted the decree to end the marriage.

Privately Eva told Jolie that there "was no way I could live in Hollywood and not become an actress. I caught the fever like thousands of others who come here. It became the most important thing in the world to me."

Whatever the original motivation, Eva was firmly committed to acting. After the divorce, she moved into a fairly presentable single apartment, went to more casting calls, and worked at the USO.

The Hollywood USO during the war was a mecca for exciting, glamorous women, dashing servicemen, and big-band entertainment. Hollywood social life switched from watering holes like Ciro's and the

Mocambo to the small USO ballroom, where the strongest drink was coffee and the most exotic menu item was powdered-sugar doughnuts. With most of America's eligible men in the service, it was just as easy to meet a millionaire in the USO as anywhere.

One Saturday night Charles Isaacs walked out of the ballroom crowd and swept Eva off her feet. Her prince had finally come. He was tall and muscular; his prematurely gray hair was turned white by the sun; and a white Coast Guardsman's uniform contrasted dramatically with his deep tan. As he walked toward the long line of USO volunteers, the women began whispering about his devastating looks. Then they moved aside as he passed through them and strode over to a buffet table where Eva was pouring coffee.

She looked up into his eyes and flushed slightly. Her hands trembled. Later she said, "He was simply the most appealing man I'd ever seen. I was drawn to him immediately."

"Hi, I'm Charles Isaacs," he said. She held out her hand: "Eva Gabor." "Like to dance? he said with an incline of the head. She walked into his arms. "Ah, but he was resplendent in his uniform," Eva wrote Jolie. "I should have locked myself immediately in the cellar, but sometimes being weak is lots of fun." There was a brief courtship and then the wedding.

Without consciously thinking about it, Eva had married a millionaire. He fit perfectly Jolie's prescription for a son-in-law. He was young enough, rich enough, and loving enough to make her daughter happy.

"Talk about your change of fortune," Eva remembered. "There I was, a girl who had learned to worry about fifty cents, suddenly the wife of a man to whom small change was a petty annoyance like stuck zippers. Charles was rich—very rich."

A real estate millionaire, Charles came equipped with a mansion, servants, and ready-made social ties in Beverly Hills. Movieland's great and famous, out of her reach before, now came regularly to her weekend gatherings. As she and her sisters would do again and again, Eva fell into the arms of a lover and landed in the wealthiest of fast lanes.

She recalled one particularly triumphant evening when Selznick's protégée and future wife, Jennifer Jones, the year's Academy Award winner and one of the hottest talents in Hollywood, walked up to her, chattily took her arm, and indulged in girl talk. "People who would slam the office door in my face were happy to come to my house as guests. That was the essence of Hollywood in those days—so many users."

On the first anniversary of the marriage, Charles and Eva set up tables and chairs under sparkling lights in their garden. And anyone who *was* anyone in Beverly Hills lined up to pass through the receiving line.

Hedda Hopper told millions of readers that "Eva and Charles are divinely in love—a rarity in this town of heartbreak and frequent divorce."

Eva, however, remained a driven woman. She wanted stardom more than domestic happiness, and she couldn't shake this albatross from her neck. If she couldn't make it in Hollywood, she would make it on Broadway. So she picked a quiet night to tell her adoring husband that she was going to New York. "Anything you want, darling," he said sadly. "Come back when you can."

"When I went to New York, I left my marriage behind me," Eva said.

She had closed another door.

5

❋ Heroine

*M*agda pulled a nondescript gray coat around her shoulders and slipped quietly down the stairs of an elegant apartment in Budapest. It was just after dawn, but she needed each of the precious minutes before the big city came to life.

On this rainy November morning in 1943, Europe was in flames; Hungary, still an Axis ally, was being threatened by the approaching Red Army. But Budapest, with its lush suburbs and riverside forests, remained a stranger to the violence and death that eddied around it.

Twice Nazi armies had crossed Hungary—first to Poland and then to Russia—and the thought of the Gestapo agents billeted on the outskirts of the city made Magda shudder.

She had a rough cap over her flaming red hair, so that she was almost indistinguishable from the truck drivers and wholesale produce men stirring on the deserted streets. Her face was free of makeup and the famous hourglass figure was bundled in a heavy sweater thrown over a flannel shirt. The deubtantes and socialites of her high-flying set would have gasped in horror at the visage she presented in the truck's rearview mirror, and this made her smile.

To those who knew her socially, and even to her own sisters, Magda was the last person one would expect to join the Hungarian underground. It was such a secret, in fact, that only Jolie knew of her daughter's clandestine activities.

The residents of her apartment building knew only that she was a driver for the International Red Cross, armed with a permit to help wounded Polish soldiers interned by the Nazis outside the capital city. In any case, she always sneaked back to her flat by mid-morning, when Budapest socialites had just been awakened by their maids for lazy breakfasts in bed.

Shrouded in early-morning fog, several other drivers—well known to her—nodded silent greetings as her truck left the secure confines of the city and headed into the darkness of the surburban forests. It took only a few minutes to leave the medieval town gates and plunge into the foothills, but it was a dangerous transition. Outside the gates was military territory where a car could be stopped and its passengers machine-gunned merely because they looked suspicious.

The destination was always the same—a prisoner of war camp hidden by trees and sealed off from civilization by SS guards in full black battle dress.

Sometimes the Nazi officers flirted with Magda, calling out to her in German and laughingly pelting her with lewd propositions.

And it was good the guards were diverted. Crammed into the van were bundles of neat, clean civilian clothes rummaged from the attics and closets of underground members. Quickly and right under the noses of the POW guards, Magda traded the clothes for Polish and occasional Austrian uniforms, which she rushed back to town where the telltale evidence was burned.

The old clothes rescued an estimated 5,000 soldiers who, out of uniform, made it out of Hungary and across the continent to Britain. In very extreme cases, badly wounded soldiers were smuggled under a false truck floor and ferried to neutral Portugal.

The return trips back through the heart of the city were the most dangerous. Since it was later in the morning, the route was cluttered with police and Hungarian soldiers loyal to the Nazis who blocked the streets with stop-and-search parties.

Magda was ready for them with the highest priority Red Cross permit signed by the Portuguese Ambassador, Dr. Carlos de Sampayo Garrido—one of the few influential diplomats left in the country and Magda's lover since 1941.

The affair, which would eventually save not only Magda but Jolie and Vilmos as well from certain death at the hands of the Nazis, began in typical Gabor style. There was the locking of glances in a crowd, the dazzle of a white Parisian gown, and the lure of forbidden fruit.

It started at the Ritz Hotel in London, where Magda was living with her husband of two years, the Count Jan de Bichovsky of Poland. And, also typically, she was bored to death with him.

The marriage had gone swimmingly for a while. The Count was tall, broad-shouldered, and thick with muscles from years of service in the Polish Light Cavalry. He was the sort of aristocrat Magda had always dreamed of marrying, the sort that populated hundreds of romance novels.

And it was nice, for a while, to be addressed as the Countess of Warsaw and to traipse around the grounds of an enormous Polish estate.

It wasn't long before Magda was hit with the Gabor curse—that brand of ceaseless sexual wandering that would eventually brand Zsa Zsa as a modern courtesan in the tradition of Madame de Pompadour and the Countesse Du Barry.

So her heart was already straying when her eyes caught those of Carlos de Sampayo in the Ritz Hotel ballroom. In those days Magda was thought of quite naturally as the most beautiful and regal of the Gabor sisters. Her hair was autumn red, her eyes were dark and flashing, and her skin was a contrasting white. To quote her father: "Magda, in her twenties, took your breath away. When she walked into a room, men had eyes for nobody else."

Carlos, already ambassador to Hungary from Portugal, fell under her spell at once. She was moving through the crowd in an elaborate ball gown when he caught her eye, and they moved toward each other. The days were numbered for Magda's handsome Count.

"Perhaps it was fated," remembered Jolie. "First Poland fell. Then the Count joined the free forces in Britain, and Magda rushed home. It had been only a matter of months when she tired of him. What happened I really don't know. He simply disappeared out of our lives, and who appeared in his place was the Portuguese Ambassador. . . . I said to her, 'Magda, who is this man?' And she answered, 'He has asked me to be his secretary.'"

Jolie's eyebrows raised only at the new suitor's age, which at the time he met Magda was the mid-sixties, several decades older than Jolie herself. On all other counts he was highly eligible. A man of considerable wealth and polish, Carlos was a diplomat of the old morning coat and gray spats school.

Even better, he was a rare liberal in a radical Europe—a man willing to overlook the trace of Jewish blood that Jolie had brought to her marriage with Vilmos Gabor. Dr. Garrido was himself the target of Nazi censure, and Hitler had already put considerable pressure on the government of Portugal to recall him and send a pro-Fascist diplomat to Hungary—a country that grew more crucial to Germany every day.

"They tried many, many times to recall him," said Jolie. "But for many reasons the Portuguese government stood behind him."

It was Magda's love for Carlos that drew her into the web of Hungary's underground. Over lunch in his suite at the Portuguese embassy in Budapest, he took her hand and asked quietly for her help. "Magda, I'm sick. I've a heart condition that could kill me at any moment. Stay here and help me; work with me to break the Nazi codes."

Magda nodded her assent, and within a few weeks was up to her beautiful neck in espionage and counterespionage. She committed to memory the secret Portuguese ciphers used to communicate with the floundering pockets of freedom surviving in Europe.

And Carlos entrusted her with seven glass vials from Switzerland. "If you see me collapse on the floor or in a chair, break off the top of one of these and pour the contents immediately in my mouth. You must do it within two minutes."

Carlos had become a powerful man in Hungary after Pearl Harbor, when all the Allied embassies closed. The Portuguese embassy in downtown Budapest and its summer villa outside of the city were virtually the only contacts with a neutral country in Western Europe.

Jolie had ignored blunt warnings from Zsa Zsa's husband, the Turkish diplomat Burhan Belge. In early 1939 he had told her, "Jolie, war is going to break out everywhere. Get out of here. Go to America. Go to Mexico. But get out of here."

She dismissed his suggestion with a toss of her ash-blond hair. "I'm not political. What has Hitler to do with me? I see no reason to leave my friends or family."

Burhan became more insistent. "Jolie, this is only the beginning. All Europe will burn. Hungary will be engulfed. All the Jewish intellectuals will be massacred by the Nazis, and the Christian elite will be murdered by the Soviets."

Jolie watched him leave shaking his head as she settled back on the luxurious Oriental divan that dominated her living room. Her closets bulged with Parisian clothes; her jewel boxes sparkled with gold and diamonds; and important friends came and went on an endless social merry-go-round.

"Mama, still as beautiful as ever, was having fifteen people to a sit-down dinner that night, and I could not see what I possibly had to fear," Jolie reminisced. "We all threw caution to the winds."

The fragility of the Gabors' position was underscored when Jolie dashed by express train to Leipzig to buy jewelry for her two stores. As the train crossed the border into Nazi territory, she noticed that the porters and conductors were replaced with uniformed attendants —most of whom were brash and rude.

She arrived in Leipzig at nine P.M. to find the streets filled with brown-shirted troopers marching to drums and hundreds of gas lanterns. They chanted over and over: "Death to the Jews! Death to the Jews!"

In just a few minutes Jolie Gabor understood what was to come in Hungary—a purge and a bloodletting unequaled since the pogroms of the Middle Ages. "I shuddered and ran stumbling to my hotel room," she said. "I never went to Germany again."

But the experience failed to jar her out of the comfort and familiarity of Budapest. Her Auntie Mamish character made her persevere and linger in the Old World like so many thousands of others. Unlike them, Jolie would have a second chance.

She stayed partly because her immediate family drew together to shut out the cold smell of fear. Every Tuesday from 1942 to late 1943, a member of her family (usually her mother or brother) gave a cozy dinner party for the rest. "It was gossip and non-stop gaiety as usual," Jolie remembered. "We gossiped and bragged about our children. Naturally, I had the most to say, since Eva and Zsa Zsa were successful in America and Magda was the consort of the most powerful man in Hungary. I put them all to shame."

Outside, the curtain was coming down forever on a free Hungary. The country was ripe for Nazi exploitation, as Germany was fast losing ground in Eastern Europe. Nazi generals decided that Hungary, fully occupied and armed, could become a buffer against the Red Army.

As early as 1938 the Hungarian government, controlled by a weak regent, had passed the first law against the Jews, but it was largely a token gesture. In February of 1939 the government, by then courting Hitler, passed anti-Semitic regulations with real bite in them. In reaction, more than ten thousand Jews emigrated in less than six weeks.

Hitler called the Regent, Admiral Miklos Horthy, to Germany and harangued him into opening the door for the growing Fascist movement within the country itself. When the Horthy-appointed Prime Minister, Count Istvan Csaky, resisted, the Nazis uncovered records to prove that he had a Jewish great-grandfather. He was hounded from office by the token laws he had written himself.

After the Russo-German war erupted in 1941, the German dictator's agents forced the Hungarian government to mobilize all its available strength to fight on the Russian front, and in some cases even the Budapest police department was raided of manpower. "Soon you will not need police," said Heinrich Himmler to Admiral Horthy. "The Gestapo will take care of all that for you."

Month after month rolled by. "And Burhan's prophecy was coming true," said Jolie. "All Europe was burning."

In February of 1944 war finally came to Budapest. At two A.M. American bombs began falling less than a mile from Jolie's apartment and almost directly behind the Portuguese embassy, where Magda usually spent the night. Jolie was jolted out of her sleep by the whistling followed by deep rumbles as the bombs tore into gardens, theaters, and centuries-old villas. She said to herself, "They won't land here. They won't land here."

Finally the Nazis began marching into the city, moving stealthily from block to block and house to house. Jolie's phone rang shortly after dusk, and a friend on the outskirts of the city told her of the quiet invasion. "They took the city without even a wail of protest and without firing a shot. Budapest seemed to wilt with sadness," she was later to write.

But this sadness failed to put a dent in Jolie's life. The night before the German occupation she gave a dazzling dinner party for her entire extended family. "Everybody was there. The conversation was brilliant, and the lights sparkled until dawn. There was nothing to spoil the mood," she recalled. "Of course, Hungary had gotten by for so long without being affected by the war that we kept our happy little heads buried in the sand."

Soon, though, even she couldn't miss the signs of terror. One evening, dressed in her furs and a new silver dress, Jolie motored into Budapest's downtown section for an evening at the Arizona Club, the city's chicest nightspot. She found the doors boarded up and a warning nailed outside by the Nazis. "Warning. Do Not Enter," said the sign. "This club is closed permanently on orders of the Gestapo."

The club, it seems, had been a hangout for the Jewish aristocracy and the country's liberal elite. Gossip soon filled Jolie in on what had happened. "One night Gestapo officers broke through the front door with machine guns," she said. "They told the owners and their guests that, in exchange for their jewels and money, the Gestapo would fly them out to safety in Switzerland. When the plane was in the air over Austria, all of the passengers were shoved out the door."

Several days later, a thousand of Hungary's Jewish lawyers (including Jolie's own barrister) were herded out of their beds, marched to the banks of the Duna River, and shot.

"Everybody was afraid," Jolie recalled. "Nobody could trust anybody, and there was no food, no water. Things were pitiful—even for the rich."

On a Tuesday evening in April of 1944 Jolie's family got together for the last time. It was business as usual—except for Jolie. She had finally realized that an end of some sort was near for all of them. Her conversation lagged and she grew tipsy, grabbing full champagne glasses from her brother and mother and emptying them. "What are you doing?" her mother asked. Tears came to Jolie's eyes. "This might be the very last time we will see each other, the very last time we can be together like this." The prophecy was correct. "It is over thirty years ago," she remembered. "And I can still close my eyes and see myself drinking all that champagne."

On a Sunday morning about two weeks later her world caved in on her. Carlos, fearful that Magda would be snatched out of her bed by the Gestapo, spent thousands of dollars on informants inside Gestapo headquarters so that he could learn in advance of any menace to the Gabors. Finally, a plain white envelope was pushed through the door of the Portuguese embassy. "Dr. Garrido," it said, "Magda Gabor Bichovsky's name has been added to the internment list. She will be arrested within twenty-four hours."

With only about twelve precious hours left, Carlos sent the embassy car with its armed guard and bulletproof glass to collect Magda at her apartment. It was 7:55 A.M., and Magda, awakened by her front doorbell, ran to the window and opened the curtains. "I saw the embassy car with the Portuguese flag flying," she told Zsa Zsa. "I had suspected that my time was up."

She did not suspect, however, that the Gestapo was already massed in barracks and empty warehouses awaiting the order to arrest dissidents, underground members, and prominent citizens with Jewish blood. Magda qualified on all three counts.

Her fur coat had been pulled over her nightdress by the time she answered the door. Carlos' driver, his face ashen with fear, faced her. "The Ambassador says you must come to the embassy now," he said. She dashed back in, pulled on a dress, grabbed a bag of jewels, and rushed out to the car. The driver locked the doors of the limo and urged Magda to sink down into the seat out of sight.

Carlos was waiting for her at the embassy. "The Germans are going to begin arresting members of the underground in several hours. They begin at about four P.M., but nobody knows about it yet. You must move in here and stay here. It's the only place you can be safe."

"My parents," gasped Magda.

Carlos nodded to the driver and told him to drive once more into the city's old quarter to collect the elder Gabors. "Come right back," he ordered. "I don't believe we're safe even here at the embassy. We'll move to my country villa in Galgagyork." Galgagyork was a Budapest suburb about thirty miles from the center of the city. The Portuguese embassy's villa was a seventeenth-century castle set on ten acres of forest and gardens. More crucially, it was adjacent to hidden pockets of Hungarian underground partisans.

When Magda reached her mother's apartment, Jolie at first refused even to see her. A maid bustled about the front hall, making hurried excuses for her mistress. "Never mind," said Magda. "I'm going in."

"Magda, get out of here and leave me alone. You *know* I don't like to be disturbed this early in the morning."

Jolie was enthroned, Gabor-fashion, in an enormous velvet-curtained bed and wore a Belgian lace nightdress. Thick sweet coffee had been poured for her on a side table, and fresh yellow roses decorated her makeup table.

"For God's sake, Mama, come with me right now. I'm not prepared to argue with you. Just get out of that bed and put some clothes on."

"To do what?" Jolie asked petulantly.

"To save your life—and Papa's," Magda snapped back.

"Oh, really, dear, aren't you overdoing it? I'll be fine. Besides, I have a luncheon date at the Hungaria."

"Listen to me," Magda continued. "The Germans are rounding up everyone with Jewish blood and everybody who has helped the underground in even a small way. Do I have to tell you what that means?"

"Oh, they won't bother me," Jolie answered. "Now get out of here and let me go to my luncheon."

Finally Magda shoved her mother out of the bed, made her dress and pack a few essentials, and got her into the car. Vilmos was less resistant and silently accompanied his daughter to the limousine.

When the limo pulled into the courtyard of the embassy villa, the Gabors found the mansion bustling with temporary refugees—professionals, underground leaders, and quite a few aristocratic Jews. Magda and her family, however, were given preferential treatment—a bedroom of their own. Magda, of course, shared night quarters with Carlos. But Jolie, who had been divorced from Vilmos for several years, created a scene when she realized that the one bed in the suite was to host both her and Vilmos.

"Dr. Garrido," she complained. "I'm divorced from this man. How can you order me to sleep with him?"

"Madame, for the time being. This is war, after all."

Jolie pulled herself up with great dignity and nodded. "For the time being . . . for the time being."

Later she admitted to her daughters that she and Vilmos renewed sexual relations that very night. "If it was good once, why not again?" She smiled.

By nightfall more than seventy persons were jammed into the embassy villa, which resembled a calm island in the riptides of confusion that stirred around it.

"We listened to the radio day and night," said Jolie. "And this became our only contact with the outside world. We walked in the garden, of course, and pined for gossip from the outside, no matter how terrible the subject."

For a few weeks late that spring the clouds of war disappeared with the warm sun of the lower Danube River. Acres of golden jonquils, purple crocuses, and scarlet tulips blazed around the garden paths at Galgagyork. Afternoon tea was served outdoors to men in dress clothes and women in afternoon gowns. "If time could have stopped right there," Jolie remembered, "my memories of Europe would have been so nostalgic rather than the terrible nightmares I often have. But doom was only around the corner."

Even Carlos was lulled into a false sense of security. It seemed as if the Nazis, after all, had forgotten about Magda's dangerous connections with the underground movement. The Ambassador let down his guard, and security measures were relaxed.

Thus an armed Portuguese guard was asleep at the gate when fourteen terrorists—clothed in black and disguised by bandit masks—forced their way into the villa and herded the residents into an upstairs ballroom. They pointed machine guns at the crowd: "Go to your rooms and bring back all your jewelry and money. Get back here within a minute or we will start shooting hostages."

Jolie, with her hair in disarray and a pink velvet robe thrown over her nightgown, ran to the room, grabbed her jewels, and then literally threw them at the bandits.

Less than five minutes later they were gone. Jolie and Vilmos had just returned to their bed when a commotion and screams were again heard in the hall. This time Nazi stormtroopers—partly in and partly out of uniform—leveled chillingly familiar machine guns at the crowd. "We heard there was an armed robbery here, and we came to help get your jewels and money back," said one of the men, shifting uneasily on his feet.

Jolie's eyes strayed to the floor, and she had to strangle a scream that was rising in her throat. She recognized three pairs of scuffed boots. They had been worn by the black-masked terrorists who had just menaced them in the ballroom.

Jolie lifted her face and saw two of the men take Magda by the arm. "We're just taking you to police headquarters, where all this will be cleared up," said one of the soldiers.

She thought to herself, This is it. This is the end of your life, Jolie. Prepare yourself.

This was the first step toward the death camps still operating in Nazi-occupied Poland. First the SS and Gestapo agents lured victims from the safety of the legation. Then they were taken to the captive Hungarian state police headquarters, and from there to cattle cars headed for Auschwitz. Others were shot immediately on the outskirts of town.

The troopers, obviously outnumbered by the refugees, backed off toward the hall, allowing their captives to sneak back to bed. They obviously had thought better of it. However, four of them followed Magda to her room. "Magda Gabor Bichovsky, we must take you in for questioning."

Magda didn't answer.

"We can use force," said one of the men.

"I'll be out in a minute," she answered.

Before Magda could close her door, Jolie came out into the hall dragging Vilmos by one arm. "If you take her, you take us," she yelled at the man. "We are her parents."

"Fine with us," said the trooper.

Wearing only nightclothes, Magda, Jolie, and Vilmos were escorted down to the main floor, where the Portuguese Ambassador had been working through the night. The lights were blazing in his open office as the Gabors were herded past.

Magda gasped as she saw his unconscious body on the floor. At first she thought he had been shot. Then she saw his hands move as his lips tried to form a word. "Let me go in. I have to help him. I'm the only one who can administer his medicine."

She pulled herself free from the Nazi agent and pulled one of the medicine vials out of her purse. She snapped the top off on the edge of the desk and poured the contents down Carlos' constricted throat.

Several minutes later he drifted back to consciousness. "Magda, stay right here until I get my strength. I must go to Budapest with you, or they'll ship all of you off to one of the death camps."

He pulled himself up onto a chair and faced the policeman. "If you are to take these people, then you take me. They are officially under the protection of the Portuguese government." The Ambassador held up his hands so the Gestapo officer could bind them with handcuffs. Flustered, the officer lowered his eyes and refused.

But a Gestapo captain nodded, and they pulled Carlos into the grim procession.

Outside, a battered Budapest police car waited. The captain, obviously infuriated that he had been forced to take the Ambassador along, grabbed Vilmos, Jolie, and Magda, forcing them into the car's back seat. He obviously intended to keep Carlos out.

Magda was quicker than that. She stuck a leg out the car door, dug her foot into the roadway gravel, and prevented the sedan's door from closing until Carlos was able to force his way inside.

Later, from the luxury of Portugal, Magda wrote Zsa Zsa: "I don't know what strength God gives to people in danger. But I didn't think. I just stuck my leg in and let him slam it until it was bloody and half crushed. I almost fainted from the pain, but I never let go."

Carlos emitted a sputter of indignity and hate, causing the Gestapo captain to raise his fist against the Ambassador. He thought better, though, and dropped his hand.

"We had gone about ten miles when the car halted, and, to our astonishment, the Gestapo men leaped out and disappeared into the fields," Magda recalled. "Then we realized that we had been followed by Hungarian police." Police during that era were almost to a man loyal to the Nazis.

At the police station, Jolie became hysterical when Magda was taken into another room for questioning. Carlos comfortingly offered her an arm and then played his final card. Having tricked the troopers into arresting him, the Ambassador now demanded his single telephone call. Then, using a code name known in diplomatic circles, he was put directly through to the Nazi Ambassador to Hungary. Carlos spoke two or three quiet sentences and hung up.

Within fifteen minutes the Hungarian Foreign Minister (in the Nazi puppet government) phoned the officer in charge of the police department's graveyard shift. The underling's face turned red, Magda was quickly brought back to her parents, and the cuffs were removed.

"You are free to go, Your Excellency," the officer stammered.

"I'll go only if these three—all Portuguese citizens—are allowed to go with me." The police were defeated.

"Please accept our car for the return trip," the official mumbled.

"Absolutely not," Carlos said. "I want everyone to see the way diplomatic officers are treated here. I want everybody to know."

The trek on foot back to the outskirts of town, where the party was met by Carlos' chauffeur, took the better part of a day. When the party finally collapsed into their beds it was six P.M.

"Somehow we made it," whispered Jolie to her daughter. Magda nodded her head in silent agreement, realizing that the Gestapo would come again—this time better prepared. The second time they wouldn't go back empty-handed.

Carlos agreed. "None of us are safe now. It's time to get out."

They learned later how lucky they had been.

Magda took Carlos' hand. "This is full payment, my dear, for everything I have done for the Allied countries and for the underground. From this moment on, I'm Portuguese. You have given me the gift of life."

6

✳ Mrs. Conrad Hilton

*H*er sleek leg emerged slowly from the limousine. The doorman extended his arm, and there was a glimpse of an extraordinary satin gown. As she stepped gracefully toward the door, a sudden gust of wind caught her blond hair and swept it backwards. Diamonds had been tossed carelessly at her neck and wrists, almost as if they had been an afterthought. The lady paused at the door for carefully calculated seconds before sweeping into Ciros's, the crown jewel of Hollywood's Sunset Strip.

"Jesus Christ, who is that?" asked a young actor in dinner dress. Paul, the club's maitre d', whispered back, "That's Eva Gabor's sister. 'Sari,' they call her."

"Married?" the actor queried.

Paul lowered his eyelids suggestively. "Divorced and hunting."

Zsa Zsa had knocked Hollywood over with her delicate beauty. Louella Parsons and Hedda Hopper had already featured her in their gossip columns—a rarity for a non-actress. And a battery of screen tests had been suggested but tactfully declined.

Zsa Zsa was after far bigger game. After taking a peek at Eva's paltry salary, she decided that life as a Hollywood actress provided too lean a budget, even if you became a star.

So when she gazed out over the crowd at Ciro's, she was definitely window-shopping—a sort of last look at what the city had to offer before trying the somewhat greener fields of Manhattan or Palm Beach. The crowd was awash with vacant-faced, too pretty actors. She was about to shrug off another evening when she saw him.

He towered above those gathered around him so that he seemed like Gulliver surrounded by the Lilliputians. His eyes were piercing in a rugged face, and his too roomy suit couldn't hide the power of his shoulders. His long legs were shod in cowboy boots.

Here, at last, Zsa Zsa thought, was the American man she had fantasized about, looking not unlike Tom Mix or William S. Hart, cowboy stars who'd impressed her back in Budapest.

Conrad Hilton had seen her also. Their eyes locked for several silent seconds. He thought she was the most beautiful woman he'd ever seen, with a finely drawn face that could have graced a cameo from Pompeii.

Zsa Zsa whispered in her escort's ear, "Who's that?"

"Conrad Hilton, the hotel man."

She pouted a little. A hotel man. Why couldn't he be a diplomat or a politician?

"But, honey, this is the biggest hotel man in the world."

Now that woke her up! Raised to bag important men, the Gabor sisters possessed the Continental training that allowed them to snare a man before he knew what hit him.

Since Conrad Hilton was essentially "hers" before the evening was over, Hollywood observers would later try to put the jigsaw puzzle together from what they had seen or bits of conversation they'd overheard.

There were those, of course, who said that it was love at first sight. The Hollywood heavens parted! An orchestra played "Love Walked In," and Zsa Zsa immediately conquered one of the world's richest men.

Some were far less kind. Columnist Sheilah Graham, for instance, acidly agreed that it was, indeed, love at first sight—at Zsa Zsa's first sight of the Hilton wallet.

Still others noted that Conrad—at fifty-four and a divorcé of some years—was already adrift in the nubile Hollywood glamour pool and just naturally tumbled into the arms of the town's most sensational eighteen-year-old.

Conveniently for history and for Zsa Zsa, Conrad was surrounded at his table by three gloriously empty chairs. Zsa Zsa got her escort settled into one, conveniently placed a beautiful girlfriend in another, and then slid naturally down by Connie.

Up close she found him even more dynamic than she had first thought. Oh God, if I could only get him to a tailor, she said to herself.

Connie was instantly on his feet to help with the Gabor chair. "Evening, ma'am," he said. Zsa Zsa merely smiled.

After he danced with her and they chatted over champagne, Zsa Zsa leaned over and whispered, "You just may be the man I'm going to marry." As impossibly foolish as this sounds, it's wise to remember that the improbable words came from a teenager who had drenched herself with romantic fantasies ever since she could read. She had been waiting for a knight on a white charger all her life.

Later, Conrad admitted that Zsa Zsa had most certainly made the naive proposal. "And I answered back, 'Well, ma'am, why don't you just do that."

Zsa Zsa silently appraised his physical assets, approving of them instantly. He was tall, older, domineering—all the things a young girl whose father had been somewhat cold and distant to her would want. "He looked like a very rich cowboy," she told Eva later that night. "Or a beautifully dressed Uncle Sam." Whatever, he looked like he belonged in the Gabor family.

Remembering the meeting and the four-month courtship years later, Connie said, "I had already heard of her. Who in Hollywood hadn't? When she sat down beside me at the party, she was a blond bewitching charmer—just off the boat from Europe. Seated next to me, she suddenly did those fascinating tricks Continental women do with their eyes. At first, I thought it was just a joke," Conrad related. "By that time I was a settled, confirmed bachelor to whom remarriage from a Catholic's standpoint was forbidden." Divorced from the first Mrs. Hilton after prolonged personal crises, Connie was often assailed by feelings of guilt.

As the party at Ciro's broke up, he laughed with Zsa Zsa as he helped escort her out. A great little joke, he thought to himself. Within a month it turned quite serious.

Zsa Zsa burst into Eva's cramped apartment and shook her sister awake. "Eva, I've just met the man I'm going to marry."

Eva grumbled, "What man? What are you talking about?"

"Conrad Hilton," Zsa Zsa said, then repeated, "I'm going to marry him."

"Isn't he a bit too old?"

"Not at all, not at all."

Several days after the party, Connie asked her to accompany him to a winter sojourn in Palm Beach. He told Zsa Zsa she would share a bungalow with him on a millionaire's estate. Sorry, Zsa Zsa told Connie at once, explaining later to Eva that "this is a man you do not go to bed with until he marries you. If you do, all his interest will be gone."

Within two weeks of the first meeting, the hotel mogul was already so serious that Zsa Zsa and Eva were whisked off by chartered plane to meet Connie's mother in El Paso, Texas. Somehow Zsa Zsa appeared guileless in her love, and family hurdles were cleared easily. Mrs. Hilton loved her new daughter instantly, and a relationship was sealed that lasted until Connie's mother died.

The Hilton homestead was, however, steeped in devout Catholic relics—a prominent crucifix, the family Bible on a big stand, and a collection of lovely antique rosaries, including one that had belonged to Mary, Queen of Scots. Zsa Zsa sensed then that religion, not age differences, would imperil the marriage. For the time being, the religious issue was evaded when Mrs. Hilton suggested a civil ceremony fully approved by the family.

The Hilton engagement ring on her hand provided Zsa Zsa with her first taste of the family one-upmanship that would become her trademark. Eva was working for $75 a week, Magda was still stuck in Hungary, but Zsa Zsa had married the millionaire they all dreamed of.

The ring also gave her instant fame, immediate social status, and prefabricated wealth. Her sayings were suddenly quoted by Walter Winchell and Hedda Hopper; and Louella Parsons, queen of the Hollywood columnists, described her to seventy-five million readers as "a radiant girl—reverently in love with a wonderful man." Privately, however, Louella told her assistant Dorothy Manners that the devout Connie was due for much private heartbreak.

Few unlikelier marriages were ever conceived in the dream city known as Hollywood. Zsa Zsa was a born hedonist: a fashion plate, a free spender, a creature of nightclubs, and a glittering social butterfly. Fashion was her religion; money was there to be spent, until it ran out.

Thrift to Connie was a credo of life. He had taken $5,000 in cash and $20,000 in credit to build his chain from a single hotel in Cisco, Texas, into an empire of twenty major hostelries by the time he met Zsa Zsa.

His first marriage had dissolved under the constant pressure and demands of his growing business. And the divorce cost him heavily, denying him Communion and much solace from the Catholic Church, another rock on which his life was built.

The engagement to Zsa Zsa was considered quite frivolous and out of character by those who knew him well. The crushing nature of it eventually hit Connie also. One afternoon, shortly after the betrothal was announced in the papers, Connie summoned an old friend to lunch at the Los Angeles Country Club. "I feel like I'm trapped in the middle ring of a circus," he told the friend. "Zsa Zsa has turned my life inside out."

"Can you live with it?" the friend asked.

"I don't know yet."

At first he hoped to find the answer within himself. He flew to New Mexico without Zsa Zsa and committed himself to an austere Catholic retreat in the city where he had once lived as a member of the New Mexico state legislature. The priests at the monastery who tended the retreat noticed him pacing for hours out in the sun, seemingly impervious to the heat of a particularly hot summer.

The monastery was built of adobe and painted a stark white, so simple and different from the flashy Beverly Hills Connie had become used to. It had a spectacular view of the red and lavender Sangre de Cristo (Blood of Christ) Mountains. It reminded him of the great distance—economically and socially—he had traveled from his roots. He also knew he couldn't step backward in time and space. He was still a neophyte in the international society that had produced Zsa Zsa. The only sounds that broke the silence were the rustling of the pine trees and the howl of the peculiar New Mexico winds. Sadly, it only made Connie recall Zsa Zsa's sparkling laughter.

The retreat didn't work. The love affair still filled his heart and made him feel warm inside with an intensity he had never before experienced. Then, just as suddenly as he arrived, he flew back to Hollywood. Early the next day he called Zsa Zsa and asked her to meet him at the Beverly Hills Hotel for lunch.

Connie was strangely silent, as if he were struggling for the right words. Across the table, Zsa Zsa's confidence failed her. She trembled, dreading what he might say.

He finally suggested a walk in the sprawling gardens of the hotel. As they walked between brilliant beds of marigolds and salmon hedges of bougainvillea, the halting words came: "Darling, the wedding is off. The Church is too dear to me, and I can't get a dispensation."

Zsa Zsa bent over to pick an orange marigold so Connie couldn't see the tears in her eyes. As hard as it may be to imagine, Zsa Zsa was at a loss for words. Connie's severity made her feel every bit the teenager she still was. The rejection broke her heart.

The Gabors, while not Catholics themselves, were steeped in Catholic tradition from the Church-dominated high society in Budapest.

She fled to Eva's apartment. "No man has ever made me feel the way Connie does," she told her sister. "I'm really in love for the first time. And if it doesn't work out, I'll be lost."

Later she told a friend, "Eva didn't truly understand. So there was nobody I could confide in. I locked myself in the bedroom and waited for the telephone to ring."

Four nights later he called. "I can't live without you, darling," he said in a voice choked with emotion.

Zsa Zsa was delirious. Then *she* had second thoughts. Here she was, an exotic hybrid from decadent Europe, about to marry a glorified cowboy. She had already married one older man—a man who had forced a cruel existence on her. Was she really hunting for a father?

She knew that most people—maybe even her own sister—believed she was marrying for money. She knew that wasn't true. Could she convince anyone else? Especially Connie's family. Forty years later, when Zsa Zsa took a battery of lie detector tests for a television series, she was asked directly, "Did you marry Conrad Hilton for his money?" "No," she answered, and was judged truthful by two polygraph experts.

"I fell deeper and deeper in love with him each week. I didn't know a man could be that gentle and kind," Zsa Zsa remembered.

Finally, the week after Easter 1942, Connie and Zsa Zsa were married in the Santa Fe Hotel La Fonda at the foot of the Sangre de Cristo Mountains. The day was favored by a crystal clear blue sky, and the patio of the hotel had been draped in gardenias, white lilies, scarlet bougainvillea, and hyacinths of blue, pink, and rose. Connie was waiting in the sun as Zsa Zsa and Eva, her matron of honor, emerged slowly. Ten minutes later she was Mrs. Conrad Hilton.

Right after the ceremony, and before they even had champagne, Connie pulled the deed for a new hotel, the Los Angeles Town House, out of his pocket. "See," he said to Zsa Zsa, "this is a package deal. Zsa Zsa and the Town House on the same day." Business! And on the most romantic day of his life. It was to become a cross for Zsa Zsa to bear. Could she ever compete against a new hotel?

The small but exquisite wedding ring he slipped on her hand dazzled the wedding party. Though only several carats in size, it was tailor-cut and set in platinum and gold fittings. Part of the ring's attraction for the wedding guests was, in fact, its conservative size.

Interestingly, Zsa Zsa was given a deliberate test of character when Connie offered her a choice of rings. On a velvet pillow he placed two diamonds—one large and a second modestly small. "You choose," he said. Secretly, she wanted the big one, large diamonds being a major weakness. He's doing this on purpose, she decided, and pointed carefully at the smaller stone.

Connie beamed. "That is just the ring I knew you would choose."

She cursed inwardly. She was *dying* to have the large one. This marked the last time Zsa Zsa Gabor would choose the smaller in any pair of gems.

Late on the honeymoon night Zsa Zsa whispered in Connie's ear, "What are you thinking about, darling?" She expected to hear rhapsodies of love."

Connie raised up on one elbow. "By golly, I'm thinking about that Blackstone Hotel idea."

Zsa Zsa, with her dreams of romance, wanted savage words of passion. He should have protested undying love, perhaps saying, "I love you, I love you," again and again.

That was never to be. Zsa Zsa was to compete with Connie's empire for the rest of the marriage in a contest she eventually lost.

A month after the wedding Connie and Zsa Zsa went to Sunday

mass at the little church in Beverly Hills where he had worshipped for years. She had risen at six A.M. that morning to dress as properly as possible for an occasion so important to her husband. She chose a dark blue suit with a dark feathered hat covering most of her upswept hair.

It was a glorious summer morning that saw the Beverly Hills set out in their finest—Loretta Young, Mary Pickford, Kathryn Grayson, and Mrs. Spencer Tracy. But Connie, usually so proud of his bride, clung to her side as if he were chained there. She felt powerless. Had she been at a party, she would have used a bit of Continental repartee to change the mood. In private she learned that her charm, properly applied, could lift Connie out of the blackest of moods.

The confines of the small church crushed in on her. She felt like an intruder, and, in a way, she was. As Connie sat through the service with his eyes downcast, Zsa Zsa realized that she represented a great sin—and not only to Connie. As a divorcé with a new wife, he was denied Holy Communion and forced to sit in the pew while the rite passed.

Later that same afternoon Connie telephoned his mother in El Paso "I've never felt so powerless," he said. "When the congregation rose to take Communion, I stayed on my knees—chained, as it were, to my beautiful wife. When I married, Mother, I wasn't really aware of what it would be like. I felt adrift, cut off, spiritually forlorn."

With perfect timing, the household explosions that were to characterize the marriage erupted several weeks later. Zsa Zsa, still so much a child, retreated to the lavish confines of her boudoir much the way her mother had done during the trauma of her marriage to an older man. As for Connie, he sank deeper into his world of hotel ledgers, construction plans, mergers, and mega-purchase deals. He found it far easier to cope with the details of a hotel in Mexico than the battle royal being waged in his own household.

The society hostess Elsa Maxwell observed that Connie and Zsa Zsa were like two magnificent ships that passed each other on the waters of life and then drifted apart, leaving a brilliant afterglow.

A thunderstorm of glamour and its trappings rained on Connie's ascetic way of life: furs, Tiffany cases full of jewels, elegant gowns. It all poured through the gates of his Bel Air house, followed, naturally, by a tidal wave of bills.

But the full impact of maintaining a Gabor didn't hit him fully until he was suddenly stricken with a virulent form of flu. Forced to remain in his New York penthouse, the hotel king watched wide-eyed as his beauteous bride worshipped at the altar of high fashion.

The ritual began at ten A.M., when a languorous Zsa Zsa, having already breakfasted in bed on lightly buttered toast and coffee, approached her antique dressing table. The trails of a lacy nightgown wafted behind her like the robe of an ancient high priestess. She touched a button and the lights of a theatrical mirror cast the most cruel of lights onto her face, allowing her to examine it pore by pore from neck to forehead. Not even a biologist would have been so reflective. Spread about her were bottles, jars, pots, and thousand-dollar flagons of perfume.

It was a shrine, Connie noticed, and his wife trembled before it as if she were a vestal virgin going out to her sacrifice. Heaven forbid that an unwanted freckle or the trace of a wrinkle be discerned. One morning, after watching from his sickbed for an hour, Connie finally asked, "Georgia [his pet name for her], what are you doing?"

Zsa Zsa's perfectly painted mouth flew open, and she looked at him in amazement. "Why, darling, I'm getting ready for lunch." The tone of her voice was a bit disdainful, as if to suggest that any civilized human would know that the time to prepare for lunch was immediately after breakfast.

A hand was clapped, signaling a maid to open one of Zsa Zsa's three gigantic closets, revealing racks of afternoon wear. She danced up to a mirror holding a blouse and brooch. A look of distress crossed the Gabor face. She discarded the brooch and picked up another.

Then came a rainbow parade of designer scarves. Holding one up, she moved toward the bedridden Connie. "You like this?" she said. Before he could mumble a single word, Zsa Zsa had already moved on to other scarves, other accessories.

At noon, Connie wrote in his diary: "Beauty took itself to an elegant luncheon club, which, I suppose, was its proper setting."

Back from lunch, she began the ritual all over again—"this time with a terribly painful decision over hats." Zsa Zsa glided back to the boudoir and spread her arms mechanically to allow a maid to remove her suit jacket. The rest of the luncheon finery was stripped off right down to the makeup, and Zsa Zsa put on still another dressing gown. The fashion show continued. Hats drifted down from a special cabinet in waves of felt, feathers, and gauze. First, a midnight blue creation was lowered onto Zsa Zsa's tilted head. "You like this?" she asked in the direction of her husband.

He opened his mouth to answer, but "Beauty" had already moved to another selection, a towering triangle of ruffled ostrich feathers and green stones. "You like this?" she asked again. He didn't try to answer the second time.

Stuck as he was in bed, Connie was forced to watch the boudoir ritual through its final—and main—event, the gargantuan preparation for dinner. "After tea, taken exactly at 2 P.M.," Connie wrote in his diary, "the finale began. Beauty emerged from her dressing closet and announced in her most solemn tone, 'I am dressing for dinner.'"

The voice was stentorian, causing time to stand still in the Hilton penthouse, waiting for the proper choice. Zsa Zsa whirled around. "Connie, darling, what about sapphires to match my eyes?"

Before he could even nod assent, Zsa Zsa rejected a sultan's ransom in blue stones and moved on to rubies. "Oh, not the rubies," she said impatiently. "Turquoise and diamonds—that's what it will be." And so it was.

By Connie's calculation, Zsa Zsa spent more than four hours preparing for her progress through the day.

It was about this time—a year into the marriage—that Connie began thinking of Zsa Zsa less as the love of his life and more as a glittering adornment of his own existence. He described the dilemma beautifully in his autobiography, *Be My Guest.*

Over dinner at the Los Angeles Country Club one evening he told a close friend, "You know, a conservative friend of mine recently wrote that 'every man should have one Gabor in his life,' but I've come to view that differently. Perhaps every woman should have *a bit* of the Gabor about them—that might be workable."

He told the same friend that the problems didn't arise merely because of Zsa Zsa's spending. "I can afford her, yes. But you have no idea how time-consuming glamour can be. And so much of the cost seems worthless. Zsa Zsa knows more days that gifts can be given on than anyone in the world. Gifts fall from her hands in a shower."

Soon, however, according to Conrad's own diary, sums of money began slipping through Zsa Zsa's fingertips, and Connie decided he had to do something about it, no matter how innocent were his wife's spending habits. He couldn't know it then, but he was in for a domestic battle of Herculean proportions.

As the days and weeks passed, he found it much easier to control the expenditures on his new hotel in Mexico City than those of his own household. It started with his Spanish Moroccan showplace high in the Bel Air hills. Zsa Zsa redecorated, from the tiles on its tower to the doorsteps in the basement. "There were some days," Connie said later, "when workmen, fabric merchants, carpet dealers, and decorators swarmed about the house like locusts."

After one particularly expensive week, Connie called Zsa Zsa to his study for a long talk about finances. He was still in his three-piece suit, but Zsa Zsa had changed into a velvet gown designed solely for domestic affairs of the heart.

As he looked into her eyes, he had trouble concentrating on what he had to say. "Georgia, I've always placed a great deal of importance on the way money is spent. Maybe I learned to be careful by holding down the costs of hotels. But I can't abide frivolity when it comes to money."

Zsa Zsa looked up, wide-eyed and innocent. "But, darling, I try to be—"

He didn't let her finish. "Hear me out, Georgia, because if we don't do something about the wild spending going on here, there could be trouble for both of us."

Zsa Zsa stifled a yawn and stretched back in her lavish housecoat.

He pulled out a shiny new ledger with leather binding and suggested that the book be used to keep track of the "Zsa Zsa funds." "Now Georgia," he said, still pacing, "I'm going to give you $250 a month spending money. I will give it on the first of the month and will consider it a payment—much like a check for the servants or to pay the light bill."

She kept silent, but her eyes widened and she gasped inside herself. She had been spending $300 a month while still a schoolgirl in Switzerland. So it was hard for her to imagine getting by on that in the Beverly Hills of 1943.

Connie loomed at his desk like a frugal character from a Dickens novel. "You are to use that money for everything, *everything* you personally need—clothes, luncheons with the girls, the beauty parlor, gas, tips—all your personal expense. Do you understand?"

Zsa Zsa nodded, a headache forming behind her eyes.

She let it sink in and drifted off to bed alone, already formulating plans to circumvent the new directive. On a small pad near her dressing table, she wrote, "Personal expenses—$250?" The question mark spoke volumes.

Several days later Zsa Zsa, with Eva, went to a small Beverly Hills shop that specialized in housecoats for the rich.

"With Connie, I spend so much time at home," she said as she tried on one chiffon creation after another, laying an enormous pile to the side—those that she intended to buy.

By chance Connie was home when this queen's ransom of gowns was delivered to the mansion. They all bore the notation "Charge to Mr. Conrad Hilton."

His face grew red with anger. "Zsa Zsa," he said, waving a bill in her face, "didn't you understand our discussion?"

"Perfectly, darling," she purred. "You said I was allowed $250 for personal expenses, but you also said that household expenses would be fully taken care of."

He was mystified. "I don't get it."

But, darling, these are *house*coats."

He had to laugh.

From then on, however, he tried to hold her to the budget he had prescribed—down to the last dollar bill. When Zsa Zsa let a few hints of her financial predicament slip while talking to Connie's mother, the elder Mrs. Hilton called her son on the carpet. "I'm just trying to instill some sound business sense into her," he explained. "She is a beautiful Circe when it comes to money, and I might as well have been talking to a concrete statue in the park. Her logic is completely beyond my limited social experience—it's so European."

Eventually, Zsa Zsa found a way to become one of Hollywood's best-dressed women and still live more or less within her husband's restraints. She coped with this considerable privation by working out lend-lease agreements with designers in Beverly Hills and Manhattan. Many of the most elaborate creations used by Zsa Zsa to bewitch an entire generation were merely loaned for the night. The designers cooperated, realizing that a dress on the Gabor back brought a million dollars' worth of advertising. Many dresses were given outright.

The contrast between Conrad's so obvious wealth and Zsa Zsa's perception of his stinginess confused her. One afternoon, Zsa Zsa said in an interview, Connie's mother sat her down for a family talk. "I don't know how to say this in the nicest way. But deprivations in Conrad's youth made him awfully close with a buck. It's just that his sense of values was formed in another era."

Looking at Connie's financial ledgers in retrospect helps explain her confusion. They were outlined in Hilton's own memoirs, several magazine articles, and a series of newspaper articles.

During the years of his marriage to Zsa Zsa, Connie earned about $5 million a year. Of that, federal taxes took $316,672; California taxes accounted for $31,393; $80,944 went for charitable gifts; $19,659 was spent on travel; insurance premiums cost $11,433; the maintenance of his homes in Bel Air and Lake Arrowhead totaled $36,526; and his own clothing allowance amounted to $4,171. It wasn't hard for Zsa Zsa to weigh her $3,000 allowance against this lush annual expenditure.

Added to the financial woes sinking the marriage was Connie's absence. He was gone an average of four days a week, flying from city to city as his empire expanded.

Zsa Zsa was at the age when most American girls were pledging sororities, going to work as secretaries, or marrying boys their own age.

One afternoon Eva found her sister sitting on a couch in the Bel Air home reading *Good Housekeeping, Better Homes and Gardens,* and *Emily Post's Book of Etiquette.* Zsa Zsa had decided that she would become the ideal American wife to her husband. "But I had to choke back my laughter. Zsa Zsa was trying *too* hard."

Zsa Zsa tried harder to hold this husband than she would ever do again. "Often when Conrad was in town, I would say, 'Connie, let's have a real nice evening at home tonight,' " Zsa Zsa told Hedda Hopper. "But he always shrugged. 'Oh, go along without me, Georgia. I'm going to bed early.' "

When Jolie finally arrived from Europe she could sense immediately that something was wrong. Zsa Zsa, greeting her at Connie's Plaza Hotel, had lost much of the zest she'd had in Europe. Her hair was indifferently styled, much of the lilt was gone from her voice, and she seemed strangely ill at ease.

Jolie waited until the excitement surrounding her arrival died down and then ordered Zsa Zsa to lunch with her in private. "What's wrong?" she demanded.

"Nothing's wrong, Nuci. I think Connie and I are both still getting used to being married. Our separation [in effect by then] is only temporary."

"Nonsense." Jolie narrowed her eyes. "You're about to fly apart at the seams."

Then Zsa Zsa confessed her worst fear: "I knew from the moment I met him that he was dying to go to bed with me, but he's so old-fashioned and of German origin. This type of man will not marry if you go to bed with him before, so I never . . ." She didn't finish the sentence. "But after he's married and gets what he wants, interest wanes."

Tears formed in Zsa Zsa's eyes as she looked across the luncheon table. "You know something, Mother? On our wedding night he talked to me about a hotel deal he was setting up. And now, in bed, he might suddenly say, 'I wonder if they will give us the ten million dollars we asked for.' The newness of the marriage has worn off, and I've been kicked into a corner of his life."

She spared her mother the worst humiliation. One evening, about eighteen months into the marriage, Zsa Zsa and the Hilton boys, Barron and Nicky, were listening to *Fibber McGee and Molly* in the living room of the house. Zsa Zsa heard her husband come quietly in and go straight to his room.

Zsa Zsa went into the hall. "Connie?" she called lightly. There was no answer.

When the boys went to their rooms, Zsa Zsa put on Connie's favorite nightgown and went down the hall to his room. She knocked softly and again called his name. There was still no answer.

Then she grasped the crystal doorknob and turned it. The door was locked. Zsa Zsa sank heavily against it. "It was such an overwhelming blow to my pride," Zsa Zsa said later. "I had been desired by so many men, desperately wanted, and now my own husband locked his door against me. Well, if he can do that, then who needs him? Who the hell needs him?"

The door between Connie and Zsa Zsa was never to fully open again.

The house on Bellagio Road that Connie had built as a monument to his glory seemed like a mausoleum with its many empty rooms. Zsa Zsa felt trapped in a gilded cage. Ambition sealed her in that house and that lifestyle. But it took her many years to admit it. Talking to George Sanders, who became her third husband, many years later, she confessed, "I came to Hollywood to be a movie star. I had dreamed of it for years. Then I met Connie and noticed that he was one of those men desired by all the beautiful women in Hollywood. Suddenly it was more important to me that this great man should die for me than that I should be a big star. It was a dreadful mistake."

George looked at her closely. "But did you ever love him, really love him?"

Zsa Zsa turned her face away.

Early one morning Connie opened the door to Zsa Zsa's room and announced matter-of-factly, "Father John Kelly is coming to see you today; nothing important, just for a little chat."

She panicked. What would she say to him? How could she bear the guilt for Connie's religious torment? Her thoughts wandered back over the wasteland of her three-year marriage. And she wondered, Was it all worth it?

It seemed like an eternity before Father Kelly arrived, and Zsa Zsa used the time to dress in a modest suit and to pin her hair into a severe bun. When the priest arrived, she led him to the formal living room, where both tea and coffee had been laid out on a silver tray. There was a bit of light patter. Finally, himself ill at ease, Father Kelly looked up. "You know, of course, that Conrad's first wife is still alive." She nodded. "Now, Mrs. Hilton, I don't want you to misunderstand what I'm going to say. Conrad loves you very much, but you must realize that in the eyes of the Church he's not really married to you."

Zsa Zsa, only twenty-one at the time, was crushed. What did he want her to do—walk out of his life as if the marriage had never existed?

The priest continued his lecture: "Mrs. Hilton, Conrad suffers a great deal from this. It's really more torment than he can bear. But no matter how much it hurts him, he can't bring himself to speak of it to you directly." The priest stopped just short of suggesting divorce. But as she watched the emotions play across his face and the hardened glint in his eyes, she knew what he wanted or, more importantly, what Connie wanted—a divorce.

The priest was just a messenger sent to end the marriage that Connie could no longer live with.

Fortunately, Zsa Zsa was able to dash off to New York before her emotions shattered. On the plane, however, she admitted to herself that the marriage was over.

She checked into the most prestigious of Connie's hotels—the Plaza. A week later, a massive California brush fire raged through Bel Air causing immense devastation and destroying Zsa Zsa's wing in the Hilton mansion. Her clothes and all her family mementos were destroyed. When a radio bulletin relayed the news to New York, Zsa Zsa turned to her sister and said, "I'm not going back. I'm not going to be trapped in that life again."

"He fenced her in," Jolie said later. "A girl as free and gay as Zsa Zsa can't be trapped in anyone else's life. It's like trapping a firefly in a jar and keeping it there until the last flicker is gone."

Divorce papers had already been drafted by Connie's lawyer. It was a miserly property settlement but one completely acceptable to Zsa Zsa. She would receive $35,000 in cash and $250,000 in alimony to be paid at the rate of $2,083 monthly for ten years. As soon as she remarried, the financial arrangement would become void. Rumors abounded that an under-the-table cash settlement was made and deposited in a Swiss bank. There was, however, no proof of this.

When Zsa Zsa finally appeared for the divorce hearing in 1946, the legal proceedings turned into a circus. She arrived to testify in a dark gray suit, her hair hidden by a cloche hat and her face covered by a veil. Looking soulfully up at a superior court judge, she solemnly said she decided on the divorce because (sobbing profusely) "Mr. Hilton came to prefer his butler to me."

Aha, the butler did it! Zsa Zsa told the judge that the butler had repeatedly treated her like a servant and at one point ordered her around. She had complained tearfully to Connie. "I'll see what I can do," Connie told her. But when the Hiltons returned from a brief vacation, Zsa Zsa complained, "the butler was *still* there. He wouldn't take my orders, refused even to speak to me. So I complained again to Mr. Hilton. And he said, 'If you don't like it, you can pack up and go.' "

There was a melodramatic dab of the Gabor handkerchief at the edge of a perfectly mascaraed eye. "So I left. Imagine a man who cares more for his butler than his wife."

Eva, on the stand for less than ten minutes, supported her sister by saying vehemently, "Conrad Hilton is one of those men who doesn't want to be married. It's as simple as that."

The divorced Hiltons continued to sweep by each other later in the entangled trail of the emerging jet set. Jolie once said that Zsa Zsa and Connie met, suffered a brief infatuation that evaporated, and "were left with only fractions of romantic memory."

In a weak moment, Zsa Zsa told *Time* magazine (and therefore the world) that she didn't find out much about the man she married until six months after the wedding. "Then I found that he was a man who refused to be influenced by a woman. He was never willing to explain himself, and didn't care what I thought or how I lived. . . . I could never compete with his real love—*hotels.*"

7

✳ Escape

*I*n Hungary, where the war cut all communication with the Western world, a gloom had settled on the Portuguese villa where Jolie, Vilmos, and Magda were huddled. The danger challenged their bravery. There was no conversation over breakfast coffee, no more black jokes about the war swirling around them.

The invisible shield of diplomatic immunity that protected the Gabors dissolved like cellophane with the Nazi occupation of Budapest. The chill of real fear spread through the villa's vast rooms as if it were a virus.

The morning after the Gabors had first been arrested by the Nazis, Magda lingered in her room until just before noon. She put on a cheerful show for her parents. But Jolie heard her sobbing quietly behind the door. She stopped to answer Jolie's knock with feigned jauntiness. Nobody knows how he will face danger until he confronts it. Magda faced it head-on with a sturdiness that was almost foolhardy.

Portuguese Ambassador Carlos de Sampayo Garrido, her lover, watched her carefully the day after the arrest. When he realized she was determined to go on with her resistance activities, he intervened. "The Gestapo hasn't forgotten you, dear," he told her. "They'll be back, and next time they'll come with arrest orders strong enough to bypass my diplomatic powers. I've got to get you out of here."

A week later, Magda was spirited out of Hungary by Carlos, using a limousine and a truck flying the flag of Portugal. Some sources claim that Magda got out of Budapest and across the border under the false floor of the truck.

Carlos made the decisive move just in time. Five hours later, the enraged Gestapo officers went straight to Berlin for an order to arrest the "dissident Magda Gabor."

As the truck carried Magda from the villa, Jolie felt fully alone and isolated for the first time in her charmed life. She was finally free of her daughters now, and she realized, too late, that life without them would be unbearable. She sank onto her bed and cried.

For more than four decades she had easily coasted through Budapest high society, pampered by a rich, adoring family; blessed with three beautiful daughters; protected by a loving husband; and desired by a string of handsome lovers.

Now she was marooned inside the walls of the Portuguese embassy's summer villa, waiting for a hopeless war to end. Then one sunny afternoon fate dealt her its cruelest hand. She was sitting in a reception room writing letters when she looked up to see a young aide walk toward her with a small white envelope in his hand. There was a stricken look in his eyes as he held out the message. Several sentences scribbled on a piece of social stationery informed her curtly that her gorgeous apartment overlooking Budapest's Elizabeth Bridge had been hit directly by an American bomb. Everything was destroyed.

It seemed an impossible irony that the United States, which would shelter her and her three daughters so happily, was responsible for wiping out all traces of her old life. She shrugged her shoulders, and a bitter smile formed at the edges of her mouth. A year earlier, even several months earlier, such news would have sent her into a hysterical swoon. Now her lovely home and her possessions were merely another casualty, and an unimportant one, of a pervasive war.

"I, who had gotten hysterical if a maid dropped a plate, now didn't care that my whole house—paintings, china, crystal—was demolished. It didn't touch me. Nothing could touch me anymore," she recalled.

She was also cut off from her daughters. The letters from Eva and Zsa Zsa stopped in early 1944, intercepted by the Nazis, who now controlled Hungary's postal service.

Carlos had tried to persuade Jolie and Vilmos to leave with Magda. He sat down with Jolie and explained: "Madame Gabor, Magda and I must leave the country, and right now. It's your daughter's only chance. I can't answer for what might happen to you after we go."

But Jolie hesitated. Her ex-husband lacked the Portuguese visa that would have allowed him to flee the country. "I can't leave Vilmos," she told Carlos. "Maybe later I will come."

Earlier, Vilmos begged her to stay. "I know the children adore you and they want you. I also know you will get out of here safely." Then he took her hand. "But without you, I will be lost. The children adore only you. Zsa Zsa, Magda, and Eva all have their own lives. I have only you."

She grasped his hands and said quietly, "I'll stay with you, and if we must leave we will leave together."

Jolie felt she could afford the luxury of time. All her daughters were now safe. From the moment that Magda was smuggled out of Hungary, Jolie relaxed into an easy acceptance of the horror around her. "My daughters are safe," she told one of her sisters. "And if I have to die, I can do so in peace."

There was, however, another, secret reason for her to remain in a country that was dissolving in terror. She had taken a lover three years earlier, and her allegiance to him was as strong as her responsibility to Vilmos. The lover, Paul Savosdy, was wanted by both the Nazis and the underground Communists because of his unorthodox beliefs. Thus he became a fugitive even before the German armies moved into the city.

His salvation was Jolie's final act of heroism. Luckily for her, the Portuguese Ambassador had turned his embassy over to a young attaché who, as a social climber of the highest order, was dazzled by Jolie's contacts and her considerable wealth (estimated at about a million dollars just before the war). When she invited him to tea, he showed up in an ill-fitting morning coat, followed by his wife in a Parisian gown that looked as if it had been decorated with a pastry tube. Jolie cooed. She flattered. She chirruped in her most cultured tones. The attaché, puffed up by his own importance, allowed himself to be led down the garden path as if he had a bronze ring in his nose.

"It wasn't all that hard," Jolie said. "The chargé and his wife were nothings, but in the Ambassador's absence they were trying to be frightfully chic and social. They saw me as the key that would let them into Continental and international society."

Madame Gabor spoke of princess this and baron that; of general this and prime minister that, and all the while she was repressing a smile as she glanced at the lady's ridiculous hat. The last of her precious prewar champagne flowed like water. It had been smuggled into the embassy by her mother.

But the flattery didn't work. It was greed that finally saved Jolie's lover. "I held out a diamond ring to the girl," Jolie remembered. The girl answered, "Oh, Madame Gabor, we don't do this for your ring." Still, she quickly grabbed the diamond and stuck it in her purse. "Okay," agreed the chargé. "We will grant this Savosdy fellow asylum, but only as far as the Swiss border." A visa was also obtained for Vilmos, and soon it was time to get out of Hungary.

It was bitter cold and snowing the morning Jolie and Vilmos left Budapest in a car bearing the license plates of the Portuguese government—diplomatic plates that meant the difference between life and death.

As Jolie remembered it, bombs had been falling on central Budapest since dawn, creating a montage of crystal and flame, as elegant townhouses and centuries-old buildings exploded, sometimes only a hundred feet from the car.

Jolie's mother, now partially crippled with arthritis, risked her life to plow through the streets to bid her daughter goodbye. Jolie felt a bitter forewarning: "You will never see her again—never," a voice inside her said. "This life, your life, is over now. You can never come home."

Jolie, ever the romantic, rejected this pessimism, but there was a catch in her throat. Even if she could return, Hungary would not be the same country. She looked out the car window at the Budapest skyline. "You've seen the best of it, old girl. You have lived fully here." Then she sat upright on the seat, tucked her hands deep in the comforting warmth of her blue fox, and looked forward. She never looked back again.

The car plowed a zigzag course through Budapest, where block-to-block fighting had broken out between advance Russian troops and the Nazis. There was death around every corner. Smoke filled the air, and several times the limousine pulled into alleyways to avoid combat. Still she looked ahead—absolutely unafraid.

"The Nazis were still herding out Jews and shooting them against the wall, while in another part of the city the Russians lined up Nazis for the same fate," Jolie said. Several times, Jewish mothers wearing the yellow Star of David ran into the street begging passersby to take their babies. Jolie's sobs finally came, and Vilmos wrapped her in his arms.

Since the diplomatic plates were stronger protection than the armor on the side of a tank, and because Jolie and Vilmos were considered "friendly aliens" by the Nazis, the car was able to take the fastest route out—through Austria, then through a corner of Germany, and then to the Swiss border.

They crossed the border into Germany shortly after dawn on the second day. The havoc and gore along the roadside were appalling, as Jolie remembered. Bombed-out cars littered the autobahn, and bodies were piled in gullies. At one point, mysterious and fast-driving cars plummeted around them, ejecting uniform jackets and insignia from the windows. It wasn't until later that they learned the cars held Nazi officers with the power (and the money) to escape through the west disguised as civilians.

Across the world in Beverly Hills in early 1945, Zsa Zsa and Eva were emotional orphans. Zsa Zsa rattled around the Hilton mansion in a dreadful malaise, weighed down with fear and worry. As for Eva, she protested about life's injustices to an empty sky.

Both girls were in their early twenties—adolescents in many ways. Eva, at least, desperately craved matriarchal approval. She filled her letters to Jolie with vague descriptions of her career and enclosed painfully deceptive still photos that showed her lounging next to pools and houses she didn't own, wearing gowns borrowed from the studio. "I thought she was a big star," Jolie said, "until I finally reached the United States.

Zsa Zsa, mired in her lonely marriage to Connie, grasped each of Jolie's letters (while they were still coming through) as if it were a lifeline.

One night Zsa Zsa was at a Beverly Hills cocktail party awash with celebrities when the conversation shifted to the war and the conflagration swallowing up Hungary. A particularly boorish man mouthed off: "Damned Hungarians, they've been playing footsie with Hitler all along. If you want my opinion, we should bomb the hell out of Budapest, and Austria too."

It was more than Zsa Zsa could stand. She let loose of Connie's arm and ran out into the night. Tears came though she knew they wouldn't help. She clenched her fists and vowed to get her mother out of Hungary no matter the cost. And power was definitely on her side; Connie was then one of the twenty most powerful men in America. (Eva's husband Charles Isaacs' $5 million real estate empire didn't hurt either.)

The sisters joined hands and stormed Washington, D.C. First Eva attacked the bureaucracy as if it were a military fort, bombarding it with telegrams, phone calls, and hundreds of letters that she persuaded friends to write.

But all the pleas met with chilly politeness. Eva couldn't believe that people could be so heartless. She had graphic evidence that time was running out in Hungary. Friends with American intelligence ties in Europe related horror stories about Budapest. (During the last two years of the war, 14,000 Hungarians were deported; 5,000 were killed, and another 5,000 sent to Nazi slave labor camps.) Eva was desperate. Why wouldn't anybody help them?

Finally, a young legislative aide leveled with them. "Look, Mrs. Hilton," he said to Zsa Zsa. "You've got to face some nasty realities here. Hungary chose to side with Germany and to ally with both Hitler and Mussolini. Your country has issued a declaration of war against the United States. This makes your parents and your sister Magda 'enemy aliens.' I don't know how much, if any, help you can expect from this country."

"Enemy aliens!" The phrase filled Zsa Zsa's days with sorrow. Her mother, father, and sister were considered enemies of the United States—the country both she and Eva had adopted wholeheartedly.

But they aren't enemies, she wanted to scream. They were just caught in the tide pools of war; their fates resting on a technicality—a mere word, alien.

"What chance do we have of getting all three of them out and to America?" she asked one official

"It ranges from poor to none," he said somewhat edgily. "We're having enough problems rescuing Americans caught in the war. There's nothing we can do."

Zsa Zsa flew back to Beverly Hills outraged. "Do something," she pleaded with Connie. "Mama will die if we don't get her out."

Thus was hatched a daring private rescue plot, involving the American Secretary of State, the dictator of Portugal, a mysterious wartime privateer named André Zalabondy, and Magda's amorous diplomat, Carlos Garrido. A lot of cash probably changed hands, and the Madrid Hilton much later may have been built on land owned by the privateer Zalabondy.

It was Connie's influence and the Gabor sisters' persistence that opened the doors to Cordell Hull, the United States Secretary of State. That he agreed to see them at all was a minor miracle.

The war was winding down when Zsa Zsa and Eva dashed to Washington. They wore sedate business suits to Capitol Hill, and when they were finally ushered in to see Hull, Zsa Zsa broke down. Speech wouldn't come to her.

"I looked up and saw this severe, elegant man," she said later. "And I didn't know what to say, what to ask for."

Eva, however, got right down to business. "Please help us," she said. "Our parents and sister are caught in a situation beyond anyone's control. Surely, you can do something."

No trace of emotion played on Cordell Hull's face, though he did seem solicitous of Zsa Zsa, bringing her water and, for a brief moment, sitting on the arm of her chair. Painstakingly he explained the hopelessness that engulfed Europe as the war ground down. "The Russians are moving very quickly in countries such as Hungary," he said. "Once under their control, there may be nothing we can do."

"Then we have to do something before the Russians take over," Eva said.

"I can't promise anything, ladies," he said. "But I will look into it and do all I can."

In fact, he did far more than could be expected. He wired American officials in Lisbon that very afternoon, telling them to clear the Gabors for passage into the United States should they get as far as Portugal. The latter possibility, however, seemed very unlikely.

Connie was far too savvy to let the matter rest there. He worked through the middle levels of the State Department until a major concession to his power was achieved: Magda, Jolie, and Vilmos Gabor were officially listed as "American allies." And an official American request, relayed through the Portuguese government to the country's chargé in Budapest, ordered him to "save twelve people." The chargé was mystified at first.

He immediately called Lisbon. "What does this mean?" he asked. "It means save the Gabors and any ten other people," a superior told him. "If we used all our power to rescue Vilmos and Jolie, it would look fishy. But as members of a group, they won't stand out so much."

"But how will I get them across Germany?" "Never mind," he was told. "Just get them out of Hungary and get them out tomorrow!"

The only other high-level war rescue to compare with this one was the earlier plot to save the heiress Barbara Hutton in the early days of the war. Since Hitler had put Barbara and her young son on a kidnap list, U.S. Ambassador to Britain Joseph Kennedy mounted a campaign that whisked her from Biarritz, across France, into Fascist Italy and then to Venice, where she boarded a passenger liner.

As the limousine carrying Jolie and Vilmos sped through Germany toward the Swiss border, André Zalabondy moved into action. A portly, rather unappealing man who made his living from real estate, he had courted Jolie when the sisters were still schoolgirls. At one point, when he claimed to be dabbling at directing films, he made an impressioned plea for Jolie's affections when they met on a street in downtown Budapest. He threw his chubby arms around her and suggested an afternoon in a hotel suite. She merely laughed and brushed him aside.

"You haven't seen the last of me," he vowed.

He disappeared from Hungary when the war began and, according to some sources, became a black-market courier, operating in both Allied and Nazi-controlled countries. Probably, Zalabondy was employed by Conrad Hilton on this mission and deployed by Magda in Lisbon. One thing was certain: he was already in Switzerland to help Jolie and Vilmos cross the border.

Democratic, neutral Switzerland loomed as a seemingly insurmountable roadblock to Jolie. The afternoon before she left Hungary, she had tried to exchange her last bit of property, a five-story apartment house, for an entry visa from the unofficial Swiss consul. The offer was nastily refused. "You are considered to be, technically, Nazis," she was told. "I hate the Nazis," she pleaded. "I'm sorry," he said coldly.

"We were terribly afraid we would be stuck in Germany," Jolie told Zsa Zsa later. "And, since we couldn't go back, I prayed silently for a miracle." The Swiss were justifiably wary. Thousands of Nazis, in all manner of disguise, were attempting to cross into the country before jumping off to South America.

The Portuguese headed his small caravan to Santa Margarita, a bustling resort, popular with Germans before the war. But, besides having an armed barrier, it was separated from Germany by a small footbridge above a deep, forbidding ravine.

"If the authorities ask for your visa, get out and run for it," the chargé suggested. "It's only a few steps." This was easy enough for him to say. He had a visa! Still, Jolie steeled herself for this run. She wondered what it would feel like when a bullet pierced her back, her arms, or her legs. Could she keep on running? But as the car pulled up, she looked at the impossibly isolated bridge, at the grim faces of the guards, and caved in.

The guards were adamant. The cars were pulled to the side of the road, where military couriers drove up to confer with the chargé. Hours dragged by.

The Portuguese were finally ordered to lead their charges, under heavy guard, to a resort hotel where Swiss policemen with guns stood outside the doors. "I was baffled," Jolie said later. "Why were the Portuguese so intent on delivering us to freedom?"

Jolie had managed to smuggle 80,000 Hungarian pengös out of the country—a fortune in postwar terms. They felt secure that they could indefinitely pay for their stay at the border.

Then Jolie went shopping and realized she was impossibly poor. A chicken (if you could get one) cost 10,000 pengös; one piece of bread went for 100; apples were 5,000 pengös each.

They hadn't enough money to pay for even five full-service meals in the hotel restaurant, so Jolie marketed, putting together a picnic-style feast in their rooms. She was called to the telephone in the midst of their first meal.

It was Zalabondy: "Listen and don't say anything," he said. "From now on, you and your group are my guests. When you arrive in Bern you will have $5,000 American dollars waiting for you. So do as I say and collect this money at the Portuguese legation. I will contact you again."

Before she could answer, the connection went dead.

The next day, right after dawn, they were mysteriously allowed to cross the border, not through official gates, but through "no man's land"—the deserted mountain ridges between Germany and Switzerland. Absolutely no record was made of their crossing. Officially, they didn't exist.

They collected Zalabondy's $5,000 in Bern and immediately headed for France.

The France through which they traveled resembled a surrealist painting. The blue cast of war's end smothered the country, and the air was tainted with the smell of death. At each border Jolie began to tremble until she felt Vilmos' arm tighten around her shoulders.

It was like passing through the nine circles of hell.

Incredibly, Zalabondy always knew exactly where Jolie was during the escape and at what precise moment he could reach her by telephone. A second call had come while she was dining in Bern. "When you pass from France to Spain, you will be taken care of at the border. From then on, you will be my guests."

"Why?" Jolie wondered. Zalabondy was like a phantom pursuing her across Europe. She was about to dismiss it as a coincidence until they reached the Spanish border. As the limousine cleared the border gates, Jolie heard sirens. "Something is wrong," she thought at first. Fear crept back in. But the police were beaming. One of them, a handsome lean man, opened the door and bowed. "Madame Gabor, welcome to Spain." He had a box of chocolates in one hand and roses in the other.

She took the gifts in amazement. It was the first joyful thing that had happened to her in two years.

Zalabondy finally met Jolie face to face in a sunny hotel dining room in Spain. He had truly become a fat cat—overdressed and smelling of men's cologne. She looked across the table and thought, He's like the Count of Monte Cristo, coming back rich after so many years.

He cleared up part of the mystery at once. "Magda found me," he explained. "She found my name in the Madrid telephone book and told me where you were." When Zala, as they now called him, was called away suddenly during the meal, Vilmos shook his head. "I don't like this guy. He wants something."

The same day Jolie joyfully reached Magda by phone in Lisbon, and they gossiped gaily for hours. "What does Zala want?" she asked her eldest daughter. "He wants you to introduce him to your son-in-law," Magda answered. "My son-in-law?" Jolie said, mystified. "Yes, Conrad Hilton," Magda explained. What did Zala receive in payment for his part in the mercy mission? Nobody concerned cares to talk about it. But Jolie, in her autobiography, claimed that Connie did, in fact, build the Madrid Hilton on Zalabondy land.

By the time Jolie and Vilmos headed for Portugal and final safety, she was sick of the unctuous, fawning admirer. Luckily, and for some mysterious reason, he was officially barred from entering Portugal.

While the rest of the world waged war, Portugal held its breath. You couldn't get nylon stockings in Berlin or London, but you could get them in Portugal. You couldn't get rich fabrics from China in America, Italy, or Austria; but you could buy bolts of them in Portugal.

The sunny little country had made a peculiar truce with the world, hosting Americans and Germans, who vacationed together. And in its seamy bars and dark, ageless streets, spies from America, Germany, Italy, and Britain buzzed together and then sent intelligence messages to their respective countries. It was not unusual to see Nazi spies lingering over dinner next to a table of American intelligence officers. This was the country that welcomed Jolie and Vilmos.

Magda sat down with them the minute they arrived and gave them the straight facts concerning their predicament. "You can't leave for America until the war is over. Get that into your head right now. We stay here and have a good time."

The Gabors' "safe place" was to be the plush resort suburb of Lisbon—Estoril. It was a lovely city where the villas were faded pinks, yellows, and blue-white. "As we drove along this exquisite bit of the world, I wondered how we could afford it," Jolie remembered.

"Portugal is cheap," Magda said. "For four dollars a day you have a suite overlooking the ocean. Butlers and waiters will serve you on silver trays and you will live like royalty."

Zsa Zsa and Eva had agreed that they would each supply $500 a month while their parents remained in Portugal.

Trouble erupted between Vilmos and Jolie the moment they were settled. An unwitting hotel clerk had the effrontery to put them in one room.

"This is uncivilized, Magda. I cannot take it."

"But, Nuci, this is the only room they have."

Jolie shook her head. "Go right down and get me another room."

Magda promised to try. Several hours later she managed it. She had used every contact she had before someone else was displaced so that Jolie could have a private suite.

But when she arrived with the news the next day, she saw that only one of the twin beds had been slept in. She glared at her mother. "You see," Jolie explained with a smile, "I went over to Vilmos' shoulder for consolation and put my head on his chest as I always used to do. He was so kind to me and stroked my hair to make me feel better. And, you know darling, one thing led to another."

"I feel like a fool," Magda screamed. "I had this fight with the manager and now you're back sleeping with Papa"—where Jolie remained for the rest of her stay in the neutral country.

The war ground to a halt, but not fast enough for Jolie. She was bored in safe but "dull" little Portugal—no excitement.

So, to pass the time, she began assembling a wardrobe for America, using pictures of gowns in fashion magazines and having a seamstress copy them. One particular ensemble seemed particularly chic: a dress, turban, gloves, and bag in a deep wine color. It was to be her disembarkation costume. She was ready to storm the shores of America.

Magda had seen to it that Jolie was placed at the top of the list for flights to America. But members of the military, spies, and wounded men had first priority.

Jolie decided one day that she had to get on some form of transportation that very week, even if it was the leakiest boat afloat. She picked almost that—a cork-carrying liner—the S.S. *Mirandello*. Even a later plane might have been faster, but Jolie refused to stay in Europe one day longer. Vilmos remained in Portugal.

The trip was interminable, and she arrived in Philadelphia on December 31, 1945.

She got up before dawn, dressed herself in the wine-colored outfit, and was ready to show America what they had been missing.

There was certainly no mistaking her as she came down the gangplank. When the girls finally finished crying, Zsa Zsa stood back and surveyed her from head to toe. "You know, Nuci, you are not at all elegant. Too much wine color."

As Jolie embraced Eva for a second time her eyes focused on a mysterious figure in the shadows. His face slowly moved into the light. It was Zalabondy, haunting her life.

Connie's majestic New York Plaza Hotel hosted Jolie for her first few weeks in America. She was greeted with a suite full of flowers. "America, it's wonderful," she told Connie. "You have no idea how bad it is in Europe."

But tears came to her eyes when she spoke of Budapest. The Russians had, by then, closed the iron curtain around it forever. She could never go home again. Could she live with the crushing homesickness that engulfed her? "I don't know, Eva. Maybe Vilmos is right to go back to Budapest whatever the cost."

Eva blanched. She opened her mouth to protest and noticed a stricken look on her mother's face. Jolie had been admiring the collection of Portuguese postcards that Magda had sent with her weekly reports. On one Magda had sadly written, "Take care that Mama doesn't see this—Uncle Sebastyen and Grandmother Francesca were trapped in the Portuguese legation and killed by U.S. bombs."

A wail emitted from Jolie, a mournful, self-accusing cry. "It's my fault." She turned toward her daughter. "Mama wanted to hide with her own concierge, but I wouldn't let her. I made them go to the Portuguese villa."

The heartbreak, once Jolie faced it, helped her turn away from the old country. She would, she decided, stay with her daughters and start life anew.

Family Portrait. Jolie, Zsa Zsa, Eva, Vilmos, and Magda at an Easter celebration, probably in the mid-1920s.

Gilded Lilies. The sisters (from left) Magda, Zsa Zsa, and Eva, were all decked out for their first formal dinner in old Budapest, circa 1927.

Budapest Belle. Mama Jolie in 1936, the height of her social elegance in prewar Hungary. The dress was by Jacques Fath.

Turkish Delight. Zsa Zsa, a very mature-looking seventeen, arrives in Berlin during the late 1930s with her first husband, Burhan Belge, powerful, superrich Turkish foreign affairs minister. *AP/Wide World Photos*

The New Garbo? Eva, still boasting hefty Hungarian poundage, adrift on a raft at Malibu, 1939. *Paramount Pictures*

Baby! Another rare photo of the original Eva Gabor in a 1940 glamour pose in what looks like a giant baby buggy. *Phototeque*

Starlet. A rare photo from Eva's days as an unsuccessful
Paramount player, 1940. *Paramount Pictures*

First Divorce. With Zsa Zsa standing at her side, Eva became the first Gabor to get a divorce when she parted from Dr. Eric Drimmer in Hollywood, 1942. Early, time-battered news photos like this one lend some weight to the claim that Zsa Zsa's nose and face were redone sometime during the 1940s.

Divorce Again. Eva and a dark-haired, buxom Zsa Zsa leaving Santa Monica Municipal Court after Zsa Zsa's 1946 divorce from hotel billionaire Conrad Hilton.

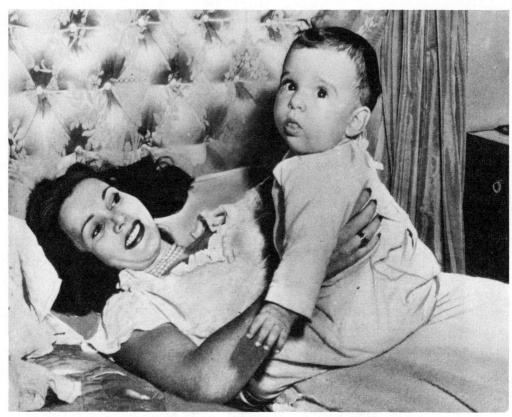

ABOVE: *Mama.* Zsa Zsa holds daughter Francesca Hilton in 1947. The only child of any of the sisters, Francesca became the darling of Mama Jolie, Eva, and Magda. *AP/Wide World Photos*

Heist. Zsa Zsa arrives at police headquarters after the "king of diamonds" robbed her of $750,000 in jewels in 1947. Arrow shows her New York penthouse where robbery occurred.

Blushing Bride. A third time. Zsa Zsa walks down the aisle with actor George Sanders in 1949. He was, she still maintains, the love of her life. *AP/Wide World Photos*

True Love. Following the wedding ceremony, a radiant Zsa Zsa, then billed as Sari Gabor Hilton, beaming at her third husband, George Sanders. This may be the last time he looked so pleased. *Phototeque*

Oscar Night. Zsa Zsa with a beaming George the night he won the Best Supporting Actor Oscar for *All About Eve.* Less than six months after this 1951 appearance, Zsa Zsa was as famous as her husband. *AP/Wide World Photos*

Children's Hour. Zsa Zsa with daughter Francesca and Kathryn Grayson with daughter Patty Kate on the set of the 1952 film *Lovely to Look At.* MGM

Suddenly Famous. Zsa Zsa as Jane Avril in the 1952 film *Moulin Rouge.* United Artists

The Buildup. A 1953 MGM publicity shot when the studio was trying, with only moderate success, to make Zsa Zsa a superstar. MGM

Onstage. Magda, Eva, and Zsa Zsa during a curtain call following their spectacular three-woman show in Las Vegas, 1953. Magda managed to steal the show.

Protégé. Eva and one of her handsome "discoveries," Jacques Bergerac, rehearsing for a 1950s NBC television show. *NBC*

On Radio. Eva and Magda share the mike on Eva's ABC radio show originating from New York City in 1952. Here too, listeners admitted to preferring Magda, who made only occasional appearances. *ABC*

Stage Star. Eva holds a script of *Sailor's Delight* the day before she opened at Hollywood's Huntington Hartford Theater in 1954.

BOOK THREE

Rich and Famous

In America, my girls were wealthy, famous, and unhappy. They were most dissatisfied with their men and with each other.
—JOLIE, 1949

8

✳ Gilded Cage

*A*n enormous nurse grabbed a fistful of keys and led E. Hamlin Turner toward a private bungalow that resembled a wartime bunker. They passed through the first of double doors and were assaulted by pine disinfectant that wafted up from the floor. Cheap drapes were thrown across prison-style windows.

"She ain't been havin' no visitors," said the nurse. "She don't even get much mail."

Hamlin knew that well enough. At first the sanitarium wouldn't even acknowledge his phone calls, much less allow him to visit.

"The family prefers no visitors," an administrator told him. But Hamlin protested: "What family? Who did this?"

"I'm sorry," the man said before hanging up on him.

Finally, Hamlin's lawyer, threatening court action, got his client a precious fifteen minutes behind the walls.

The nurse looked sideways at him. Here was this guy in his beautifully tailored Brooks Brothers suit, a silk club tie, and shoes buffed to a mirror shine. Putting the key into a final door, she pulled it open.

The visitor's mind reeled. His eyes closed invoiuntarily before he was able to focus on the gloomy sight. The lady was folded on the corner of her bed as if some great heat had wilted her there. Her burnished red hair was matted with sweat, and darker roots were showing through. A terrible blue-black bruise formed a triangle stretching from her left eye to her neck. Her dressing gown, which ended at the top of her thighs, revealed open festering sores apparently created by hypodermic needles stabbing again and again in the same place.

"Zsa Zsa," he cried. "What the hell happened to you?" He turned on the nurse. "What the hell have you done to her?"

She shrugged. "Insulin shock treatments," she explained matter-of-factly. "Mr. Turner, I know you don't think so, but this is a very dangerous woman—dangerous to herself."

Zsa Zsa leapt up and grabbed Hamlin's arm, "Get me out of here! Promise you'll get me out of here. If you don't help me, nobody will."

"Count on it." He threw his arms around her. She clung to him as if he were a life buoy, her fingernails digging into the Egyptian cotton of a button-down shirt. Reluctantly, because he could feel her helplessness, he eased her out of his arms and walked back through the locked doors to freedom and sunlight.

As he looked back over his shoulder at the gray fortress of a sanitarium, he wondered how Zsa Zsa Gabor, the most vibrant woman he had ever known, had ended up a tormented prisoner.

Six weeks earlier when she had been spirited into the New York City sanitarium, Zsa Zsa was, physically at least, an unlikely candidate for a strait jacket.

She arrived draped in mink, wearing an exquisite silver jersey dress, a small strand of understated matched pearls, and leading a pampered boxer, Josephine, with a real diamond collar. Truthfully, Zsa Zsa had never looked better. She was slim as a reed, with a flawless complexion; and her hair, transformed into a soft, deep ocher red, gave her a distinctive, startling beauty.

Mentally, however, Zsa Zsa was either the victim of cruel therapeutic overkill or in such shocking condition that commitment to a maximum-security locked facility was the only answer.

Her troubles started in December 1944, when her marriage to Conrad Hilton began to unravel. Showing a brave face, she moved briefly into one of Connie's hotels and defiantly refused to get off the Beverly Hills merry-go-round that had imperiled her marriage.

But friends suddenly noticed a new, harder edge to her personality, an obsessive energy that would never let her rest. Her days often began at seven A.M. and ended with predawn breakfasts at a club in Malibu. Her conversation, normally so brilliant, now came in incongruous bursts.

She drifted around Bel Air in a perpetual haze. Often close friends came up to her at a party only to find that Zsa Zsa didn't recognize them. "So nice to meet you, darling," she said to several. And those friends she did remember were appalled when she stumbled away from them with glazed eyes. Columnist Hedda Hopper, a close friend of Eva's, tried to talk to Zsa Zsa at a party given by Marion Davies. "I asked a couple of questions, tried to get her to tell me about Hungary," Hedda remembered. "She only gave me a blank stare and asked how I liked the party. I watched her lurch through the crowd and realized that she was in bad trouble."

Eva agreed, telling friends that Zsa Zsa might be close to a nervous breakdown. "But what can I do?" she said to one. "I'm not her mother."

Apparently nobody recognized the telltale symptoms of drug addiction or understood that Zsa Zsa, unwittingly, was on that disastrous emotional seesaw of uppers in the daytime, downers at night, and horrible panic and uncertainty in between.

It started quite innocently. She went to a highly regarded Beverly Hills doctor, complaining of chronic exhaustion. Sometimes, morose, she would stay in bed all day, lacking the strength even to take telephone calls. The doctor, with a golf-course suntan, a handsome face, and a "Father Knows Best" bedside manner, soothingly offered a vial of pastel pills.

"You're just worn out, Mrs. Hilton," he said. "Now these little pills will get you through the day. Perfectly safe, my dear. And these" —he held up bright red capsules—"will allow you to sleep."

"Before I knew it I was in a drugged state for days and weeks on end," Zsa Zsa recalled. "The red pills were supposed to let me sleep away my fears, my guilt, my own wretchedness over a broken marriage. I thought all my troubles would simply drift away."

At first she rejected the uppers, or diet pills, entirely, being ordinarily so hyper that they seemed superfluous. But the sleeping pills, the downers, she embraced.

The barbiturates that hung around Zsa Zsa like a cloud seemed like the cure for all of American's tensions, and doctors prescribed them as such.

"They said I needed sleep," Zsa Zsa told Jack Paar. "And boy did I get it. I slept on into the day, remaining lethargic until night, when I would then gulp down another fistful of them. I stared at people like a zombie and sat silent through long, glittering dinner parties in Beverly Hills. Other people noticed something was wrong. But not me. I thought I was doing just great."

Zsa Zsa decided she could run away from her problems, but she carried a satchel of wonder pills with her when she flew to Manhattan.

One evening when Zsa Zsa was sitting glumly at a party given by society hostess Elsa Maxwell, a friend from Hungary eased down beside her and told her about a doctor all the girls called "Mr. Magic." "Now, he has just what you need, Zsa Zsa—a happiness pill. Just everybody is taking them now, darling. You try it and just see how fast they work."

The friend pressed the physician's business card into Zsa Zsa's willing hand.

She was in his upper Manhattan office the next day. He was an elegant man, fatherly, with dark hair silvered at the temples. "They call it Benzedrine, Mrs. Hilton. And it literally injects life into you."

Zsa Zsa frowned. Hadn't she just been all through this before with her doctor in California?

The doctor picked up on her mood. "Oh, don't worry, Mrs. Hilton. With this drug there are no side effects. All you do is take a very mild sleeping pill at night and the Benzedrine when you get up."

Zsa Zsa had never heard of this strong, dangerous amphetamine. What the hell, she thought. Things had been pretty tough lately. She slid further down the drug ladder.

"I'm *Mrs. Conrad Hilton,*" she told herself. "And I deserve to live like Mrs. Conrad Hilton."

"I swept into my new life, giving party after party. Soon I was the toast of New York cafe society. It was fun, and I was starved for the gay life as it had been lived in old Europe." And the darker side of old Europe haunted her. She wasn't sure if her mother had escaped the Nazi death camps, and she fully believed she might never see Jolie again.

One morning she looked around the Plaza Hotel suite that Connie had provided rent free as a financial cushion and decided she deserved a lot more. She may have been separated, but she was every bit a millionaire's wife.

Like an Indian pasha she summoned interior decorators, dealers in fine antiques, carpenters, framers, and purveyors of fine fabric. In less than a month, Zsa Zsa redecorated the compact suite at the then phenomenal cost of $15,000. "I spent entire afternoons drifting through the showrooms of the importers," she said. "My pride was the bed of the French Empress Josephine. "It cost $5,000, but what the hell."

The free-spending Mrs. Hilton roamed the couturier houses with equal abandon. Clinging jerseys in a rainbow of colors were custom-designed for the Gabor figure; pelts of rare fur were sculpted to accent her long neck and slim ankles, and cosmeticians treated her hair with three blended shades of red and applied a flashy makeup style to match.

The superchic Zsa Zsa of today was born during this desperate search for affection, love, and attention in the mid-1940s.

"And I was very much the party girl," she admitted to Jack Paar on one of his early *Tonight* shows. "People who knew me at this period said they had never seen such energy, such wakefulness, such vivacity. Out on the town I was gayer than anyone in New York City."

Even her monthly food bills soared above $2,000 and boasted such delicacies as caviar, steak fillets packed in ice and shipped from Kansas City, and out-of-season raspberries brought by air from South America. Her phone bill usually topped $600, and her demands on the Plaza Hotel staff were staggering.

Nobody can pinpoint when Zsa Zsa began her slide from a drug-fed existence into a bona fide nervous breakdown, but warning signs were there. One night she was holding court in a New York nightclub when a young reporter from a New York tabloid slipped into the booth and asked brashly, "Are you and Conrad Hilton considering divorce?"

Zsa Zsa nodded arrogantly.

"Will you ask for alimony?" he demanded.

She nodded through her barbiturate haze.

"How much?" he questioned.

Zsa Zsa made a grand, sweeping gesture. "I will ask for ten million dollars." There was a gasp from her companions. One of them whispered, "Zsa Zsa, be careful. Divorce hasn't even been filed for yet, and you might screw it up in advance." There was a wave of the Gabor hand as she ignored the advice and plunged forward. "Not that I want a single penny for myself," she said. "I don't; you must believe that. I plan to give every cent of the ten million to homeless European refugees."

Several days later, she told another reporter that she was periodically locked up in her room at a California Hilton hotel on Connie's orders. "They're trying to make me a permanent prisoner," she said, wild-eyed. "Who is *they?*" the reporter asked. "I can't tell you that," she answered fearfully.

Then she showed up at one of her own parties with her head and neck swathed in hospital bandages. "The wife of a Washington, D.C., big shot chased me away from her husband with a brass poker," she explained gaily to her guests. "You can't believe how jealous she was." But rumors quickly surfaced that she had had her nose fixed in an expensive operation.

The single decisive act that led to her commitment was apparently her irrational attempt to have the legal separation from Connie nullified. Less than a week after that action she was confined in the sanitarium.

One lovely spring day she was lolling in her Plaza suite. The next morning she was locked up in the private hell of a sanitarium.

"How did I get here?" she screamed, realizing for the first time that her arms were pinned behind her in a strait jacket, and a needle was dripping something into her left arm.

She repeated again and again: "How did I get here? Please, please get me out. I've been kidnapped!" She looked at the gloomy bunker with its dirty fireplace, bed, and chipped chair; but her cries for help only echoed back to her. Slowly, however, the horrors drifted from her mind as the elixir from the needle drugged her to forgetfulness.

In interviews and lawsuits over the years, Zsa Zsa has variously claimed that she was clapped into the sanitarium by Eva, by Conrad Hilton and his lawyers, or by a combination of both in which Eva was doing Conrad's bidding. Jolie, who got the story secondhand after arriving in America, refused to pin down the blame, saying only that "Zsa Zsa may have needed a firm hand and some help. She never would have ended up in that place if I were there."

Some friends of the sisters point out that Zsa Zsa may have, partially at least, gone willingly, so desperate was she for some sort of help. "But I'm pretty sure of one thing," said an old friend. "Zsa Zsa had no idea she would be locked up and the key thrown away."

Once Zsa Zsa told New York columnist Earl Wilson that "Connie had me drugged for six weeks. They put me out in this place where I suffered hallucinations and nightmares. It was terrible darling, simply terrible. . . . I was seldom awake during the entire time. They put a constant flow of drugs into me and gave me as many as eighteen sleeping pills a day. I would wake up at night and hear the other patients screaming. It was like being in a concentration camp right in the middle of New York City."

On another occasion she said, "I was in there alone with one dress, a coat, and a hat. In the end, I weighted only eighty pounds." (A fact confirmed by E. Hamlin Turner.)

Zsa Zsa, of course, told other versions, in which the blame is invariably laid on her sister Eva's doorstep. In a long interview with the New York *Post* she said that Eva and a family friend from Hungary, Bundy Solt, came to her Plaza Hotel suite with a man they introduced as a producer. She quoted Eva as saying, "He's interested in starring you in a play."

Something was wrong. "I knew immediately that he was a doctor," she told the *Post*. The physician in disguise came over and sat next to her on a sofa: "How long has it been since you have slept?" he questioned. Zsa Zsa had to admit that she didn't know. "You're a very, very tired little girl," he allegedly said. "Why don't we get you into bed."

She testified later in court that the doctor was a "psychiatrist Eva and Bundy Solt flew in at Connie's urging. They told me I had to go into a sanitarium and talked me into dressing in an afternoon jersey and mink coat."

Through all the versions, Zsa Zsa has never varied the story of what happened to her inside the mental hospital, even though she has told it several hundred times to people as varied as Earl Wilson and several of her private secretaries. Zsa Zsa said she tried to regain control of herself as the car taking her to the sanitarium sped down a freeway to another part of the city.

"The limousine finally entered an enormous park and headed down a long, dark lane ending in a driveway surrounded by tawdry little bungalows. . . . The car stopped at one of these. Bundy led me to the door and said, 'Go in.' "

Inside she found a barren room with an unused fireplace, narrow bed, and a chair for a nurse who would remain with her constantly. As she inspected the room she heard a door slam and found herself alone. The doctor who checked her in, Eva, and Bundy Solt had vanished.

After what seemed like an eternity, a man in uniform unlocked her door and entered. He was dressed all in white and had a hypodermic needle in one hand. Zsa Zsa heard a nurse whisper to the man, "Be careful. Look out. They say she's very violent."

How preposterous was this description. The frail, trembling girl, not yet twenty-five, was docile, defenseless, and quite harmless. Quoting E. Hamlin Turner: "To see her that way made you want to cry."

"Then the nurse and the orderly both leaped on me. I felt the needle in my arm. Seconds later, I blacked out." She came to the next day, her silver dress tangled about her and soaked with sweat. "I lived alone in a world of strait jackets, insulin shock treatments, and coarse treatment by the hospital staff," she recalled. "Nobody came to see me—not even Bundy or Eva."

She was watched constantly, by male attendants in the daytime and a registered nurse at night. "The hours were leaden and endless."

Finally, an Irish night nurse befriended her. "Honey, you don't belong here. All you need is a little rest. Tell me how I can help you."

Zsa Zsa reached under a mattress, where she hid any personal belongings, and pulled out the name and address of a New York couple she had known since she arrived in the United States. "Tell them everything that has been going on," Zsa Zsa pleaded. "And tell them not to go to Eva, not if they want to get me out."

Within hours a difficult legal maneuver was under way to get her released. The next afternoon E. Hamlin Turner, a recent Zsa Zsa consort, engaged several attorneys, the most important of them being Barnet L. Arlan, the man who finally got Zsa Zsa out.

The day he visited Zsa Zsa, Hamlin gave a deposition about her shocking condition. "She was physically in terrible shape," he said. "She had apparently been brutally beaten about the neck and face and was, according to one nurse, submitted to severe insulin shock treatments three times a week. (E. Hamlin Turner's description of Zsa Zsa's physical condition comes from court records, since it figured in four separate suits.)

Arlan immediately applied for a writ of habeas corpus from the New York Supreme Court. Zsa Zsa was brought to a private court hearing several days later.

Judge Lloyd Church met her outside and escorted her to his private chamber. For once there would be none of the circus publicity usually surrounding a Gabor. He put her in an overstuffed chair and sat next to her, questioning softly: "Who are you?"

"Sari Gabor Hilton," she answered, accentuating each word.

"Where is Hungary?"

She gave a concise, precise answer.

"How did you come to America?"

"From Turkey, through India—it took four months," she answered, gaining optimism from the kindly look in Judge Church's eyes.

He leaned back in the chair and took one of Zsa Zsa's hands in his. "You're fine. Just fine. The writ is sustained."

Zsa Zsa was free!

Later, however, Zsa Zsa wasn't entirely grateful. Shortly after her release, she initiated three lawsuits: a renewed effort to have her separation set aside, a suit against the sanitarium, and a third against Barnat Arlan, the man who got her out.

Arlan, furious, countersued for payment of his uncollected $20,000 fee. "It took me three months to even make sense of her tangled financial affairs," he testified in court.

He also said that Zsa Zsa had been in danger of losing her resident-alien identity card and mortally frightened of being deported to Turkey when he began representing her. "It was only through a difficult series of negotiations that we got the new card," he said.

Then he related perhaps the most peculiar version of Zsa Zsa's commitment. While still in the sanitarium, she supposedly communicated to Arlan that Eva had her locked up because she threatened to publicize her sister's affair with John Perona, the handsome owner of New York's Club Morocco.

Arlan told the judge during his countersuit, "Zsa Zsa told me she had an altercation with Perona over the fact that he was ruining Eva's life by living openly with her in New York. Eva reacted by having her committed."

"Let me get this straight," the judge in the case asked Arlan. "Eva had been living with Perona?"

"That's right," Arlan said. "And in order to escape the threat of being exposed, Eva allegedly had her shunted into the sanitarium."

Eva has always refused to comment on this, and Perona at the time laughed out loud when reporters queried him. "Of course it isn't true," he said.

But Arlan said his investigation (which included work by two attorneys) revealed that a fight actually occurred between Zsa Zsa and Perona and that it happened just before his client was committed.

"The entire episode was wrapped in scandal," Arlan concluded.

In all the tangled court cases involving the commitment, Eva is always given the ultimate blame, since Zsa Zsa apparently was not coherent enough to solicit help for herself at this time. In *Zsa Zsa Gabor, My Story,* written in 1961 with Gerold Frank, Eva is likewise given responsibility.

Today, Zsa Zsa sticks to her guns. "Eva had me committed," she said recently. Why? "Jealousy."

And Eva clings to her silence.

The sisters apparently were estranged for only a very short time.

Shortly after Zsa Zsa's release Eva called, announcing matter-of-factly that "Mama and Magda are on their way from Portugal to America." Zsa Zsa hung up coldly. She brooded on the conversation. She was glad, certainly, to hear about Jolie and Magda. But Eva was acting as if the past dreadful months had never existed, would never be discussed.

"But that's the way the family is," Jolie explained. "When something's over, it's over. We just go forward."

9

❋ Actress

$\mathcal{F}$ ame finally came to Eva Gabor in 1951. You couldn't overlook her if you tried. Her sunny little face smiled out from newspaper ads, winked from the faded backs of buses, and peered from nifty cardboard cutouts in 20,000 department stores. But her public renown came about in a most peculiar way. America learned about "Zsa Zsa's little sister" not because of her beauty, nor for her talent, but because she was dubiously crowned Miss Valen-Tie.

After a flurry of live television performances, the American Men's Necktie Foundation decided that Eva was just the ticket for their spring advertising campaign. It seemed like a good idea at the time. "This was another sign that I was at least recognizable in my own right," Eva told Louella Parsons.

"My public debut as Miss Valen-Tie took place in that retailers' Valhalla, the Astor Roof," she wrote in her 1954 autobiography, *Orchids and Salami.* "Before all this was over I was convinced that the nation's economy was based on my photograph, and if I should lose my front teeth, the Board of Trade would have to close the stock market."

A tidal wave of publicity engulfed her, leaving her with a bitter-sweet aftertaste. She realized that such notoriety wasn't necessarily professional validation. After working seriously for twelve years, she was still only an asterisk in the annals of entertainment, a footnote on the Broadway scene.

Her predicament was underscored by an outburst from Jolie. "Darling," she told her daughter, "you have a millionaire husband, you have three Cadillacs, you have a raspberry-colored bathtub. You could have anything in this world, yet you are still working in small parts for a few dollars."

Eva had, however, made some laudable progress, particularly after she finally gave up her dream of becoming a Hollywood superstar. Her first breakthrough started with a kiss. After languishing in mediocre straw-hat theaters, Eva was cast in a live TV production, *L'Amour the Merrier,* with Burgess Meredith, then one of television's brightest actors. It was a silly pastiche, but Eva's kiss and the romantic aura she projected caused sparks to fly.

In true Gabor fashion, the stars were in proper alignment. The composer Richard Rodgers, in the throes of launching a new production, was watching. Sitting in his Manhattan penthouse surrounded by rewrites of the play *The Happy Time,* his attention was diverted by Eva's charm. "She's the one," he said to himself. "I've found my Mignonette"—a central character in the new play. He called her later that evening.

"The day before *L'Amour the Merrier* I couldn't find work; the day after I was rejecting offers and fighting off agents."

Rodgers asked Eva to read for him at the Majestic Theater, where the production was to be staged. Like all tryouts, which can make or break a career, this one was traumatic for Eva. Onstage, she was a blond vision, her hair and delicate features silhouetted by a tiny spotlight. Even far back in the theater her beauty was obvious.

But Eva had no way of knowing this. Her voice was tremulous and her hands shaking. She was surrounded by impenetrable darkness and assaulted by distant, disjointed voices. The thought that Richard Rodgers was judging her on each word left her terrified.

"God, she's beautiful," said Rodgers to an associate. "The stage lighting seems to make her transparent. A glow surrounds her." An assistant director threw lines at her in a bored and uninterested voice. It seemed to Eva that her voice was a hoarse whisper, certainly inaudible in the vast theater. There was no comment—just a few moments of silence. Then several key pages of the play were thrust at her and she was told to read two very long scenes. As she finished, only silence greeted her.

"Nice, my dear. Very nice," said Rodgers. "I'll call you later."

She sat by the phone in her Manhattan apartment for twenty-four long hours. When the call came, she was told to fly to Boston to read for *The Happy Time.* It was a frightening replay of the first one: the same pages and a similar but larger theater. When she walked away from the audition she felt weak. Her voice was tremulous.

She could have spared herself; the part was hers. From the moment *The Happy Time* previewed at the Shubert Theater in New Haven, it was an unqualified success and a personal triumph for Eva. At one point on opening night she looked out toward the packed house and lost all composure—not to mention her memory. The girl who talked a mile a minute couldn't find words. Luckily, Leora Dana, the veteran screen and stage actress, fed her her lines slowly and one by one brought her through.

Several months into the run, Eva appeared on the cover of *Life* magazine. The article described her as a "glorious success" and prophesied an auspicious Broadway future. And for a year or so it seemed that this might actually be the case. New York television offered her a nightly one-woman production, *The Eva Gabor Show,* which inconveniently aired from eight to eight-fifteen each evening—a time schedule that left the star gasping for breath. Her mad dash from the television studio to the theater became a humorous fixture of the Broadway scene during the run of *The Happy Time.* A car with the motor running waited outside the studio for Eva, who at exactly eight-fifteen and trailing the long lace dresses she wore on television jumped into the back seat as the car jerked off down the jammed streets.

Several blocks from the theater, a cop named Frank O'Shea stopped traffic at a key intersection, allowing the car to clear the last hurdle on the way to the stage door. Two dressers met her at the door and began stripping her as she rushed up a flight of stairs to her dressing room. There, she gulped down a chocolate malted, slid into her Hungarian maid's uniform, and becam Mignonette.

Eva calculated that through television she could trade fleeting Broadway fame for a healthy bank account. "I was never one of those TV snobs," she said. "And I already knew about the scads of money to be made in that medium."

Television, at the height of its "live" golden age, cast Eva in a series of productions on the order of *Leave It to the Girls.*

"Never in my life had I known a star who wanted so badly to be considered a serious actress, nor one who deserved it more," said Leora Dana. "She was never content to coast by on her considerable glamour. She would have gladly shaved her head and gained fifty pounds if the part required it."

Then quite suddenly Eva's dream of a great part, the part of a lifetime, came true. And she hesitated, fearful of failure. She was offered a major part in an expensive TV production of *Uncle Vanya,* the Chekhov masterpiece. "I was scared to death," Eva told a New York *Times* reporter. "I turned it down."

But the producers wouldn't give up. "I finally told myself, "It's just a play about two men who are after a girl (me) and one of them gets her.' " When *Uncle Vanya* aired live, the critics were knocked out of their seats. Every second of the many hours Eva had spent studying drama showed on the screen.

Television executives, in their infinite wisdom, decided to show off their newest star in an inane fifteen-minute series called *Famous Women of History,* in which Eva had only a few minutes to capture the essence of some of history's most vivid ladies. When Eva did *Marie Antoinette,* she found her own head on the block. At a sponsor's party after the show, an executive sidled over to her and said, "We're in big trouble. The ad men are ready to cut bait."

Eva choked on her champagne. "Why?" she said. "Beats me," answered the producer.

She circulated through the crowd, trying to sidestep the guillotine being sharpened by the sponsors. She finally uncovered the cause of her dilemma, and it was ludicrous. She had been done in by the studio's elevator operator. The nice little guy who always greeted her so cheerfully had been carrying one of the sponsors down from the screening when he volunteered an opinion. "I hated her as Marie Antoinette. I just hated her."

The elevator operator had almost cancelled Eva's show! "So you can imagine how seriously I took ad men after that."

After eighteen months, *The Happy Time* closed, leaving Eva with a desire for glory on the Great White Way that would never be satisfied. Her continued success in the straw-hat theater circuit, no matter how lucrative, was no substitute for Broadway.

She blindly chased this dream for decades. Ironically, Eva, the baby of the Gabor family, the one Jolie most often shunted aside, ended up with the most drive. "Starring Eva Gabor" became the guiding theme of her life. In her haste, Eva stumbled into two massive Broadway flops.

First she twittered onstage in an eighteenth-century farce, *The Little Glass Clock.* Opening night in 1954 was quite unforgettable, although for the wrong reasons. The young lover of the piece tripped on his sword, a leading character actor's knee breeches split, and Eva was virtually drowned in satin, so voluminous were her costumes.

The critics roasted the play as if it were a mammoth turkey. One of them even suggested the play as an effective antidote to insomnia. "Why take a sleeping potion?" he asked. "The same effect would be easily achieved by merely listening to this play's dialogue." Mercifully, the production had a short run.

She didn't get off as easily several years later in 1958. She generated a whirlwind of publicity for an Off Broadway clinker called *Lulu.* To prove her infinite faith in the play, she accepted a paycheck of $75 a week in the hope of establishing herself as a bona fide stage actress. "They even took out seventy-five cents for Social Security," she said later. Derived from a bad turn-of-the-century play, *Earth Spirit,* it was a sad little production that required Eva at one point to recite singsong lines while pirouetting about the stage in toe shoes.

Eva put one tiny foot ahead of the other, her hands waving wildly about. And though the lines she spoke were quite serious, the audience rocked with laughter. Later, during scenes of supposed high comedy, the playgoers audibly groaned. There was a great sigh of relief when the curtain finally descended.

Both Eva and the play's producer, David Ross, displayed false bravado backstage. Ross expounded to the press about hiring Eva's services for such a bargain price. "She took only $75 because she realized what a great part it was." Reporters looked at him quite skeptically. "But," he said, gesturing toward the star's dressing room, "I spent $2,000 making her dressing room more comfortable."

Eva likewise was holding court in the dressing room of the Fourth Street Theater. First came Jolie in a whirlwind of lime chiffon. "Let me kiss my triumphant daughter," she gushed, winking at journalists. The door opened a second time, revealing Magda bedecked in ermine and white satin. "Oh, let me kiss my brilliant sister," she cooed. "What a triumph, darling, what a triumph."

Then came Eva's flame of the moment, the actor Ben Gazzara. "Congratulations, Eva," he said between kisses. He turned toward the columnists: "I trust this little Hungarian. She's got a lot of power."

An electrician moved in and out of the dressing room trying to repair a socket. He grumbled to nobody in particular: "I don't give this play a month." Actually, it closed in a matter of days.

Later, when the Gabor party adjourned to Sardi's, Eva was snappish. "I don't care what it looks like," she said to one reporter. "I'm *not* here waiting for the notices. I'm here because I'm hungry."

10

✻ Cokiline

*T*he voice was gushy and oversweet: "Oh, Mr. Sanders, I've been waiting so long to meet you. I've got such a terrible crush on you."

George Sanders opened his eyes wide and arrogantly looked down over his patrician nose. "How perfectly understandable, my dear, how perfectly understandable."

For a few precious seconds, Zsa Zsa was at a loss for words. The giant of a man towering over her was so distant and imposing, so handsome and distinctive, that she lost all traces of composure.

She first met George Sanders at one of those little cocktail parties in Manhattan—a glide-and-smile affair of the kind so popular in the late 1940s.

"Everybody there was *somebody,*" George later recalled. "But it wasn't polite to ask *who* you were."

There was a slight rise of stairs in one corner of the immense penthouse. And it was there, on the third step, that George Sanders held court. At forty-one, he was an extraordinary specimen, with a sun-bronzed face, silver hair, and the body of an athlete.

That night he was wearing Old World dinner clothes: a boiled shirt, pearl studs, a black silk suit, and black tie. A circle of adoring women surrounded him.

Suddenly there was a vibrant flash of scarlet at the door. Zsa Zsa had arrived. As a valet received the beige mink stole she let slide off her shoulders, her eyes focused hypnotically on George as he towered over the crowd.

It was April 1947. Zsa Zsa was legally free of Conrad Hilton and had become a very gay divorcée riding atop the wave of high society. Hostesses soon learned that she was a magnet, attracting all that was glamorous. Even the dullest party was enlivened by her sparkling wit.

Several weeks had elapsed since the birth of her daughter, Francesca Hilton, the only child from any of the Gabor marriages (who was conceived after the legal separation), so the party marked her return to the Manhattan social wolf pack.

She arrived alone, nudged cheeks with the hostess, and continued staring at George. "He was like a pasha, listening to the praises of the women, yet obviously so bored," she said later.

"Take me to him," she ordered the hostess. "I must meet him."

"George looked up, and his blue eyes swept over me," she remembered. "He was even taller than Conrad Hilton, a powerful man of great, great elegance, and so very, very handsome."

Both of them were among the most beautiful human animals in the room. "To look at Zsa Zsa full face caused you to almost fall into it," Ali Khan once said.

George's physical attributes were heightened by his brusque manner. Many people automatically felt inferior the minute they met him. He was aloof to the point of eccentricity. Zsa Zsa immediately thawed this reserve and, from all accounts, it was love at first sight.

When Zsa Zsa met him, George was an important character actor in films, having played villains in more than sixty movies. His screen voice had just the proper edge of nastiness that could elevate even the most mundane of characters. Supposedly, Zsa Zsa decided to capture his heart after seeing him on the screen in *The Moon and Sixpence.* While watching the movie with her mother, she had turned to Jolie and said, "That's the man I'm going to marry." (This version appears in both Jolie's and Zsa Zsa's autobiographies.)

If all this seems like an excerpt from a romance novel, it's only because Zsa Zsa has always conducted her life as if it were sugary fiction, with her as the heroine. Unlike a dime novel heroine, however, Zsa Zsa took George home that very night.

Zsa Zsa suggested that George and his companion, the author Erich Maria Remarque, accompany her home for a nightcap and early breakfast. The three stayed into the morning hours, each sipping a drink.

"George, I think I must go now to leave Zsa Zsa time to sleep," the author said just before dawn.

George looked up impassively and continued to sip his drink.

Remarque put on his coat, kissed Zsa Zsa's hand, and waited. George merely kept his seat, staring into his drink. The author cleared his throat.

"Oh, yes indeed, old boy, yes indeed," said George. "You go. I'm staying."

Zsa Zsa heard the exchange over her shoulder as she headed up to check on Francesca. She blushed and grasped at the banister: How does he dare? she thought to herself. He dares to say that in my presence. He must think I'm a common tart—an easy conquest.

It was too early for Zsa Zsa to know that this little exchange was to be the theme for their life together: George would lead; George would select. George would decide, and Zsa Zsa would obediently follow.

But on this first occasion, as on all others, she merely recovered her poise and returned to do his bidding. George was leaning across a couch, carefully spreading caviar on the last piece of toast. "We need more toast, my dear," he said, popping the last bite into his mouth. His British voice continued, increasing in loudness so that she could hear it in the kitchen. "There was really nothing fit to eat at that dreadful party," he said, stretching his frame so that it spilled over into the chair as well as the double divan. When he heard her buttering the toast, he bellowed, "And you might bring me a glass of milk too, my dear. . . . And, by the way, I'll call you Cokiline from now on." (Which meant, more or less, "sweet little cookie" in Russian. Sanders, son of British parents, was born in St. Petersburg and spent his first eleven years in Russia.)

This caught her attention. She was mortified and spilled the milk she was pouring. Nobody, not even Burhan the Turk, had dared address her in this manner. What was this—*Taming of the Shrew?*

"Just what does that mean, exactly?" Zsa Zsa asked.

"It's just a term of endearment, Zsa Zsa. You're my sweet little cookie."

As Zsa Zsa delivered more toast, caviar, and milk, George grabbed her waist with both hands, causing her to tumble breathlessly into his lap. As he kissed her, she felt the excitement that had been missing in all her other romantic encounters. (And certainly in both her marriages.)

She slipped away and dimmed the lights. George made one more demand before joining her in the darkness of her bedroom. "Cokiline?" he asked.

"Yes, George."

"Do you suppose you have any more milk in your refrigerator?"

So began a love affair that would wax and wane, a friendship that would endure the blackest of periods, and a twosome Hollywood would never forget.

About as quickly as it took to get that second glass of milk, George Sanders had mapped out Zsa Zsa's life. She would sell her penthouse in New York, trade in her luxurious Bentley car, and swear off high society. She would put away her Paris gowns, store the king's ransom of furs, and lock up the jewelry. She was to be, it must have been quite plain, a quiet obedient adornment to George's life. She would wait at home with his slippers and pipe.

Suddenly, all the male chauvinism she had escaped in leaving Europe crashed down on her again. But she must have wished for this domination. On that hot afternoon in New York when Zsa Zsa watched George emote in *The Moon and Sixpence,* she had experienced shivers of delight when he verbally abused the heroine.

After one particularly nasty scene in the film, Zsa Zsa claims that she grabbed Jolie's arm and said, "This is a man I understand. This is the kind of treatment I call love."

Since the Gabors have fairy-tale explanations for all their love affairs, this one deserves no more attention than her premonition about having an affair with the Latin lover Porfirio Rubiroso, or a fortuneteller's prediction that she would marry the world's most important hotel man. Still, Zsa Zsa has a masochistic desire to be knocked about by her lovers. She now claims that all of her husbands, save Conrad Hilton, struck her.

Jolie said she could tell what kind of marriage it was to be from the first time she met George Sanders. "I always called George 'the deep freeze' because he was so cold. When Zsa Zsa married him, I went out to California to visit them for three days," Jolie recalled. "They had a long, black mirror table in the dining room. Zsa Zsa sat at one end and George at the other. I addressed him as 'King George.' Anyway when Francesca's nanny brought her down to say goodnight, she skipped over to him. 'Georgie, Georgie, I love you," Francesca said. Without looking up from his plate, he said, 'Good night.' "

When describing those years to a talk-show host, Jolie poured out a torrent of venom for the late actor (though she said, grudgingly, that she liked him). "They went to bed at nine. And Zsa Zsa preferred being at home with him than being taken around the world by anybody else. And George? All he wanted was a housewife. And that's what my glamorous daughter became. She waited on him hand and foot, rubbed his back and flattered his ego. He always inferred, 'I'm helpless. I need someone to mother me.' "

The marriage caused gasps of incredulity from the very beginning. An hour after the ceremony, Hedda Hopper asked the usual banal question: "Where will you go on your honeymoon?"

Zsa Zsa patted Hedda on the shoulder. "What a silly question to ask, Hedda. We just came back from it." The vitriolic den mother of Hollywood was about to strike when Zsa Zsa explained: "I don't say this to shock you, but it *was* the honeymoon that led us to marriage. George and I were both in love; that much we knew. But marriage really frightened us. . . . The honeymoon convinced us that marriage would work."

Economically, Zsa Zsa realized that the marriage might be fool-hardy. First, her Hilton alimony stopped the minute she married. Second, George was a relative pauper by her standards, and so much a skinflint that Connie was Daddy Warbucks in comparison.

When George asked for her hand, it was her bank account—not her heart—that made her hesitate. Before accepting, she demanded a week to think it over. But the next night she phoned George at two A.M. "George, I want to marry you anyway."

He paused. "You had better think about it twice. I have many problems, Cokiline. I've been in analysis for years. I might come home to you fine one night and return the next day as somebody different —maybe a psycho."

As Zsa Zsa told Hedda, "George suggested that we slowly motor from Hollywood to New York. George said that he wanted to show me America. If the trip worked out, he explained, the marriage might have a chance."

The trip was a bucolic little affair. They stopped for sausage and bread at little mom and pop stores, sat in the car looking at the Mississippi River for hours, toasted each other with apple wine, and dressed in jeans to meander on country back roads. On one of these little picnics, George fingered the edge of a wilted paper plate and looked up shyly at Zsa Zsa. "Am I making you miserable?" he asked tentatively.

"On the contrary, darling, I love every minute of it. And, by the way, if you plan to make me miserable, then go ahead. So much do I love you."

Decades later, the jaded, pampered Zsa Zsa of the 1980s would look back on this simple trip and recall that it was the happiest time of her life. "George was my true love," she told a reporter in 1980. "He changed my life, made me enjoy simple things such as a Pacific sunset or the beauty of roses damp with the morning fog."

Once back in California, the Beverly Hills country bumpkins had to lie low. Since George's citizenship was to be granted in several weeks, he had to keep his slate clean. Publicity about his premarital and open affair with Zsa Zsa had to be avoided for the moment. After he became a bona fide American, George became a Lothario who would have caused any woman to swoon. He buried his deep-seated neuroses and became—for a short time—an ardent lover.

He splurged on an exquisite wedding, showered Zsa Zsa with flowers, and even chartered a plane to fly in the rest of the Gabors.

But it was a dumpy little "rent-a-minister" who helped them tie the knot just off the Las Vegas Strip by stuttering, "You are now man and wife."

George leaned over Zsa Zsa and lifted her veil. His eyes were moist and full of love. "My dear," he said, "you are no longer Mrs. Conrad Hilton."

Zsa Zsa blushed and continued to hold up her face for the traditional kiss. But George hesitated so long that it became embarrassing. "Cokiline," he finally said, "now that we're married, I'm not sure if I will be able to make love to you anymore."

The Sanders neurosis was showing itself.

"So they spent their wedding night playing chess," Jolie told a reporter for the New York *Times*. "Sometimes I would phone them up at ten P.M. and find them already in bed."

For the Zsa Zsa Gabor of today all these minor insults would prove impossible. The Zsa Zsa of today would tell George to make his own toast, spread his own caviar, and, more importantly, to put away the damn chess set and get into bed.

The Zsa Zsa of 1949 was quite different. She was not yet a public figure and had no solid identity. Her only fame was as the consort of famous men—as Mrs. Belge, Mrs. Hilton, and now Mrs. Sanders.

Other than wearing some of the world's most beautiful clothes, sporting a fortune in diamonds, and undergoing a painfully public "nervous breakdown," Zsa Zsa had no claim to fame. (For that matter, only Eva had any public identity.)

Zsa Zsa was adrift and hunting for an identity. The newlyweds started with a little nothing of a flat on Hollywood's Shoreham Drive, a modest address in class-conscious Hollywood.

"George lived in the small apartment house he had always rented on Shoreham," Zsa Zsa once explained to Merv Griffin. "One apartment was empty. George gave it to me . . . and I dressed in little peasant outfits, cheerfully worked over a hot stove, and decorated the apartment with materials from the corner hardware store."

It was during her "hausfrau period," however, that Zsa Zsa came face to face with her true nature. "George insisted that we were two of a kind. And we *were* two of a kind. We both lived in a very special world. In time I was to discover that, like George, I saw things not as they were but as a play within a play in which I was always waiting for a prince to awaken me with a kiss and lead me away from sadness, suffering, and from the terrible truth that beauty vanishes as youth grows old. George and I both wanted to live a dream."

So, the apartment house in the Hollywood flatlands proved far too confining for the heroine of a grand romance. George also longed for the proper setting for his wondrous bride. One morning he looked up over the eggs Benedict Zsa Zsa had carefully prepared. "Cokiline, you need to buy a little place out here now that you have sold the brownstone in New York."

She was house hunting that very afternoon and found what she wanted in less than a week. Her dream house was a staggeringly large Bel Air mansion with fourteen rooms, three acres of gardens, and a guesthouse. The grounds meandered about a knoll and possessed an Old World charm. A week or so later George motored over to have a look. He saw the huge living room. Nodded. Saw the master bedroom. Nodded. Then there was the swimming pool of "early movie star" design. He stopped to look at it, screwed up his face, and moaned. "Oh, Cokiline, I'm happy in my little apartment. I don't like big houses. I would be lost here. I'm happy in my little apartment. But for you this is perfect. I insist that you live here."

Zsa Zsa was crushed. This dream house was to be for them both. But she arranged a compromise that, unwittingly, was to start her on a long road to divorce. "We decided that he could move some of his stuff to the house and keep many of his possessions in the apartment. Therefore," said Zsa Zsa, "he would have two homes to run back and forth between. I didn't realize the heartbreak this would mean."

When the mood struck him, the lord and master could partake of Zsa Zsa simply by making the small journey to the mansion. If not, he would stay down in the flatlands, playing the piano and indulging in his obsessive hobby—the crafting of furniture in an expensive workroom stocked with saws, lathes, and finishing benches. In time, Zsa Zsa became a widow to that hobby.

In addition to an absentee husband, even more stinging insults were in store for Zsa Zsa. One afternoon she returned to the mansion and found her house full of photographers. It had just been announced that George would star in *All About Eve,* and the studio, Twentieth Century–Fox, was preparing a series of magazine layouts. The theme was "George Sanders at home." And it was significant that he chose his wife's sprawling home, not his bare apartment, as the proper setting. Zsa Zsa was at first overjoyed and dashed upstairs to dress imposingly. Within fifteen minutes she was all ready for the photographers. Every time she ventured near one of them, George waved her aside disdainfully.

At one point he bitingly suggested that she drift upstairs and remain in her boudoir. Her presence, he whispered, was detracting from his own persona.

During a break in the photo session, Zsa Zsa sidled over to George and suggested, "Shouldn't I be included in the pictures? I *am* your wife."

He gave her a look fierce enough to wilt a turnip. "My dear Cokiline," he said acidly. "I know it's very hard for you to understand, but this story is about *me.* I am an actor."

Embarrassed and betrayed, Zsa Zsa turned on him in fury. "George, this is my house and if you want to be photographed in my house, you include me. If not, take them down to that dowdy little apartment of yours." This time, George acquiesced. But he got even.

"I was so proud to be on his arm the night he won the Oscar for *All About Eve*," she said. "The ceremony was at the old Grauman's Chinese Theatre. We sat there in the dark as the nominations were announced, and I was hoping so hard for his victory that my nails dug into his arm. When George's name was announced, I grasped his hand and said, 'George, I'm so proud of you.'"

George yanked his hand from hers, looked coldly down at her face, and walked up to collect his Oscar. Needless to say, he didn't mention his wife in the victory speech.

Zsa Zsa's eyes filled. He refused to share even a bit of this triumphant moment with her. He disappeared behind the curtain for the usual Oscar press conference. But unlike the other winners, he didn't return to collect his partner after the show. "I sat there until all the other awards were announced," she said. "Then everyone began to leave. Finally, the theater was empty and I was crushed. Then I heard George laughing with some of the other winners and realized he had completely forgotten me."

At least he *took* her to the Oscar ceremony. This was atypical. Normally when he went out of the country for location filming or when he crossed America on publicity tours, Zsa Zsa remained at home warming the hearth.

Zsa Zsa worked hard to be the ideal "Mrs. George Sanders," perhaps harder than at any other time in her life. She roamed the markets and pored over cookbooks, hoping to please her husband's discriminating taste. She even kept her mother and sisters away to devote herself completely to George. "She was blind to the truth— to the truth that she wasn't really getting anywhere with George," Jolie said later. "It was heartbreaking to stand by and see her hurt so often and so deeply."

Of course, George had his own version. In his autobiography, *Memoirs of a Professional Cad,* he wrote, "My life with Zsa Zsa was a kaleidoscope with large areas of fun in it. Yet there came a time when I simply had to get away. Providence came to my assistance in the form of an offer from the brilliant Italian director Roberto Rossellini."

The day Rossellini cabled him that he had a part for him, George said he went looking for his wife to tell her the news. "I finally found her under the hair dryer, going over the guest list for her next party," he wrote in the memoirs. "She saw me come in and must have known that I wanted to talk to her, but she was under the hair dryer and under the hair dryer she stayed."

Her fingers, nails newly polished, stretched out in the warm air, and there was expensive cream on her face. George tried to attract her attention with a serious grimace and a crude attempt at sign language. Finally he waved his passport in front of her face and vainly tried to convey that he was leaving for Italy.

"She regarded me indulgently for a few moments with a sunny social smile and then returned to the sober scrutiny of her guest list," he recalled. "In no time at all I was on an airliner headed for Rome."

Zsa Zsa's version is, of course, contradictory. "I didn't even know that he was going to Italy until a few hours before he left." She pleaded with him, she said, almost on bended knee. "Oh, George," she wailed, "why don't we go together. It's so glorious in Rome."

Once again he sniffed, looking down the long nose. "You can't go. How could you expect to go when you know you would just ruin it for me?"

Psychiatrists had no small role in crippling the marriage. Insecure, nervous, and a hypochondriac, George contracted that addiction so common in Beverly Hills—complete dependence on psychiatry. After thousands of hours on the couch, he would come home with a different neurosis every month. Some weeks he was an "obsessive-compulsive," running madly about the city, accepting every movie role in sight and working around the clock on his hobby. Then, convinced by the analyst of the moment that he was a reclusive neurotic, George would skulk about Zsa Zsa's house, closeting himself in the bedroom and piling great quilts over his body.

"I came to hate the analysts," Zsa Zsa remembered bitterly. "Every time he went for an appointment, I shuddered, not knowing who would come home."

George, on the other hand, claimed that he suffered constant trauma in Zsa Zsa's home. "I was welcome only as a second class guest. During the five years I was married to her, I lived in her sumptuous mansion as a sort of paying guest," he told Louella Parsons on the occasion of his divorce. "My presence in the house was regarded by her press photographers, dressmakers, and friends with violent amusement. The joke was always on me."

Zsa Zsa, he claimed, allowed him only one small room in which to keep his personal effects. "And I was even kicked out of that room when more space was needed to store Zsa Zsa's mounting stacks of press clippings and photographs. . . . Unless my working hours on a film were excessively long, you would find me at home, standing at the bar—just beneath a huge portrait of Zsa Zsa—fixing drinks for her newspaper interviewers and photographers. But the most rewarding experience came when I had the pleasure of driving her dressmaker home. She, at least, was grateful."

George, it became obvious, protested too much. He was peculiar to the ultimate degree. Zsa Zsa would go for weeks without seeing her husband. Then he would call her up late at night and ask her to rush down to his apartment with milk and sandwiches. She always went to sleep uncertain whether she would be called into action as a volunteer supply sergeant. One night after a vicious fight with George, in which he told her to keep out of his life, the phone rang at three A.M. "Cokiline," said the neurotic husband, "I've got no milk here and no bread. I'm starving."

Sleepily, Zsa Zsa got up, packed up bread, chicken, and milk. But just before she rushed out the door, the phone rang again. "And Cokiline," he said, "do you have any of those wonderful little cookies on hand?" "Yes, George," she said wearily. "I'll bring them."

"When all was said and done," said New York columnist Earl Wilson, a major Gabor expert, "you can believe only about two-thirds of what George Sanders said and only half of what Zsa Zsa tells you. Some formula. If you can figure it out."

Every once in a while George would call on Zsa Zsa to bask in his heady fame as a film actor. He would phone, usually very late at night, to take advantage of cheaper telephone rates, and ask her to fly to his side. One time it was Bermuda to which she was summoned.

One midnight Zsa Zsa picked up the phone, and it was an overseas call. "Cokiline. Cokiline, are you there?"

"My heart began to pound," she recalled. She feigned peevishness. "I don't want to talk to you, George," she said, not meaning a word of it. "So I talked to him and talked to him and talked to him. He had just finished a film in London and wanted me to meet him in the Bahamas. But I don't *want* to meet him, I thought. I don't want to be hurt anymore."

Soon George was pleading. "Cokiline, I know this will sound absurd to you, but please, please come. I can't get by without you." Those were the magic words.

"Recoiffed, reoutfitted in the best resort wear available in Beverly Hills, I flew off to be with him in the Bahamas. Every night we danced in the light of the moon—George in his British whites and I in my blue and pink organza gowns. At the end of two glorious weeks, George said, 'Darling, we must go now. I'm going off to Cuba and then to Mexico. You may come with me to Cuba, but I must go to Mexico alone.'"

"Why?" Zsa Zsa asked, taking the bait.

Her husband almost sneered at her. "I promised Dolores Del Rio that I would visit her, my dear. And it's purely business. She's a big star down there and can be difficult. You would only complicate things."

Zsa Zsa was crestfallen. But she flew back to Beverly Hills resolving never to be humiliated again. She was ready to fly on her own.

11

❋ Overnight Sensation

*T*he folds of a beige brocade dress cascaded off her
shoulders, tapered in at her eighteen-inch waist, and
then flared out again toward the rich carpet. Three matched diamond
circlets caught the glow of an overhead light that also illuminated her
platinum hair.

Zsa Zsa wondered how something that looked so great could feel
so wrong. George had gone off on location and left her alone again.
But what else was new? And time—in lost weeks and months—was
slipping through her hands. This was frightening. "Mrs. George Sanders" wasn't a big enough role for her. There had to be more. She
needed more. So she swore to find it.

It was during this period of immense personal crisis that fame
crashed down on Zsa Zsa, bringing an avalanche of glory, a fountain
of money, and a runaway acting career so frantic that it would eventually ravage her nerves—a second time.

There was no warning. Indeed, the summer of 1951 started out
dismally. She had purchased an expensive summer wardrobe in the
hope of traveling to England with George, who was to be there for
four months. He had hinted that this time she would be allowed to
go. But at the last minute, George said sternly, "You stay home.
You would just be bored and would make it impossible for me to
work."

Zsa Zsa pleaded, warning that he was about to leave her at home
one time too many. "Nonsence, Cokiline, you belong here."

When he left for the airport, Zsa Zsa collapsed in tears. Eva was
busy on the summer theater circuit, Jolie was making her fortune with
an immensely popular jewelry boutique in Manhattan, and Magda was
busy with a collection of romantic suitors.

She was stuck.

Then, several days after George left for London, Zsa Zsa was thumbing through a *Vogue* magazine when George's brother, the actor Tom Conway (famed as the Falcon in a series of very popular films), called up with an offer. "Look, Zsa Zsa, I'm stuck. The actress who was to appear with me on a TV guest panel has suddenly cancelled. It's a new show, *Bachelor's Haven.* I'm a regular panelist. We're really stuck, on the spot, and I suggested you."

This offer, at first, alarmed Zsa Zsa. A couple of months earlier, Pamela Mason had asked George to let his wife appear on her talk show. George answered nastily, "Oh, Pamela, Zsa Zsa's just too dumb for that."

It was understandable that she panicked when faced with Tom's offer. "I can't do that. What would I say? I'm no actress."

Conway explained that it was a simple little affair. "All they do is read husband and wife letters, allowing those of us on the panel to give advice. Each week we showcase the wife of a celebrity. Believe me, darling, you'll be great."

Reluctantly she agreed to appear. But after hanging up the phone, panic again engulfed her. What would she wear? What would George think? Zsa Zsa was so intimidated by her husband that she was almost crushed. The ravages of the Hilton divorce, the hangover from her weeks in the sanitarium, and the rigors of daily bullying by George had all but destroyed her normally buoyant self-confidence.

She paced the house psyching herself up for the public appearance. Finally she said to herself, "What the hell. Maybe I can carry it off." Characteristically, she scavenged through her closet for an outfit that would show her in the best possible light. She chose a simple black gown by the designer Balenciaga, and sprinkled it lavishly with diamonds. Later she told Louella Parsons, "I thought that I might not be able to knock the TV world on its ear, but if I flopped, I was damn well going to fail beautifully."

She drove to the studio with an almost crippling case of stage fright, but Tom Conway calmed her down. "Zsa Zsa," he advised, "you are one of the most naturally witty women I've ever seen. All you have to do is be yourself."

A makeup man trotted up to apply finishing touches and shrugged. "Honey, I don't think I could top what you've already done." Before she had time to work up any more jitters, she was shoved onstage and the taping began. Her diamond bracelet and a twenty-carat solitaire ring sparkled brightly, causing one of the hosts to whistle.

"Oh, darling," she said disdainfully, "these are just my working diamonds."

With her very first remark on TV she brought down the house.

"Exactly what happened that first evening is still vague in my mind," she recalled. "All I know is that I was handed a career on a silver platter. . . . *Bachelor's Haven* called me back week after week, and week after week my fame seemed to multiply. I was in the right place at the right time."

From that first line, Zsa Zsa displayed a razor-sharp wit. "Zsa Zsaisms" rolled off her tongue in an endless verbal torrent. For instance, one letter was read from a young woman: "I'm breaking my engagement to a very wealthy man. He gave me a beautiful home, a mink coat, diamonds, an expensive car, and a stove. What shall I do?"

Zsa Zsa's hand caressed her own diamond bracelet and she looked innocently at the TV camera: "You have to be fair, darling. Give back the stove."

Then another: "My husband is a traveling salesman, but I know he strays even when he's at home. What should I do?"

"Shoot him in the legs," Zsa Zsa said.

By this time the studio audience was in tumult, with calls from fans already flooding the Hollywood studio's switchboard. "I ad-libbed constantly," Zsa Zsa explained. "My original stage fright vanished as I said the first things that came to my mind."

Someone else asked, "Can you cook?"

"You bet," Zsa Zsa answered. "When I was courting George Sanders, I cooked three meals a day for him in his own apartment. Now I don't cook for him anymore. . . . I don't have to. We're married."

Within minutes after the show went on the air, producers were talking of a long-term contract for Zsa Zsa. "Would you consider it?" asked one of them. "Sure, why not?" she answered. "This is fun."

Nevertheless, she went home thinking of the experience as a nice innocent lark—something to pass the time away while George was on the Continent filming. The next day she awakened to a hurricane of attention. Agents began calling at eight A.M. followed by phone interviews with Louella Parsons and Hedda Hopper. Sidney Skolsky led his newspaper column with the Gaborisms. Shortly before noon copies of the show business trade papers—*Daily Variety* and *Hollywood Reporter*—were sent out to her. Both hailed her as an "instant star" and ran hastily acquired photos of her taken by the Associated Press.

Also, and unknown to Zsa Zsa, Hollywood's most prestigious studio, MGM, was preparing to make her a movie star. One of the studio's top directors, Mervyn LeRoy, had watched her TV show and remarked to an associate, "Look at the way the camera caresses her. She has that special sort of screen glow that comes along rarely, very rarely." Since Zsa Zsa had no agent and still wasn't thinking in terms of a screen career, LeRoy was thwarted in reaching the future actress.

Ten days later, however, when Zsa Zsa was dancing at the Mocambo nightclub, LeRoy asked her to his table and offered her, right there, a showcase role in the studio's newest and most expensive musical, *Lovely to Look At,* which was already filming with Ann Miller, Kathryn Grayson, Howard Keel, and Red Skelton.

"They didn't even want to test me," Zsa Zsa told her mother by phone. "He told me I was a natural and that I didn't need a test."

"I've seen all I needed to on the first television show," LeRoy told MGM producer Jack Cummings. "I think we should grab her up before anyone else does."

In one half hour, Zsa Zsa achieved what Eva hadn't been able to do in twelve years. She had an acting career and was offered ten movie roles, twenty-five television appearances, and immediate national publicity.

More importantly, she hadn't been forced to starve or to make demeaning screen tests. Her new career wrapped comfortably around her like one of the many minks in her closet.

A week later she met the P. T. Barnum of Hollywood, the city's most successful publicist, a man who could make a change in hair color so important that it knocked international stories off the front page of America's newspapers. His name was Russell Birdwell, the man who made Carole Lombard a household name and the genius behind the contest to find an unknown actress to play Scarlett O'Hara. He had been tipped off in advance that Zsa Zsa was to grace the cover of *Life* magazine and the same week the Sunday supplements of the 225 Hearst newspapers. To quote Zsa Zsa, "He smelled money."

Later, when Hedda Hopper asked how the Gabor-Birdwell liaison had come about, Zsa Zsa explained: "He called up and told me that the entire country would soon be talking about me. But unless I knew how to prolong it, I'd be a flash in the pan."

Zsa Zsa was skeptical. In the first place, she had no real money yet from her fifteen-day-old career, and George's Scrooge budget wouldn't pay for two restaurant lunches.

Birdwell sensed the reason for her hesitation. "Look," he said, "I'm reopening my New York office after some time. As part of the deal I'll take you on speculation. You pay me nothing. Just make sure the word gets around that Russell Birdwell is handling you."

An agent warned: "Zsa Zsa, you don't really need a press agent. You're getting by without one now. Be careful with Birdwell or you might find yourself overexposed." Zsa Zsa, typically, kept her deal with the press agent. There was no way for either Zsa Zsa or Birdwell to know that the mammoth tidal wave of publicity would backfire and put Zsa Zsa on a one-woman blacklist. The infamy of her love life, her wild spending habits, and a gypsy lifestyle would cause studios to shun her as unsuitable for family film fare.

The afternoon she concluded her agreement with Birdwell, she had him over for tea. His wit was a match for Zsa Zsa's. To him, nothing was too outlandish, nothing so insignificant that it couldn't be traded for thousands of dollars in free publicity. "My aim is to impress the whole country, but we also want you to wow the top ten moviemakers right here in Hollywood," he told her.

"The publicity campaign opened up a new life for me," Zsa Zsa recalled. "Russell began taking me to all the important openings in baronial style with a chauffeured limousine and hired cameramen to take my photos. And at last I was able to use the magnificent clothes I had bought during the past five years."

About the time this flood of publicity hit the country, George flew in from London, his picture completed. It was a touch of high irony that Zsa Zsa's face on the cover of *Life* greeted him as he glanced at the airport newsstand. Ever the hermit, he had received no word of the transformation of his little Cokiline. Certainly he never expected to find a star.

Two show-business egos now operated within a marriage that was already damaged by the pressures of George's career. "Now there were two big stars sitting by the same hearth," Zsa Zsa said. "Separations and kissy reunions began to dominate our lives. Although we were still very much in love, we tormented each other constantly."

The fact that George continued to live in his apartment and spent only an occasional night with Zsa Zsa certainly didn't help the crumbling marriage.

"Somewhere in me was a woman who wanted to be dominated by a man like George," Zsa Zsa remembered. "But now there was also in me a restless, driving, ambitious woman who *had* to have a career."

Zsa Zsa got her wish. In 1951 and 1952 she made four major films, *Lovely to Look At, Moulin Rouge, Lili,* and *The Story of Three Loves.* In October of 1951 she graced the cover of *Life,* followed by the covers of *Look, Collier's, Paris Match,* and the *London Picture Post.*

It was the London cover that earned her a featured role in *Moulin Rouge,* the highly acclaimed film about the life of the painter Toulouse-Lautrec. The London photographer coated his camera with an almost invisible veneer of baby oil, creating an indistinct mist about Zsa Zsa's face. The haunting quality impressed British producer James Woolf, then assembling the cast of *Moulin Rouge.* Again Zsa Zsa was signed sight unseen.

Her angelic beauty, however, failed to impress director John Huston in the least. In fact, after seeing Zsa Zsa stumble through *Lovely to Look At,* he asked Woolf to recast the part with "somebody who can act."

Woolf refused—and with good reason. Zsa Zsa was to play the legendary chanteuse Jane Avril, an impulsive and impossibly beautiful woman who became Lautrec's favorite model. At one point during the negotiations, Woolf placed the *London Picture Post* cover alongside a Lautrec portrait of Jane Avril. "Uncanny, isn't it?" he asked Huston. "Not particularly," said the director. "But it's your film."

Just before she was to leave for London, George drew her aside. "My dear, do you realize that you will be a major figure in one of the most distinguished pictures of the year? You have a great, great responsibility."

Trembling with the uncertainty of her own talents, Zsa Zsa contacted Hollywood drama coach Elsa Stanoff, who had coached her the year before, and began rehearsing scenes from the script. As if this weren't enough, she engaged the antique but prestigious British actress Constance Collier for additional aid. Failing to realize that Woolf had cast her to be herself, Zsa Zsa was confused and imbued with a sense of her own shortcomings when she reported for rehearsal with Huston.

The day the company moved to Paris, the news magazine *Paris Soir* featured the headline "Zsa Zsa Gabor—The Most Fashionable Woman in the World."

Gruff, unapproving, and sometimes fueled by vodka and tomato juice, Huston put Zsa Zsa near the windows of an immense rehearsal studio and made her recite lines from the film script. She tried vainly to be heard, failing eaach time to meet Huston's standards.

"For more than a year I had been told to speak softly since the studio microphones pick up any sign of shrillness," Zsa Zsa said. "Now here was Huston telling me to scream—sometimes in competition with the Paris traffic just outside the windows. This would become a dilemma for most of my career. I was hired because I am Zsa Zsa, but when I go to work directors try and force their methods on me. John Huston's intense, precise directions tortured me."

Worse, he often humiliated Zsa Zsa before the entire cast. Once, when a group of important visitors were on the set, Huston said to nobody in particular, "Goddammit, she's dropping the ends of her sentences."

Finally the director found an approach that would work, one that Zsa Zsa could easily understand. "Zsa Zsa," said Huston, "forget about acting. Just make love to the camera."

"Now I knew very little about acting but a great deal about making love," she recalled. "It worked."

During a key scene in the film, Zsa Zsa scored a triumph. Wrapped in a gorgeous crepe dress, her angelic face framed by a picture hat, she moved slowly down the stairs mouthing the words to the prerecorded "Song from the Moulin Rouge." Her eyes burned with fire, her movements were sensual, and the camera seemed to picture her with the same color and intensity Toulouse-Lautrec had used to depict the real Jane Avril.

Huston had filled the set with an oily fog to simulate the conditions of the gaslight era, so the tableau was like watching an entire world come back to life. When Zsa Zsa paused on the bottom step, the cast and crew, including a grudging John Huston, burst into applause. It remains one of the screen's great moments.

With two of the Gabor sisters already acting and the third, Magda, doing occasional summer stock, the money men in Las Vegas thought they saw a golden opportunity. There were four bids for the three sisters from the gambling palaces, but the Frontier, in 1953, offered the most—$500,000 for a planned series of three appearances. (Only one was completed, but the paycheck was still in six figures.) Since none of them could sing or dance, the Frontier devised a little ensemble entitled "The Gabors—This Is *Our* Life." The main topic, naturally, was lightly veiled sex. Eva, always the most sensitive about being lumped together with her two siblings, demanded that the Frontier add a clause to the contract forbidding the club, in any way, from advertising them as a "sister act" like the McGuire Sisters. "We are *not* the McGuire Sisters," she snapped to the general manager of the hotel.

The day before the three-sister act was scheduled to open the Frontier staged a massive press conference, for which almost a hundred reporters were flown to Vegas, adding to the ballyhoo that erupted when the Gabors descended on the gambling capital. Except for appearances by Marlene Dietrich, the city had never seen such luxury, such glamour. It was made all the more potent by the fact that all four of the Gabors were in place at one time and lavishly on display.

Magda and Jolie were unknown publicly until the sell-out Vegas act made them instant celebrities. The champagne that flowed freely at the press conference put the reporters in the mood for the Gabor invasion. Then, fashionably late, a curtain was parted in one of the banquet rooms, and the Gabor sisters glided into view. Dressed in identical gowns but of different colors—black, red, and white—the sisters stepped up onto a small stage riser, fluffed out the full skirts of their gowns, and leaned back dramatically into amber spotlights.

Quite unintentionally, Magda stole the show. Her natural red hair was accented by the stark contrast of her black gown. While Zsa Zsa and Eva were publicly overexposed, Magda had remained a shadow figure since she arrived from Portugal in the late 1940s. She had drifted in and out of very forgettable marriages, done a bit of summer theater, and survived more or less on money brought with her from Europe.

"This is the most exciting thing that's ever happened to us," Magda answered press inquiries. "My excitement, of course, is more intense than that of my sisters; I'm the quietest of the three."

Just as the press conference was about to break up, Jolie entered on the arm of a friend. "Nuci, Nuci," Magda cried in greeting, causing the press to turn in unison toward the vision at the back of the room. Jolie, her figure reduced to a svelte shadow of its Hungarian, Old World plumpness, appeared to be an older sister rather than a mother. And she soon captured a lion's share of the attention with her unaffected charm. The reporters learned, as would the world the next day, that Jolie was fast becoming wealthy from the jewelry boutique she had established in Manhattan and that she didn't fully approve of her daughters' audacity.

Cannily, she had chosen several of the best pieces from her boutique to display in the photos and had coaxed her daughters into doing likewise.

After this appearance the Gabor foursome, despite their individuality, were forever linked together publicly.

12

❋ Runaway Ego

*T*allulah Bankhead's enormous mouth formed an angry grimace as she turned toward her director. "I've been doing radio for twenty years without a hint of trouble. And now one delicate woman is pulling the studio down on top of me."

She took a hefty drink of bourbon, giving the director another withering glance as she applied some more ghastly flamingo-colored lipstick. "Where the hell did she go, anyway?" Tallulah's manner became more imperious. She had twisted her red-orange hair into a hopeless tangle and spilled coffee down the front of her Christian Dior slacks.

Her quarry had apparently disappeared into the shadows of NBC's West Coast studio.

Tallulah's foghorn voice bellowed again. "Go get her!" she barked at the harried young assistant director."

"I'll try, Miss Bankhead, I'll try," he stammered.

As he started off on the run, Tallulah grabbed his sleeve and nearly ripped the cuff off his shirt. "What did you say her name was?"

"Zsa Zsa," he said wearily.

"Za Za?" questioned Tallulah.

"No, Miss Bankhead, Zsa Zsa."

The actress quickly pulled a silver flask of bourbon from her purse. "Forget it, kid. We'll just call her Mrs. George Sanders."

"But Miss Bankhead," he stuttered, "that's part of the problem."

"I don't give a goddamn what the problem is; I *said* we'll call her Mrs. George Sanders. After all, he's a star—at least."

It should have been the easiest thing in the world. George and Zsa Zsa were engaged to appear in a fifteen-minute skit on the nation's highest-rated radio program, *Tallulah Bankhead's Big Show.*

Tallulah presided over a rather informal hour of air time, a sort of predecessor of the talk shows that were to command vast audiences on television a decade later. The star, a veteran of thirty years' stage and screen experience, talked with four or five major guests—all of whom were allowed to shamelessly promote their current book, record, or movie.

There was only one catch. *Everybody's* patter was written and then ruled upon by the star, who insisted that she prescribe the direction any conversation was to take. And she was probably right. For one thing, the program, all sixty minutes of it, was broadcast live after four complete rehearsals.

It was Tallulah herself who decided that George and Zsa Zsa were just what was needed to set off the parade of singers and dramatists who dominated the show. But it had been misrepresented to Zsa Zsa. She had been told through her agent that she and George would be presented in just the right light, reflecting his status as a character actor and her newfound fame as a film actress.

"Don't you worry, honey, we'll take care of everything," an associate producer told Zsa Zsa. "It's very, very simple and over in several minutes. Trust me, you'll be great."

Zsa Zsa wasn't convinced. As charming as her voice had come to be, it was the total Zsa Zsa, the gorgeous human animal, that set her quickly apart from the rest of the Hollywood parade. She cannily realized that radio audiences would get nothing of this breathtaking effect.

Still, it was a chance to act with George, and he seemed so truly pleased about it.

If Zsa Zsa had known the reason for George's confidence, she would have cancelled at once. It never occurred to her that their sketch was already prepackaged and presented a certain viewpoint— George's. He was determined to again cast his beauteous wife as the little woman at home. As for Tallulah, she thought that was a hoot.

Another thing Zsa Zsa never knew was that George, always the meddler, had worked with the team of *Big Show* writers to add a certain Sandersian humor to the skit. And that meant rampant chauvinism.

A week or so before the show was to air, a messenger drove out to the Bel Air mansion and deposited Zsa Zsa's copy of the script. It couldn't have made her happy that George had already approved the script—a fact indicated on Zsa Zsa's copy. As written, it had that certain husband vs. wife slant that was so popular on radio and television during the early 1950s.

It introduced Zsa Zsa this way: "Who was *that* lady with you, George?" asked Tallulah. And George, with venom dripping from his voice, answered, "That was *no* lady, Tallulah, that was my wife." And there were other slurs. Such as "We've been married for two years, and I haven't spoken to Zsa Zsa since she said yes."

Tallulah asked, "Doesn't Zsa Zsa speak to you?" "Only in Hungarian," the actor replied. "What does she say?" Tallulah pressed. "I can only guess," he continued. "Do you understand Hungarian?" said Tallulah. "Not this one," he answered.

Then Tallulah's voice assumed its well-known arrogant tone: "Well, Mr. Sanders, I don't see how you could possibly put up with that sort of domestic setup."

"Well, Tallulah, she's perfectly happy. After all, she can catch glimpses of me as I walk in the garden or dive into the pool. And we do have a certain intimacy. We both share the top drawer of *my* dresser."

None of this could have possibly pleased Zsa Zsa, who by herself bore the entire expense of the house, pool, and gardens surrounding it.

She read the lines again and again, trying to see if there were any way her pride would allow her to go on network radio and listen to such degrading nonsense. It was not unlike the chauvinistic put-downs so common on cheap vaudeville stages in the 1930s.

Zsa Zsa was deeply hurt that these lines had been written for her but was stung even more by the fact that George thought they were just fine. "Just the thing to bring out that little Hungarian's personality," he told Tallulah.

Lovely to Look At, Zsa Zsa's first film, was before the cameras at MGM, so she was concentrating on turning that one movie into an entire career. She couldn't imagine herself being humiliated in such a way on national radio, but the film took all her energy, forcing Zsa Zsa to ignore the script.

Mervyn LeRoy, director of *Lovely to Look At,* had decided to allow Zsa Zsa certain freedoms in portraying the high-fashion supporting role to Kathryn Grayson and Ann Miller's lead performances. For one thing, he let her choose her own dresses, an almost unheard of privilege at MGM. (Garbo, for instance, was never allowed to influence her costume designers.) Luckily, Zsa Zsa and the designer, Adrian, thought along similar lines. The bell-skirted, bare-shouldered look that she had made her trademark was continued in the film.

One afternoon Zsa Zsa, in cocktail black with a bare wisp of diamonds at her throat, dropped in on Adrian in his fashion workshop. Spread around him were the bolts of pastel silk, satin, and velvet that had been personally purchased in France by the designer. "Black is my color," she said. "It would allow me to express perfectly the effect you want in *Lovely to Look At.*"

On film, Zsa Zsa's simple black gowns were startling when compared to the overripe Easter egg colors worn by Ann and Kathryn. The rigors of acting before the camera for the first time, however, drained her, and she quite naturally forgot about the *Big Show* script. Therefore, Tallulah, George, and the show's directors assumed that the format was fine and dandy to Zsa Zsa and that she would show up happily on the arm of her husband.

They failed to realize that her fledgling career was in a precarious state. Since she had not one day of experience at straight acting, she had rushed quickly into the arms of a Hollywood drama coach, one of the best, Elsa Stanoff, realizing that some would be looking for her to fail.

"You would never have known about this inner turmoil by watching her on the set," said Kathryn Grayson. "She went right into her scenes, was thoroughly convincing, and, of course, was the most beautiful woman I had ever seen."

After a particularly trying day at MGM, the studio limousine deposited Zsa Zsa at the door of her Bel Air house to find it ablaze with lights, riotous with cocktail party laughter, and with Tallulah's whiskey voice booming above it all. Inside she confronted the cast of the *Big Show* partying. A couple of them looked up as if to say, "Who's this," but most of them paid no attention as she got a glass of milk from the kitchen and wearily went into her bedroom to study tomorrow's scene for the MGM cameras.

"I felt like the brunt of a bad joke," Zsa Zsa said later. "And I didn't particularly understand, or agree with, Tallulah's sense of humor. She was treating me like the little hausfrau George wanted me to be."

Zsa Zsa ran to Elsa Stanoff with the radio script. The coach read it very carefully and asked Zsa Zsa to sit down. "Look, darling, you can never say those lines. You have a natural charm which is completely at odds with this crude dialogue. Nobody would put up with this. You fight 'em."

Still, she hesitated. It seemed, after all, to mean so much to George.

The Wednesday before the broadcast, George and Zsa Zsa met at NBC for the run-through. As usual, Tallulah was more than an hour later. But finally she arrived in a flurry of moth-eaten mink, reeking of perfume and bourbon.

"Hello, dahlings," she said to nobody in particular. She sidled over to George as if they were old college drinking companions. The awesome thatch of Bankhead hair dropped sexily over one eye, her makeup was thick and overwhelming. "George, dahling, I love you. It's such a great honor to have you on my show." Then she looked down her mink at Zsa Zsa and, knowing full well who she was, drawled, "Who are *you?*"

There was no one to counsel Zsa Zsa that Tallulah always spoiled the men and spat venom at the women. "Just self-protection of a woman falling apart," Tallulah herself once described it.

The cast began the read-through. George was up first: "Oh yes, *we* have a wife. But she quietly washes my socks. We *never* meet."

It's hard to imagine Zsa Zsa Gabor with an image problem. The Zsa Zsa of today would have undoubtedly eaten Tallulah alive and ad-libbed her own hysterically funny lines. But at the time she had been in show business only about eighteen weeks. Still, she had guts enough to look Tallulah in her bloodshot eyes and say that she would not do the show.

There was an awesome silence as everybody looked at Tallulah. Sitting in a high director's chair with a laser beam glare to her eyes, she nodded a signal to a handsome young man, her adoring assistant director.

He rushed over and whispered, "Now, Miss Gabor, these lines sound awkward to everybody working on radio the first time around. You'll get used to it."

Zsa Zsa's swan neck stretched upward. "No," she said acidly, "I won't get used to it. I won't say this line. It humiliates me and makes a fool of my husband. It has to be changed."

The young man rushed back blushing to Tallulah. "She refused, Miss Bankhead."

Again sipping from her silver flask, the star leaped up from her chair like a black widow spider ready to pounce. She said coldly, "Nobody changes lines here. This is a funny skit. It stays where it is." Then she poked a bejeweled finger in the assistant director's chest. "You waltz back over there and tell 'Mrs. George Sanders' to bloody well say her damned lines."

The normally bored cast and crew, used to La Bankhead's haughty airs, sat up with sudden interest, hoping that Tallulah had finally met her match.

The assistant gulped and timidly approached Zsa Zsa. She said, "If you don't change it, I'll walk out."

Tallulah, no longer content with the intermediary, began to shriek. *"Nobody* walks out on Tallulah Bankhead!"

Zsa Zsa whirled around. "Well, I'm the first. And, Miss Bankhead, I'm sure there will be many others."

George began eating humble pie immediately, gulping it, in fact. "Cokiline, Cokiline. How can you do this to me after I got you the job? This will be good for both of us."

Zsa Zsa turned on him. "George, I will not say those lines." Then, with George still pleading, she walked out.

"You did right," said Elsa Stanoff. "Now stick to your guns."

Zsa Zsa was proud of herself, certain that she had done the right

thing. So what if George didn't come home that night. He was probably suffering, hungry, and lonely down in that little apartment he so
conveniently kept. Give him a day, she thought to herself. He will be
right back here.

And the problem was George's damned permanent apartment. It
gave him an easy escape from full commitment to his marriage. He
just drove off rather than face the heartache building at the mansion
on Bellagio Road.

At first, Zsa Zsa couldn't sleep. She tossed, tried some hot milk, and
called Eva and her mother. Finally she drifted off, certain that the
entire issue would be dead the next morning.

She awakened to a furor. Reporters from all the wire services
called. Dorothy Kilgallen had devoted an entire column to the walkout and suggested that "Zsa Zsa be named woman of the year." A
radio poll of listeners to radio station KFWB in Los Angeles showed
that public opinion was running nine to one in favor of Zsa Zsa. And
the New York *Journal American* offered $50 to the reader who best
answered the question: "Was Zsa Zsa right when she resented the slur
on her marriage and then violated her radio contract?" Response was
four to one in her favor.

George, however, told the Associated Press that he had been "discarded like a used lemon." He had returned to the mansion briefly
the day following the walkout and collected his clothes. Ironically, it
happened while Zsa Zsa was in the midst of an interview with a
McCall's magazine reporter whose first question was "How do you
keep a man?" At about that moment her housekeeper entered the
room. "Mr. Sanders is upstairs packing his suits," she said. "Never
mind. He will come right back," said Zsa Zsa defiantly. The
housekeeper shook her head. "But, Miss Gabor, he has a truck, and
some men are moving out the piano."

"I knew right then that George was no longer pretending; he was
heading off for good," Zsa Zsa said later. "But false pride kept me
from saying a word to dissuade him."

Within a week, life was miserable for her. She had to remind herself
time and time again not to phone him, to let the anger run its course,
both for her and for him.

But at two A.M. on the sixth day she couldn't wait any longer. She
called him. "Are you coming home?" she asked.

"Never," he replied tersely.

"What are you doing right now?" she queried.

"Watching television," he answered.

Zsa Zsa wisely let several silent minutes pass before she said,
"George, I miss you terribly. Come back home."

"Do you know what I miss?" he asked. "What?" she replied softly.

"I mostly miss those little sandwiches you make in the middle of the night. Uh, by the way, Cokiline, do you have any of that crustless bread?" "Uh-huh," she said. "What about that imported ham?" "Uh-huh," she replied. "And some nice fresh milk?" "Yup," she said.

George's voice became a caress. "Cokiline, darling, would you like to bring me a sandwich and a bottle of milk right now?"

Zsa Zsa was out the door, trailing bread wrappers and juggling ham, mustard, a bottle of milk, and some cookies flown in from Paris several days earlier. As she drove to his apartment, she could see George's door open and his spare figure.

She found his embrace glorious. Remembering that night and the sweetness of reconciliation, Zsa Zsa's eyes still mist up as she talks. "Ah, George. He perhaps was my only true love; in many ways the only man to make me fulfilled."

Another quarrel had been swept under the rug. But a time was to come when Zsa Zsa's emotional broom no longer worked. The stage was set for perhaps the most tempestuous and famous love affair of this century.

❋ BOOK FOUR

The Billion-Dollar Stud

Zsa Zsa became obsessed with Porfirio Rubirosa.
She was drunk on love, but the infamy
and notoriety changed all our lives forever.
                    —JOLIE, 1962

13

❋ The Lover

*H*e pushed through the jungle of people in the hotel lobby with long, predatory strides, much like a panther on the prowl.

The superb cut of his blue pinstriped suit couldn't hide his raw physical power. The thick muscles in his shoulders, arms, and legs betrayed his passion for macho sports such as polo and boxing.

His eyes were dark and offset by tousled black hair, sunburned cheeks, and the splashy cerise of his tie. He squinted a bit at the hotel's registration desk. Ha, he thought, there's a woman at the registration desk. It was his day!

He leaned across the marble counter so that his irresistible face was only inches away from that of the preoccupied registration clerk, a thin, nervous blonde. "Madame," he said. She whirled around and felt herself drawn toward the dazzling man. "Madame," he repeated, "would you tell me the room number of Miss Zsa Zsa Gabor?"

The girl was flustered as his eyes stayed on her own. But after being tempted to answer, she shook her head.

"I understand, madame." An anguished look clouded his face. He thought for a second and slid a hand through his mane of hair. "Since you can't give the room number, perhaps I can have the room adjoining Miss Gabor's?"

The girl stammered, "But that suite is booked starting tomorrow evening. I can't . . ."

The man batted his eyelashes and discreetly slid a small stack of hundred-dollar bills toward her hand. "I will only need it for one night. I promise."

Her hand slid out and accepted the money. A registration form was pushed toward him.

Slowly he wrote, "Porfirio Rubirosa, minister plenipotentiary, the

Dominican Republic. Temporary residence, 19 Rue de Bac, Paris."
When the girl held out the key, Rubi allowed their fingers to entangle
electrically. "Tell me," he said, "do these suites have connecting
doors?"

"Certainly," the girl answered.

Rubi bit his lower lip. "Ah, wonderful! Have my bags transferred
from room 505. I'll be in the lounge for a while."

He took a high stool in the corner of the lounge, a drafty, noisy
location that had a strategic view of both the elevators and the hotel
entrance.

About an hour later, there was a flurry at the front entrance. With
a tangle of yapping poodles, winter furs, a gigantic hat, and swirls of
snow, all of which was followed by a shrill but not unpleasant voice.
"It's horrid, darling, horrid," she said to the doorman. "What a day
to be in New York!" Zsa Zsa Gabor had invaded the hotel lobby.

Luckily there was an empty elevator, giving Zsa Zsa a chance to
slip upstairs with relatively little unwanted attention. She pushed the
poodles into a corner and fell back wearily against a velvet-covered
wall.

Not until several seconds later did she sense the other person who
had slid into the elevator with her. She heard the rustle of wool, the
muffled scrape of his shoes on the gritty floor, a muted scent of manly
cologne.

But in no way was she prepared for the encounter that followed.
Her eyes were still closed when he finally spoke. The voice was deep,
resonant, and sexy. "Good morning, madame. What are you doing in
New York?"

She was startled, opening her eyes suddenly. His face and immense
shoulders shimmered into view. Zsa Zsa gasped inwardly. "He's even
more sexy than I'd heard."

Here, leaning against the wall, was the Don Juan of the twentieth
century, renowned for the quality of his lovemaking and the stormy
turbulence of his nature.

She managed to pull out of the daze and answer his question. "I'm
here for the opening of my film *Moulin Rouge.*"

He bowed. "Are you here for long?"

"Several days," answered the blushing Zsa Zsa.

"Then perhaps you will have a drink with me?"

"I really don't know. . . ." Zsa Zsa fell back on coyness for want
of any other method.

"I will hope for it," he said, slipping his diplomatic card into her
gloved hand. Then he vanished into the murk of the hotel corridor.

Exhausted, Zsa Zsa threw herself on the bed in her hotel suite and
fell into a deep sleep. When she awakened two hours later, her suite

had changed drastically. Even before she opened her eyes, the thick odor of roses drifted over her. She opened one eye and looked out into a bower of rose blossoms. Long-stemmed and short, red and cerise, they overpowered the huge room. Every table and bureau was crammed with the flowers, and large standing baskets dominated the corners of the suite.

Zsa Zsa wasn't entirely surprised. "I was flustered and distracted in that elevator with Rubi. It was all over so quickly. I knew, however, that something had already ignited between us. . . . Still, I had never seen so many roses in my life. You got drunk on the fragrance alone." She leaped out of bed and hunted for a card, hoping against hope that they might be from George. She finally found the message in a tangled tree of blossoms: "For a most beautiful lady, Don Porfirio Rubirosa."

Minutes later the phone rang. The voice was ardent. "Can I come over for a drink?" he asked. "No," Zsa Zsa said. "It's impossible."

"I had already decided, of course, to have a drink with him," she said later. "But I couldn't let *him* see me with my hair still tangled" —unfortunately a regular sight for George Sanders.

"Let me know when we can meet," he said. "It is simply a matter of you opening your door and I mine. We are in adjoining suites."

Zsa Zsa thought him audacious, arrogant, and not just a bit rude. Rubi was acting more like a high school student in the throes of puppy love than a sophisticated international lover. If he thought she was an easy conquest, then he had a surprise in store. The card slipped from her hand onto the floor, forgotten as she began dressing for the New York premiere.

Two hairdressers sculpted her hair into an elaborate platinum swirl, and makeup artisans lightly accentuated the porcelain loveliness of her face. When they had withdrawn, Zsa Zsa looked dubiously at the outrageous gown the studio had borrowed for her to wear. Made from the lush hide of infant lambs, the $50,000 dress had been tailored so tightly to Zsa Zsa's body that it was like a second skin. After she slid into the gown, she had to pull up the zipper, running from the waist to the neck. She managed only a few inches. She screamed for the maid, but immediately remembered that she was off duty. Her hands now struggled frantically behind her back. She was about to call the bellman when she saw Rubi's card on the floor.

A premonition of trouble made her hesitate. But she looked at the clock and realized how late it was. She grabbed the phone. "Please connect me to Mr. Rubirosa's room."

He was in her suite in an instant. As he slowly pulled up the zipper, she could feel his intensity. At one point, in the middle of her back, Rubi's fingers lingered on the bare skin. It made Zsa Zsa dizzy. His lips moved near her right ear as he pulled the zipper the rest of the way up. "At least let me buy you champagne after your triumph," he whispered. "I'll be waiting here for you."

"Yes, certainly," she said huskily. But it was against her better judgment.

This fated meeting might have come to nothing had it not occurred precisely at the right time. If her career hadn't catapulated her to instant fame; if George hadn't gone off to Rome and left her again; if Rubi were already married to his next conquest, Woolworth heiress Barbara Hutton—-then the blazing affair that was to rage across three continents might never have happened.

But Rubi *did* play on all these factors, pushing his way into Zsa Zsa's heart and beginning one of the more notorious romances of this century. The ardent Latin lover was to chase Zsa Zsa across America and Europe, creating a scandal that focused not merely on Zsa Zsa but on her sisters as well. He finished off her marriage to George Sanders, crippled her career, and helped transform Zsa Zsa into a queen of the tabloids.

The man who zippered his way into her life was about forty-two at the time, had the body of an Adonis, and a savage nature just barely concealed by his cultivated exterior.

South American author José Luis Villalonga once watched Rubi play polo on a Dominican field. "He became a savage, covered with blood and displaying a macho competitiveness in the extreme. You could tell that he would gladly give up his life rather than face defeat," the author wrote.

The son of a well-to-do Dominican military leader with important connections to the country's dictator, Rafael Trujillo, Rubi rose to prominence as the lusty leader of the Dominican Republic's young elite. He slept with the right women, played with the right polo teams, and did his best to attract Trujillo's attention.

Finally, opportunity knocked. He was summoned to the dictator's place, given an army commission and a secure income. It seems certain that the dictator selected Rubi from the crowd because of the young man's success in the bedroom. This man, Trujillo reasoned, could build support from the Dominican aristocracy simply by sleeping with the right wives. And it worked to such an extent that Rubi was eventually made a diplomat and sent to Europe to ply his seductive trade.

But when Rubi openly courted Trujillo's daughter, Flor, the dictator quickly had the handsome young man demoted and confined to his military quarters. Pleas from Flor, however, quickly freed him, and they were hastily wed.

Then Rubi, whose main talent appeared to be filling out a tuxedo, was sent as a minister to Nazi Germany. Rubi, naturally, didn't set the diplomatic world on fire. In fact, when Trujillo tried to send him to France, the French government refused to accredit him. His victories in the bedroom had become so scandalous that Flor rushed home to father. But Rubi proved so adept at bringing import and export business to his country that Trujillo turned a deaf her to his own daughter's complaints. Keeping Rubi on was simply a matter of good politics. So he remained in Paris as a cloak-and-dagger unofficial envoy, maneuvering a slippery course between both Nazi factions and the Allies. After the war, the French government supposedly assembled evidence proving that Rubi sold Dominican visas to endangered Jews, but there was no official action.

Back in the land of sugar cane, Flor Trujillo Rubirosa divorced her husband on grounds of desertion, leaving him free to marry French film star Danielle Darrieux. However, she was only able to hold him for a few stormy years. Apparently, she just wasn't rich enough to support him. She filed for divorce in 1946.

His third wife was more than just rich; she was probably the richest woman in the world. Doris Duke, a tobacco heiress, had an after-tax income of $4 million a year, was moderately beautiful, and willingly signed a prenuptial agreement giving Rubi his first taste of international freedom. Alice Leone-Moats, whose book *The Million Dollar Studs* paints the most accurate portrait of Rubi, believes that he got $500,000 in cash, a private plane, the deed to a Parisian penthouse, and probably $25,000 a year for life.

But, as usual, Rubi began to stray two years later. Doris booted him out, although they remained friends. It was a rich, free Rubi, therefore, who crashed into Zsa Zsa's life.

Her dress zipped, her shoulders draped with ermine, Zsa Zsa tore herself away from Rubi and headed for the theater. It took a chauffeur and a studio representative to get Zsa Zsa in and out of the limousine; the lambskin gown was so tight that she had to sit on the edge of her seat as the car drove through New York. Three blocks from the theater, she saw five searchlights stabbing the damp sky. Soon the limousine was engulfed by fans. A Technicolor cutout of Zsa Zsa as Jane Avril, almost two stories high, shimmered into view.

The door was opened. Zsa Zsa drifted into the spotlight and basked in a great roar of applause. The light from scores of press flashbulbs heightened her incandescent beauty and sent a warm glow through her body. The sweet thunder of applause from her fans washed over her as she moved through the theater to her seat. In the midst of the screening there was an audible gasp when the camera moved over Zsa Zsa, as Avril, descending a long staircase. "I was drunk on my own power from that moment—infused with pride at my own achievement for the first time."

"At the same time, I was yearning for George, wishing that he was at my side." His last words rang in her ears: "Don't come to Rome, you will just spoil my work—and my fun."

Zsa Zsa fell into Rubi's arms after the opening. "There was Rubi, the most pursued of men, the only man whose name made George grow pale. And because I was overexcited and overmiserable, because I was lonely, I said yes to him."

So it began.

Jolie, always an impartial if slightly embittered observer, noticed within days that Zsa Zsa was drifting into waters over her head. "He was a sickness to her . . . a rage in the blood. You know, I knew a lot of men just like that in the Old World. I knew that this love between my daughter and Rubi would eventually crash down on both of them."

The first night Zsa Zsa spent with Rubi, George Sanders, halfway across the world in Rome, sent his wife an urgent midnight cable. "I am leaving Rome for London. I miss you terribly. I love you, I love you, I love you."

It gave Zsa Zsa an eerie feeling. "He's psychic," she said on the phone to her mother. "He knows about Rubi and me. I don't know how he does, but he knows."

Zsa Zsa and Rubi might just as easily have met on the wild moors of *Wuthering Heights*. It would have been just as appropriate—he a wild and roguish Heathcliff and she a starry-eyed Kathy.

"I caught a glimpse of them at the edge of Central Park one morning," said Elsa Maxwell. "They reminded me of two flames shooting toward each other—yet having no control over their plight."

This was certainly the way it seemed to Zsa Zsa. She was caught in a trap. "He was, I always told myself, a man always in control. I watched him walk toward me . . . moving like a cat but balanced on his toes in the manner of a bullfighter. He was a gift from heaven which fell into my arms. There was no possible way I could resist."

For the next three fantastic years, Zsa Zsa felt as if she were moving within a dream. "I said to myself, 'I am no longer Zsa Zsa Gabor. I'm a character in a play by Pirandello. On one hand there was my husband—indifferent, supercilious, and hurting me far more than anyone knew. . . . Then there was Rubi, one of the most jealous men I ever knew. He resented even the time it took me to go to the powder room. And after George's take-it-or-leave-it attitude, Rubi was a gift sent to me from heaven."

It could all have been perfect, could have been over in a matter of months. Zsa Zsa and Rubi, both on fire, could have walked away together, moved on, and graciously spared the twentieth century one of its more tawdry soap operas.

Two things prevented this. First, there was buried deep in Zsa Zsa's psyche a kind of Victorian mentality that protected the warm, comfortable love she felt for George. Each time Rubi yanked her across the world and into his bed, this morality called to her, and she found the courage, just in the nick of time, to run back to George.

Second, Rubi's heart was gold-plated, diamond-studded. To him, Zsa Zsa was a wild and beautiful plaything. She was the love of his life. But his soul hungered for wealth, deference, and protection only a rich woman could give him. He needed the comfortable greenbacks that heiresses like Doris Duke settled onto his shoulders. When he ran into Zsa Zsa at the Plaza Hotel in New York, he was dressed and ready for the final cavalry assault on the world's "second richest heiress," Barbara Hutton, a frail, confused woman who had already been taken in by a trio of fortune hunters (among them Prince Serge M'Dvani, who fleeced her out of about three million, and Danish Count Haugwitz-Reventlow).

It was a good thing the jet set era was dawning. Rubi and Zsa Zsa needed it desperately—he to commute between Barbara and Zsa Zsa, she to commute—often weekly—between Rubi and George, patient old George who welcomed her back again and again.

But even his patience was finally tested. As they were about to take small cups of strong coffee on a quiet afternoon in Rome, George, acting uncharacteristically harshly, told Zsa Zsa to sit down. He reached into a drawer and tossed a lapful of letters and cablegrams at her. All were from friends, warning George about the blazing affair that was making him the laughingstock of cafe society. There was even a photo showing a bathing-suited Zsa Zsa on a private beach with Rubi in Cannes.

That same afternoon, a wire came from Rubi, delivered mistakenly by a maid to George on his antique letter tray. "Open it and then answer it, Zsa Zsa," he told her. "Let's see what you're made of."

"No, no, no," she wailed.

George looked up with a sneer and said, slowly and nastily, "Then *I* will."

She turned on her husband. "You shouldn't do that, George. I'm through with Rubi. I'm not that deeply involved with him—not yet. Don't throw me permanently into his arms."

George was visibly impressed and moved over to put his arm protectively around Zsa Zsa. A rose-colored sunset settled on Rome's seven hills. "It was a peaceful moment," George said later. "I was never more in love with Zsa Zsa than at that moment."

Then the phone rang. The maid answered, came out onto the balcony, and beckoned to Zsa Zsa.

"Don't take it, Cokiline. Stay out here with me."

But she grabbed the phone. It was a fateful call. She was offered a major part in a French production—if she could start almost immediately. Zsa Zsa took the earliest flight out of Rome the next morning.

Paris, of course, was where Rubi maintained his seventeenth-century town house—a monument to seduction in all its guises. Unable to resist, Zsa Zsa met him in the lair and was treated to a private fashion show of Rubi's bullfight outfits. "And you fight bulls?" Zsa Zsa questioned at one point.

He nodded, smiling. "If the mood strikes." Then he walked across to her, pushed her onto a bed, and his costume melted away.

The Parisian idyll between the lovers lasted only as along as Zsa Zsa's location filming, and then she flew quietly back to Hollywood.

For more than a year after this, the fabled romance faded from the pages of the world's scandal sheets. Gossip columnists, for all their vast networks, were unable to track the pair down.

Rubi's only public appearances were at the side of his quarry, Barbara Hutton; and in late 1953 the pair announced their engagement. "It's over," Jolie told George. "I'm not so sure," he answered. In fact, he had secretly hired a firm of private detectives to get evidence of his wife's continued affair. Soon it paid off.

George leaned back in the cavernous luxury of a hired limousine and mumbled angrily to himself.

"Sir?" questioned his chauffeur.

"Never mind," answered the preoccupied actor. "I was just thinking out loud about what an old fool I'm becoming." He looked over to the pair of buffoons next to him and suppressed a shudder of distaste.

Private detectives they called themselves, but they looked for the world like a grimy imitation of Laurel and Hardy. One of them was fat, unctuous, and had an annoying habit of twiddling with the few shreds of hair circling his bald head. The other—a greasy, gangly giant —sat looking open-mouthed at the Christmas decorations moving past the car window.

As the car purred up the hilltops of Bel Air, George became increasingly jumpy. "Turn off those damned Christmas carols," he barked to the chauffeur.

Finally his destination, the sprawling mansion of Zsa Zsa Gabor, drifted into sight—a pastiche of rich glowing crystal, thick brocade drapes, and tasteful white holiday lights encircling carefully manicured trees.

The limo was about to pull up in front of the house when George noticed three expensive cars in the darkness next to the garage. "Oh, God," he moaned. "The sisters!"

"Beg pardon?" asked the chauffeur.

"The sisters are there," he groaned. "We've got to keep driving until they're gone."

One of the detectives, the skinny one with the scratchy voice, broke in. "But Mr. Sanders, this might be the perfect time to go in. If she's willing to flaunt her lover before the rest of her family, that's even more incriminating."

George silenced him with a withering look. "Look, it's bad enough to face Zsa Zsa alone. If we break in when Magda and Eva are still there it would be like confronting the Spanish Armada in a rowboat."

"So?" said the chauffeur.

"Just keep driving. The time's not right. We've got to keep moving until those downstairs lights are off."

The car hung in front of the mansion for a few seconds and then moved off in the quiet of a beautiful California Christmas Eve.

Inside the luxurious Zsa Zsa Gabor home on Bellagio Drive, the hostess was presiding over a traditional Gabor Christmas gathering. Goose in rich orange sauce, turkey with truffles, and a rack of lamb nestled on the heavy oak table between a bouquet of candles and masses of yellow roses and tulips.

Magda, Eva, and Jolie, in Paris gowns and dripping with diamonds, indulged in the usual Gabor repartee and tried to ignore the unwanted guest at Zsa Zsa's side.

The guest himself, sporting faultless dinner clothes, couldn't have cared less. He was, body and soul, concentrating on Zsa Zsa, allowing his eyes to roam across her face and her shoulders. What few words he spoke emerged as passionate whispers that could be heard only by his hostess. It was obvious to all but Zsa Zsa that his passion was about to bound out of control.

Once, between the salad and sherbet, he had allowed his right hand to drift up her arm and his fingers to lightly touch her lips.

Zsa Zsa, her hair a crown of platinum, her shoulders an expanse of alabaster, and her face, that gorgeous face, a portrait of sensuality, let her eye drift over toward her lover's. But just as quickly the emotion faded and she concentrated on the disapproval showing on the faces of her family.

To Mama Jolie, her daughter was courting disaster by openly sheltering her lover on Christmas Eve while awaiting her husband, George Sanders. Still, Jolie couldn't deny the effect Rubi was having on her daughter. Never, not even in the bloom of early youth, had Zsa Zsa looked so beautiful. The rich green velvet dress by Balenciaga draped rakishly off her daughter's shoulders, and the diamonds given to her by Conrad Hilton were no match for the fire in her eyes.

After dessert was finished and the family drifted into the living room, Jolie caught Zsa Zsa's arm and pulled her into a small den. "Zsa Zsa, you get this man out of here and get him out before we leave. This man is dangerous."

"I know what I'm doing," answered her daughter.

"You do not, and you know, it, " Jolie said. "You've never known what you are doing. So why should this be an exception."

"Nuci, you just thrive on melodrama, don't you?"

"Yes," answered Jolie. "And so do you."

Jolie couldn't have known that Zsa Zsa had already relegated George's clothes to the corner of an upstairs closet and filled the rest with Rubi's considerable wardrobe of dark suits, Italian shoes, polo clothes, and tennis wear. Rubi, for that holiday season at least, was not only Zsa Zsa's illicit lover, he was the master of the house.

Jolie lingered as long as possible that Christmas Eve, hoping by her mere presence to head off the disaster she felt was impending. Finally, though, the last brandy was drunk, the last present was opened, and Zsa Zsa was looking up at Eva with imploring eyes.

"It's time to leave, Mother," Eva said, ignoring the angry look in her mother's eyes. "I guess so," Jolie sighed. She kissed her daughter on the cheek, and offered a weak handshake to Rubi.

As soon as the hum of the engines of the departing cars faded, Zsa Zsa dismissed the servants, turned down the lights, and dropped onto the floor next to Rubi. He flicked open the first stud on his dinner shirt and kissed her on the cheek.

Little Francesca, still up and waiting for the electric train Rubi had promised her, leaped in between the lovers, giggling and pulling on Rubi's tie. He tossed her in the air and then pulled a huge box from behind the tree. In a few minutes the European-made train was in full operation, plying its way around the tree and into a station next to Rubi's elbow.

After several trial runs, Francesca, to the relief of both Zsa Zsa and Rubi, finally trundled up to bed and left the lovers in the darkened living room. Her head fell onto his shoulder, and she looked up into his eyes. If I could freeze a moment in time, she thought to herself, this would be it. Her alliance with the world's most famous lover had blossomed into a romance even she hadn't thought possible. But at the same time she realized with tugging sadness that such a fire would burn itself out and that Rubi, as her mother warned, was a dangerous man.

This thinking evaporated as Rubi took her hand and led her slowly up the stairs to the master bedroom Zsa Zsa had outfitted and decorated for another man—George Sanders.

The lights were extinguished and the house plunged into darkness. Only Christmas lights on the outdoor trees bathed the room in a muted glow.

Outside and about fifty yards away, George sank in momentary sadness in the back seat of the limousine. Maybe he had been hoping that this moment wouldn't come, that Rubi would leave and give him a reprieve.

Lord knows what George was out to prove that night. He surely needed no proof of his wife's flamboyant affair with Porfirio Rubirosa. She had lived with her lover openly in a dozen hotels as they pursued each other across the world.

George's friends felt that he might have just been playing another role. For years the actor had hilariously confused his own life with the lives of the men he portrayed on the screen. For instance, when he played the vicious gossip columnist in *All About Eve,* he had, himself, acted like a bastard during the time the picture was being filmed.

So George perhaps was merely playing that intrepid detective, the Saint, which he had assayed so often in B-grade movies of the 1930s and 1940s. Never mind that the Saint would have been horrified at the comedy of errors about to erupt on Bellagio Drive; there was a quarry to net. The time had come.

George had begun the quest dressed in a ridiculous Philip Marlowe trench coat and Bogart fedora, but changed his mind after several glances in the mirror. By the time Zsa Zsa's lights dimmed he had stripped to a turquoise turtleneck sweater, faultless gray slacks, and loafers.

The fat detective was the first out of the car, carrying an expandable ladder and a flashlight the size of a small suitcase. The detective stalled, trying to button a sport coat around his enormous belly. Then came George, trying to creep across the lawn like a cat burglar.

Suddenly he was transfixed. His eyes were on the shadows playing on the Venetian blinds of the boudoir. It was like a lovely pantomime from a silent movie. Zsa Zsa, her velvet dress billowing around her, moved slowly toward Rubi as he shed his coat and let it fall to the floor. His arms stretched around her, and their faces, now only an inch apart, hung in space and then blended together.

"Bastard!" cursed George just as his loafer caught in a sprinkler head that pitched him head-first into one of the carefully tended Gabor flower beds. The fat detective, looking for the world like a water chestnut in a hundred-dollar suit, leaned down to pick up his boss. "Careful, Mr. Sanders," he cautioned. "We wouldn't want to give ourselves away now, would we."

The skinny one grabbed the ladder and started to fit its parts together, aiming the top rungs at the lovers' concerto playing against the blinds. There was a loud creak as the final extension was made.

"I'll go first. I've done this before," chirped the fat one, putting a chubby foot on the bottom step of the woefully inadequate ladder. Then he pointed a finger at George. "You come next. It's important that you see everything first. Of course we'll have the pictures, but there's nothing in court like first-person testimony."

George looked up at him with disdain, but nevertheless began to climb the ladder.

The creaking and groaning was ungodly as the pair moved past the ground-floor window, past elaborate window boxes, and finally to the bottom edges of the bedroom windows. There was a sudden shift in the ladder that almost tossed Sanders and his partner back down onto the grass.

The actor hooked his foot on the edge of a flower box, however, and saved the day. Within seconds, George was able to peer through the slats in the blinds and see Zsa Zsa collapse into Rubi's arms. He was so enthralled that a small cracking noise didn't register. He and the detective were both even with the windows now. There was a second crack—this time loud and popping.

"Jesus Christ!" Sanders said. "The windows are breaking."

"Nonsense," said the detective.

The detective's camera was hoisted to window level and was about to flash as a third creak—this time loud and unmistakable—echoed through the still night. Then all at once the camera flashed, Zsa Zsa screamed, the boudoir window crashed apart, and the fat detective and George were pitched through the glass and onto the thick carpet surrounding the Gabor bed.

George found himself lying among splinters of glass face up. The detective had rolled across the floor, coming to rest just below a cedar chest. And Zsa Zsa with a half-undressed Rubi ran into the dressing room and shut the door.

There were a few seconds of silence as George, embarrassed and stunned, pulled himself up off the floor. "Well, Cokiline," he yelled in the direction of the dressing room.

A breathless Zsa Zsa shouted back, "George, how could you? Go away," she pleaded.

"No, you come out," George ordered.

There were careful whisperings inside the dressing room, and slowly the door opened and Zsa Zsa, her hair already straightened and her diamonds back on, swept into the bedroom.

She glided over to George and took his hand. "Why did you have to do this, George? What were you thinking of?"

The actor lowered his eyes, then looked up defiantly. "I had to, Cokiline. I had to. I couldn't stop myself."

Zsa Zsa's mind began turning with its usual calculated, controlled speed. What did he want? she asked herself. Lord knows, I've already flaunted this affair before the entire world. No court in the world would give me a cent of alimony from George. There would be no way to contest any divorce proceeding he brought. Then it dawned on her. He wanted her back. He needed her.

Her face softened. She flew to her husband's side. "What's the matter, George? You're out of breath. Are you sick?"

George assumed a miserable demeanor. "No, my dear, I'm just an old man now. I've absolutely no business climbing ladders."

Zsa Zsa supressed a giggle. George was only forty-seven and in perfect shape, having completed the rigorous *Knights of the Round Table* a week before.

Somehow in the confusion, Rubi had slipped out of the dressing room and disappeared into the back reaches of the mansion. This paved the way for Zsa Zsa to take her husband by the arm, kiss him warmly, and then lead him downstairs.

On the way out, she turned a withering glance toward the fat detective. "Oh, you can come on down too, if you wish." The man demurred, beating a retreat on the ladder that had caused all the trouble.

"You are simply terrible, darling, " Zsa Zsa said, descending the stairs. "At least come down and have a drink."

"Well, perhaps one," George said.

In the few minutes that followed, Rubi's name was never mentioned, nor was the estrangement that had marred their marriage during the past months. It was all banter and parry, flirtation and renewed romance.

Zsa Zsa looked up at George's face—tanned from screen dueling and horseback riding through film locations—and thought that he had never looked so handsome. "Rubi's face faded for a while, and I asked myself, 'What am I doing? Is it too late for me to turn back? Or can I regain control over my life?' "

It was the first time perhaps that Zsa Zsa felt the paranoia and helplessness of a life veering out of control, of an existence that was belonging more and more to the world of publicity and less and less to herself. This was a feeling she would never again be able to deny.

Her eyes filled as she and George looked at each other longingly. Then she shook her head and led him to the front door. She let go of his arm and ran into the living room to scoop up a large ungainly parcel.

"It was perfectly awful of you to come, darling," she cooed. "But since you did, please take your Christmas present. It will save me the trouble of delivering it."

"Certainly, Cokiline," he said.

He headed out and was ready to close the door when he leaned back in and smiled. "And this visit is my Christmas present to you."

Zsa Zsa kicked the door shut but couldn't shut out George's wicked laughter. She collapsed on the stairs, sobbing softly.

Rubi had come to the top of the stairs and watched the heartbreaking scene. Back in his dinner clothes, he dropped to his knees next to her, taking her chin with one hand and tilting it up.

"I'm sorry, darling," she said. "I don't know what came over me."

"I do," Rubi answered softly. "You're still in love with him. You may not know it yourself, but he's really the love of your life."

He then drifted off to the far reaches of the living room, leaving Zsa Zsa with her sobs and regrets. He filled a beaker with Scotch and stared out the window, waiting for morning and his departure for New York.

This drama, however, was played out in relative privacy—only emerging publicly when George finally filed for divorce from his wife.

14

❋ Denouement

*T*he day after Magda, Eva, and Zsa Zsa opened their show in Las Vegas a gaggle of reporters gathered raucously in the banquet room and waited for still another press conference to begin.

"I wonder what that broad has to say this time," said one of them. "The last time I wrote about her was during that trial when she divorced Conrad Hilton. I've seen 'em all, but I've never seen anybody who can make a grandstand play better than her."

A man from Associated Press nodded. "Whatever she has to say, it's worth a couple of inches. People can't get enough of her."

Cocktails and appetizers were passed around by waiters at the Frontier Hotel, where Zsa Zsa, Eva, and Magda were set to open that night. As usual, Zsa Zsa was fashionably late, allowing the reporters to warm up on several free drinks.

Suddenly a curtain at the front of the room was drawn, and Zsa Zsa walked slowly out on the arm of a hotel executive. There was an audible murmur.

Walking as if she were in pain, and wearing a $5,000 lace gown, Zsa Zsa faced the journalists with an extraordinary black velvet patch over one eye.

The dress, she explained quite demurely, was one of the costumes she would wear in the Vegas review to open that night. The black patch, she explained just as demurely, was to cover up major damage to her eye from a "beater of women, a blackguard, a coward."

"And, darling, who could this have been?" Hedda Hopper asked coyly.

"His Excellency Porfirio Rubirosa," Zsa Zsa answered, just as coyly. "Imagine, flying out here after setting wedding plans with another woman, Barbara Hutton, and demanding that he had rights over me. I couldn't take it; I tell you, I couldn't take it."

Of all the silliness surrounding Zsa Zsa and her Latin prince, the "affair of the black patch" was probably the most ridiculous.

Her press conference was a Victorian playlet in three acts. First, she sobbed and trembled as if she were a vestal virgin and as if Rubi had violated her person for the first time. "This is the first time *any* man ever hit me," she cried at the press conference, dabbing her handkerchief at her unpatched eye. "I don't even know whether his fist was open or closed." Great sobs racked her body.

"Can we see the eye?" asked a reporter from the Los Angeles *Herald Examiner.* "Oh, God, no." Zsa Zsa shuddered. "I couldn't allow my fans or the public who come here for glamour to see such ugliness. I would never allow *anyone* but my doctor to see this."

She tried to explain: "I have been refusing Rubi for eight months, but still he has followed me all over Europe and the United States. And he came here just after Christmas, although I asked him not to."

Zsa Zsa again dabbed the hanky at her good eye. (The patched eye, apparently, was unable to shed a single tear.) "I turned him down flat and for the final time yesterday. He lost his temper and hit me, but I still cannot believe he meant it. . . . He called me three times from New York to tell me that there was still time to reconsider before he married Barbara. How foolish of him. For a very rich woman, he would be like a full-time hobby. He will be the best pastime Barbara could ever have."

There was another sob. "But I think Barbara would have to be very brave if she actually married him." Her left hand brushed across the patch dramatically. "I had thought of going on stage with just greasepaint to cover up the bruises, but they were so dark, so mottled, that I had to miss the first-night performance. Finally I got this eye patch and am feeling much better." In actuality, Zsa Zsa did miss the preview performance of the Gabor act, pleading that she was "too woozy to perform."

At the press conference, Zsa Zsa spoke directly to Hedda: "The sheriff's office here is outraged. They told me that Las Vegas is still the Old West, where men do not hit women. It just isn't allowed."

It was Hedda who suggested that Zsa Zsa call Jerry Giesler, Hollywood's top lawyer, to sue Rubi. "By then I was flipping," she claimed later. "But I managed to get Giesler on the phone. I told him to sue for a million dollars. It's not very nice when a man gives the woman he loves a black eye."

The "official" version of the fight—the version that would be used by Zsa Zsa in her books, on talk shows, and in news interviews over the years—depicts Zsa Zsa as pushing Rubi first, telling him to get out of her hotel suite. "Then he struck me," Zsa Zsa said. "I fell sharply against the bathroom door. It was ajar, and I hit it with my forehead."

For the next several minutes, Zsa Zsa pleaded temporary amnesia. "I was out for a while, and when I awakened, Rubi was holding me tightly in his arms and pressing a silver dollar against my forehead—just above the right eye. I pulled away from him, screaming, 'Are you mad?' and ran to the mirror. Above my right eye was an ominous swelling. I yelled, 'My God, we're having a preview show tonight.' "

Zsa Zsa, ever the little scrapper, leaped to her feet and pushed Rubi out of the room. "Magda, Mother, and Eva were all there in a second, and far more outraged than I," Zsa Zsa told Hedda. "Then the Frontier's hotel doctor, Edgar Compton, came, gave me a sedative, and applied ice packs. There was no question. I would miss the preview."

The wronged woman drifted off to sleep and says she didn't awaken until eight hours later. Then she rang room service and ordered breakfast. "I was still groggy and weaving about the room when I heard the waiter's knock."

When she opened the door, Rubi, in skin tight bellman's pants and short jacket, was in the hall, a breakfast tray held in one hand. "I was still angry but had to smile. I let him in, and he sat by me on the bed, speaking comforting words."

"I'm so sorry," Rubi said, letting his hand play on Zsa Zsa's neck. "I tried and tried to call, but they wouldn't put me through."

"And they damned well shouldn't have." She pouted. Then she again evicted him from the Gabor presence.

"Rubi, frustrated after our battle, got drunk and saw Marlene Dietrich's show and then Lena Horne's. Then he gambled all night." A hefty bribe had got him the bellman's suit and another obtained Zsa Zsa's breakfast.

With Rubi gone, again Zsa Zsa fell into a deep sleep. "When I awakened, the room was full of red roses—all of them sent from the airport before he flew back to Barbara Hutton," Zsa Zsa explained. She was still reading Rubi's card when Marlene knocked and came in. "Darling," said Marlene, "let me get something for that eye."

Marlene, in a startling black dress, took Zsa Zsa's hand. "This man is a beast, darling. But he must love you very much to strike you like that."

At her press conference, Zsa Zsa looked as cool as a debutante at her first garden party. But her private world was crashing down around her. Divorce actions were already in the works—George filing his and Zsa Zsa countersuing. Magda and Eva were furious at the disruption and embarrassment surrounding their Vegas opening. And agents warned from Hollywood that Zsa Zsa was very likely to end up on a "morals blacklist" if she continued to carry on with Rubi.

With both Hedda and Louella Parsons in town snooping, no switchboard call got through to Zsa Zsa without first being leaked to the press. After the conference, but before the Gabors opened as a threesome, Rubi called three more times to let Zsa Zsa know that it was "still not too late." Go fly a kite, Zsa Zsa answered in so many words.

In New York City, Rubi's wedding was very much "on." It was a tacky little affair, considering the press would eventually call it "the wedding of the decade."

The invited guests, a menagerie of dubious members of cafe society, sensed something was wrong the second the bride appeared. She wore black. And not just a chic, basic style of black. She flaunted "funeral black," which draped around her scrawny body in clouds of taffeta, bloated pendants of velvet, and pregnant hummocks of widow's netting.

Barbara Hutton may not have been the smartest heiress in the world, but she certainly wasn't without a certain native cleverness. She was well aware of the stir she created as she walked among her wedding guests.

White, after all (or at least a safe pastel), was the stuff of which romantic brides are made. However, lace and white satin would have been sorely out of place here, since Babs wasn't conquering her lover with passion; she was buying him with American dollars totaling several millions.

And she knew from the moment she signed away her own dowry that she had title only to Rubi's body and, to put it bluntly, the temporary use of his considerable sexual equipment. There was no question about even the smallest section of his heart. Zsa Zsa had that.

As the Woolworth heiress moved out of the dressing room of her suite, she was immediately pinned down by Hearst reporter Suzanne Oliver. "What about the uninvited guest at this wedding—the guest by proxy?" Suzanne queried. "I don't know what you mean." The heiress lowered her eyes in a gesture that showed she knew exactly what the reporter meant.

"I mean Zsa Zsa Gabor," said Suzanne. "What do you feel about her?"

Barbara pulled a newspaper clipping from a pocket in her Balenciaga dress. "See, even she admits it. I won." The reporter stared at the clipping for a few seconds, noting that Zsa Zsa, in her melodramatic press conference, had publicly relinquished all right to Porfirio Rubirosa.

"He's Barbara Hutton's problem now, darling," Zsa Zsa had proudly said. "And I wish her the best of luck; she's going to need it."

The reporter looked around for Rubi, expecting to see him in the crowd of Latin American diplomats gathered around a small temporary bar. She checked her watch, keeping an eye toward her looming newspaper deadline. Ten minutes to countdown and still no Rubirosa. This is the beginning of a great heartache, she told herself.

Barbara herself looked in anguish through the crowd, as if to reassure herself that the sexiest man in the Western world was, in fact, here and about to become hers. She grabbed the wrist of her social secretary and snapped, "Where *is* he?"

"In the bedroom," the secretary indicated with a nod of her head. Barbara edged over to the door, held her hand out toward the knob, but thought better of it. Too bad, because Rubi, behind the closed door, was making a final desperate play for Zsa Zsa. "It's still not too late," he implored on the phone to Vegas. "I can't call it all off—and right now."

"You do that, and who is going to pay for you?" Zsa Zsa asked. "You and I are through. You knew it when I kicked you out of here. You're Barbara's problem now."

Rubi, sprawled across the bed in his exquisite London-tailored morning clothes, tried to whisper a few final words into the phone when he heard a click. Zsa Zsa had hung up. Outside the door, tension was building to a crescendo. Barbara herself was no big attraction, and this was only one more wedding for an heiress who had been drifting through one matrimonial disaster after another since she was a teenager.

But Rubi, the man who turned the jet set into a private playground of lust, was well worth waiting for. When he appeared, the women twittered, the men barely concealed their envy, and the press was poised to greet the man who managed to have his heiress and Zsa Zsa at the same time, without missing a romantic beat.

"Well, you won, didn't you," whispered Barbara's cousin Jimmy Donahue as Rubi finally slithered into view. "You tell me," Barbara replied. Wisely, Jimmy decided to drop the subject.

She acted more confidently to a group of society reporters who awaited her at a buffet table. "I'm finally happy," she announced to them all. "I finally have a man who loves me for myself, a man who is willing to make me happy."

The strange thing was that nobody laughed at the comment. Nearby, a radio reporter, broadcasting live for a New York station, announced in a hushed tone, "They say there is no female on earth strong-willed enough to resist a calculated approach by Rubi."

Finally, the Associated Press bulletin reached Zsa Zsa saying that Rubi and Barbara had, with finality, tied the knot.

"Ahh. No more trouble," Jolie said with a sigh.

She could not have known what was to come.

It seemed that Rubi barely had time to get Barbara into bed before he was again lusting after Zsa Zsa. It was the morning after the wedding, and the bride was probably miserable, taking into consideration the whispered phone calls being made by Rubi in the sitting room of their honeymoon suite. There is the possibility that Barbara Hutton was perfectly satisfied. After all, she had collected Marie Antoinette's private commode, but she didn't use it. It was fine as it was, sitting in the corner of her Palm Beach suite, a place in which it attracted considerable attention.

The same might be said of Rubi. Barbara had bought him—that is the only appropriate description—as part of her husband collection in much the same way in which she had added Count Reventlow to her string of husbands. They were *status* husbands—proof again that the best of anything can be obtained if you have enough money. And while her third husband, Cary Grant, was probably the best deal Barbara ever got on the husband market, because he would take no money from her, Rubi was not the worst. Count Reventlow cost her as much as three million dollars. Rubi came slightly cheaper.

In any case, Barbara considered him a bargain. Doris Duke, whom she envied above all other heiresses, had sent Rubi along with an A-plus recommendation. So maybe he was just another pretty thing to buy, meaning that he did not necessarily have to perform in bed.

It was the opinion of Barbara Hutton's multimillionaire aunt Marjorie Merriweather Post that "nothing did happen." The fling lasted for seventy-three days, and then it was over. "It could have been a lot worse," Mrs. Post said later.

Barbara may not have cared about performance, but she did care about personal pride, a trait ingrained in her family background. And both her pride and that of George Sanders were to undergo ultimate tests in the ensuing weeks.

15

❋ Escapades

*P*hoenix, Arizona's, Sky Harbor Airport in the 1950s was hardly on the itinerary of the jet set, and it wasn't hard to create a stir at the airport terminal. Therefore, a supposedly discreet arrival in the spring of 1954 turned into a circus of publicity.

A drowsy air traffic controller snapped awake when a quite peculiar announcement crackled over his radio: "Sky Harbor Control, this is the Rubi One requesting land instructions."

What the hell? The controller whined back, "Repeat please!"

"This is Rubi One," came a now frantic voice. "We have your runway in sight. Request landing instructions."

The controller was baffled as he searched through the log, at his fingertips. No "Rubi One," nothing like it. Now the deep voice on the air pleaded, "We are almost out of fuel. *Please!*"

By then, chief controller Walter Lang had looked out the tower's windows toward the west. "Put him on Runway Two, taxi left," Lang directed.

The instructions were given by a still baffled radioman.

There was an audible sigh of relief from the pilot in the sky above them. Lang put his hands behind his back and strode out onto a ramp. It was a brilliant day. Suddenly, Lang heard a coughing roar, the unmistakable steady whoosh of great paddlelike propellers scooping up gusts of air.

"What the hell kind of plane is it?" Lang asked nobody in particular. "Sounds like a whopper." With immaculate timing, a doddering titanic of an airplane dropped into view. The wing span, which could have easily held the cast of a Broadway musical, threw a massive shadow over the runway.

"Jesus Christ, it's a goddamned B-25," Lang said. The World War II plane was indeed a sight, varnished a white-beige, equipped with burnished props, and outfitted with white-wall tires. It glided down the runway and stopped in the shadow of a commercial hangar.

The plane's door was opened a crack, but that was the only activity visible from the control towers. Lang couldn't take his eyes off the aircraft as it shimmered in the heat, a giant caricature, a hallucination from a destructive war.

He grabbed a pair of binoculars and trained them on the plane's door. Shadows seemed to stir in the bowels of the plane but failed to reveal even a clue about the mysterious passengers inside. The controller finally said, "I'm going down to see who it is. I'll only be a minute."

As he approached the plane he marveled at the modifications that had converted it from a bomber into a skyborne Dreamliner. He moved up toward the partially open door, fascinated by the sounds that emerged: the clink of crystal, the muted sound of a Bach concerto, the deep voices speaking Spanish.

Lang reached his hand up as far as it would go and rapped his fraternity ring against the plane's side. "Hello!" No answer. "Hey, I'm Walter Lang from Phoenix traffic control. We're just checking ownership. May I come up?"

A thick fist reached out to open the heavy door, a burly physique towered above Lang, an insolent face pulled into a half smile. The man was like those executioners who show up on late-night television movies, all muscle and few brains. This was real, physical intimidation, Lang thought to himself. He said, "May I please come in?"

The giant continued to stare him down. The seconds trickled by slowly until a voice speaking excellent English commanded, "Roll down the ramp. Show him in."

Lang quickly hoisted himself up and through the door. Unbelievable splendor was spread out before him. Aubusson draperies covered one large side of the interior, highlighting a gold-inlaid card table. The sun streamed through a leaded window. Much further back in the liner and behind a crystal bead hanging, Lang saw a double bed draped with a velvet quilt. When his eyes became accustomed to the light, he saw a man reclining on a Moroccan leather sofe. He wore a painfully snug aviator's outfit from World War I, and his shoulders strained at the jacket.

As Lang stepped forward, the plane's owner leapt up snappily and clicked his riding boots smartly together. "I'm Porfirio Rubirosa." He held out his hand in greeting.

Lang was bowled over by both the man *and* his plane. "Wonderful plane," he said. "Beautiful!"

"A gift from my wife," Rubi explained.

"Forgive me for asking how much all this cost." Lang's hands gestured broadly at the splendid appointments.

"Conversion and furnishings cost in the neighborhood of $300,000." Rubi yawned. "I'm not sure about the plane. I am sure that it was never flown until I got it. They made it up for the war, but it was over by the time the plane came off the assembly line."

A valet stepped out of the bedroom holding up two suits: a gabardine in tan and a blue wool pinstripe. "Which?" asked the servant. "The tan," Rubi said instantly. "This is Phoenix, after all."

Land backed toward the door, somehow uncomfortable in the surroundings. "Thank you, Mr. Rubirosa. Have a nice visit."

Later, as he watched Rubi dash from the plane into a waiting limousine, Lang said to a secretary, "I wonder what he's doing here."

"Don't you know?" the secretary replied. "He's here to meet his lover, Zsa Zsa Gabor."

"But he's married. He told me she's the one who gave him the plane."

"He sure is married," the secretary said. "He's sneaked off to meet Zsa Zsa." She waited until Walter went back upstairs and then grabbed the telephone. On the other hend of the line, a gossip columnist listened carefully.

Thus began a hilarious case of journalistic cat and mouse as reporters tracked an elusive Rubi across the desert, leaving a trail through th cactus.

When Zsa Zsa left Hollywood for Phoenix to film *Three Ring Circus* with Jerry Lewis, her former press agent Russell Birdwell, who had dropped her from his client list, warned the actress that she was in danger of becoming blacklisted. "And not by just one of the studios, but all of them." After almost a year of the Zsa Zsa–Rubirosa antics, Paramount had notified Zsa Zsa's agent that this "unhealthy publicity must cease."

Heeding the advice for once, she forbade Rubi to follow her. "It could ruin my whole career," she told him. "It's already ruined my marriage. Please, please listen to me and stay with Barbara."

With foreboding, Zsa Zsa registered at the Jokake Inn in Scottsdale, where a society friend, Mrs. Mary Lou Hosford, was staying while she constructed a desert mansion. But no sooner had Zsa Zsa checked in and dutifully reported to Arthur Wilde, the Paramount publicity man sent to guard her, than she received a call from the airport. "Darling," he whispered earnestly into the phone. "Rubi!" she screamed. "Where are you?"

"At the airport, darling. I had to see you. I'm coming right out there."

"Don't you dare," she ordered. "Go right back to Palm Beach. Go right back and become 'Mr. Barbara Hutton.'"

Rubi began to appeal to Zsa Zsa's sensual nature, to trade on the passion he always excited in her. Hoarsely, he began whispering to her about sharing his bed. He entreated, describing how glorious it would be when their bodies melded. And she had to face it: he was goddamned irresistible.

"Look," he whispered. "We'll register me as William Perkins. Who's to know?"

"Okay, okay," she said. "But don't come out here until after dark."

She turned to Mrs. Hosford. "It's too late to stop it. All we can do now is try and keep it under wraps."

Mary Lou, now Mrs. Cornelius Vanderbilt Whitney, agreed to handle "operation illusion," as reporters eventually called it. She booked an adobe bungalow at the inn in the name of William Perkins (Rubi's recurring pseudonym), a Wall Street financier specializing in South American investments.

A clerk asked pointedly, "When may we expect him to pick up his key?" The lovely Mary Lou looked him in the eye. "I'll take it."

"I understand."

No you don't, Buster, she thought to herself. Oh, no you don't. She carried the key to a waiting Zsa Zsa.

"When's he coming?" Mary Lou asked.

"Soon. He said sometime after dark." Mary Lou quickly got lost.

Zsa Zsa bathed in Egyptian oils, dressed in filmy and seductive red, and sat back to wait. The smell of sweet olive trees wafted on the night air. Soon she heard the urgent knock at the door.

She took her time opening it to Rubi. They crumpled onto the Navajo rugs.

The reunion was idyllic at first. "Somehow, it was all as it had been before," Zsa Zsa remembered. "I thought, this is my man, after all. This is a *man.*"

But at six-thirty A.M., forty-five minutes after Zsa Zsa had left for the film location, Rubi was lying naked, wrapped partially in a sheet, when he heard the maid turning the passkey in Zsa Zsa's door. "Dammit," he swore. He sprang up, scooped his clothes into one hand, and then skidded across the bathroom's tile floor.

In the shower, he slid on his pants behind the frosted door and then flattened against the tiles while the interminably slow maid worked on the suite. Thank God she was sloppy and bypassed the shower. By the time he heard the door close, he'd sweated through his pants. The run to his own bungalow through bright sunlight embarrassed him greatly. The privacy of his own room was blessed.

Late that afternoon, after Zsa Zsa had returned from location, Mary Lou suggested a picnic. "Let's take barbecued chicken, crisp green peppers, and a fine bottle of wine out to the site of my new house. The workers will be gone by now, and the view is spectacular."

Out under the stars, which always seem so close in the desert, Rubi and Zsa Zsa gazed at each other for hours. A bright moon traced along their classic profiles as they kissed. Her eyes had a warm glow that Mary Lou would never forget.

When they returned to the Jokake Inn, all hell broke loose. The inn's bungalows meander through a veritable forest of pungent flowering bushes, oleanders fifteen feet high, and occasional orange trees whose branches are so laden they touch the ground. This meant that the returning party had to walk one after the other on seemingly endless trails. Zsa Zsa led, followed by Mary Lou and then Rubi, who hung back in the shadows.

Zsa Zsa screamed. A reporter leaped out in front of her, blocking the walkway. "Mr. Rubirosa's here, isn't he? Is he staying with you?" The actress swung her purse at the man's lean form. "How dare you suggest such a thing!"

She began shrieking to alert Mary Lou and the hapless Rubirosa. Zsa Zsa pulled herself up haughtily. "Mr. Rubirosa, as you call him, is happily married to Miss Barbara Hutton, and I am here making a film. Now get out of my way, you idiot!"

Rubi, in cavalry twill slacks and a sweater, skittered under a sweet olive tree. The prickly blossoms rained on his head, cascaded down his sweater, and brushed over his face. With reporters prowling the bushes like the Gestapo, the world's greatest lover had no choice but to bide his time in the dark.

It was humiliating; all this was becoming too much. He heard his cotton sweater rip as he slid further back into undergrowth. Then he heard a gardener progress methodically through the grounds with a long-handled metal prong. "Oh no. Oh God, no," Rubi swore. "Not the sprinklers."

The rubber-booted footsteps drew closer and, after an agonizingly long time, the dastardly water spigot was turned. At first there was a little spurt, then a fine spray and, eventually, a thick, enveloping rainstorm. Rubi was kneeling just behind it. The water soaked up into his pants, rendering them transparent, then doused his mane of black hair and trickled down over his handsome face. He blushed a thousand shades of red. He couldn't escape now—not even if the coast were clear.

Mary Lou, in her own room, called for the manager, who burst in several minutes later. "There's an incredible rumor," he said. "That Mr. Rubirosa is right here in the Jokake Inn. My office is surrounded by reporters and photographers, and the switchboard is jammed." By now, the manager was trembling. "There are a hundred reporters here—a hundred reporters."

Zsa Zsa bit her lip: "It's true. He's here."

"Here?" questioned the manager. "Where?"

"Out in the bushes," Zsa Zsa answered, not without a trace of amusement.

The manager's hands flew up to his cheeks. "But why?"

"*Why?*" Zsa Zsa said furiously.

His eyes widened. "Ah, yes, I see. Sorry. I'm sorry. But what're we going to do?"

"Easy," reasoned Mary Lou. "We'll get the Paramount publicity man, Arthur Wilde. He'll pose as Rubi. Then he, Zsa Zsa, and I will run to the car. Believe me, the reporters will follow."

Arthur, perhaps even more handsome than Rubi, agreed. "Let's go," he said. The trio sauntered leisurely through the lobby, made sure the newshounds saw them, and then drove off in a car that was parked at the hotel's entrance. Several carloads of reporters followed.

The manager sent a secretary to rescue Rubi and spirit him to a conveniently empty house in the hills above Scottsdale.

Meanwhile, the decoy car drove through the Phoenix suburbs for almost three hours—at one point allowing the party to switch to another car—and zigzagged until they lost all the journalists.

Finally free, the car drove up to the dark house where Zsa Zsa found Rubi bathing in self-pity. He was sitting at the unfinished bar, brooding, his eyes black with anger. "Where the hell were you?" he spurted.

He was a real bastard, lost on his own egotistical planet, Zsa Zsa thought.

Jolie had believed it was over after the Las Vegas experience. Well, that's that, she told herself, flying back to New York after the bout between her middle daughter and the great stud. Bad as it had been, it was over.

What else could happen? Rubi was married and at the beck and call of his wife. Zsa Zsa was obsessed with her career. Yes, it was over.

Manhattan was Jolie's haven from her tempest-torn daughters. Her posh jewelry emporium had blossomed, and she was becoming a fixture of New York society. After deplaning, she settled back into the deep satin comforter in her bedroom and planned to read the New York *Times*.

The phone rang. "It's me, Rubi. I'm at the Hotel Pierre with Barbara. Can I come over? Can Zsa Zsa meet me?" (How did he know her daughter was in town? Who told him? Zsa Zsa?)

Jolie hung up on him. He called back. "Are you absolutely mad? Or are you just drunk?" she asked. "Can Barbara hear you?"

"No, she's in the other room." Then Rubi began to moan and alternately woo. "Oh, Jolie, I die for Zsa Zsa. I can't live without her. I must see her. Please, please arrange it." Again she slammed down the receiver. She rang for the maid. "An aspirin, dear, and hurry." She wondered if she might need something stronger, much stronger.

The phone rang again. Reluctantly she answered. "Do not call me again. If you call me again there will be more trouble than even you know how to deal with."

Over the next several weeks, Jolie urged Zsa Zsa to purge herself of Rubi. "He is not only a disease, Zsa Zsa, he's an epidemic. Call it off now! Let it end."

Then hesitantly Jolie asked, "Zsa Zsa, it *is* George that you love, is it not?"

"Oh, yes, Nuci, yes. You know that," Zsa Zsa answered.

For two and a half months after that, there was an amorous cease-fire. The shooting had stopped, but it had to begin again.

Fifty days into his marriage to Barbara Hutton Rubi made another move.

Again Jolie was relaxing in her Manhattan bedroom. She took the call. "It's Rubi. This time I'm coming over."

"But I'm in bed," answered Jolie.

"I can't help it. Get up," he said.

So Jolie rose, dressed, ordered breakfast, and waited for him to dash up her stairs. "Zsa Zsa is cold to me" were the first words out of his mouth. "What can I do?" Jolie shrugged.

"This was the period when they were running all over the world after each other," Jolie said. "The press followed. Zsa Zsa was ruining her career by courting such scandalous publicity. Plus, she was exhausted. Eventually, we all were."

With the George Sanders divorce case proceeding through the courts, Rubi decided he had to have three last nights with Zsa Zsa even if it ruined both their lives.

So Jolie took them in. "Even though I didn't approve of their relationship, even though I was ashamed of what they were doing, I kept Rubi hidden in my Sixty-third Street house for three days and nights so they could be together without anybody knowing."

As for Jolie, she stayed at a hotel. "I might be their instrument," she told a friend, "but that doesn't mean that I have to watch it."

The street in front of Jolie's brownstone became increasingly blocked by reporters, since Rubi and Zsa Zsa had virtually dropped off the face of the earth.

This meant Jolie had to keep up a ridiculous charade of entering her own house from the back early in the morning only so she could publicly exit the front door and drive to her boutique. She had to elbow her way out each time. "Where are they?" Jolie shrugged. "Will they get divorces in order to marry?" Jolie shrugged again.

She was tempted only once, seeing Zsa Zsa and Rubi peering out at her from behind her curtains, to tell the whole story then and there. Zsa Zsa saw this expression and said later, "I know how you love to talk, Nuci, but you must not say anything now . . . think how difficult it would be for me."

Then reporters discovered the back entrance, and the threesome was stranded.

Rubi had to fly back to Palm Beach. "I can't get out. What can I do?" he asked Jolie.

"I can think of only one way, but you're not going to like it," she said. "Yes, yes, anything," he answered.

"Very well," said a somewhat gloating Jolie. "Tomorrow morning I will leave in my huge black hat, fur coat, and boots. After several hours at the boutique I'll return for lunch. You will wear my disguise and slip out freely."

Rubi puffed out his chest. "Never, never will I do that." Fine. Jolie shrugged. "Stay here!"

Of course he relented, and the charade was enacted.

As she watched Rubi dash out in her garb, the veil flowing around his handsome head, Jolie was a bit sad. What a finale to a glorious love, she thought. Now it's tarnished.

16

❋ But I Love Him So

*I*t was a spectacle cleverly designed to evoke pity. There she came, the heartbroken wife wearing a black dress and leaning on the arm of her private secretary. Every step or so, she would dab at her eyes with a lace handkerchief. When she reached the table in the center of the courtroom, she seemed to melt into her chair. She emitted a sob as her delicate fingers ruffled through the divorce papers.

But she really didn't fool anybody. Hedda Hopper, in the front row to watch Zsa Zsa divorce George Sanders, squinted her eyes and said, "This may be her *only* performance—all things considered."

George wasn't there, wasn't contesting. He was off in Spain making a movie and had told his lawyer to let Zsa Zsa play it to the hilt. "She seems to need some kind of passion play to restore her life," said George by long-distance phone. "I guess it helps her ignore the massive failure that was our marriage."

It was April 2, 1954, and Judge Stanley Mosk sat down to preside over a legal soap opera. But he was merely putting his seal on a fait accompli.

The entire divorce, as a matter of fact, was anticlimactic. The world had known it was over countless months ago when Zsa Zsa's extramarital tumbles with Rubi provided fodder for the tabloids. If anything, the drama being enacted before the stern facade of Judge Mosk was really only a way of letting Zsa Zsa tell her side of a fairly tawdry story. And it was a story she desperately needed to tell, being in trouble with the Hollywood establishment over her amoral affair.

In the strange year preceding the final decree, George Sanders had his say. He was clever and took the highly unchivalric route, filing ahead of his bride of five years. She had been off somewhere with Rubi when George and his attorney slipped into Santa Monica Superior Court and filed against Zsa Zsa, claiming, among other things, that she had humiliated him mercilessly before "the entire world."

"My mental anguish has been unbearable. I have been embarrassed beyond help. And she has even caused my health to deteriorate," Sanders told reporters who had rushed out to cover the surprise move by George's attorney.

"There will certainly be no property settlement," Sanders said. "And that is for the simple reason that there is no property to divide."

George had been restrained about Rubirosa's massive and unabashed cuckolding, but the sting from the affair was evident in the divorce action. "Married life with Zsa Zsa was one of the great humiliations of my life," he said. "I suffered severe mental anguish and countless embarrassments."

Louella Parsons said that Zsa Zsa had told her the day before Sanders filed that she intended to file for separate maintenance within a week. "Yesterday, when I talked with her, she said she was hurrying home from New York in order to arrive here Thursday."

Louella claimed that the "whole thing started when George sent his wife a letter of nonresponsibility on October 30, 1953." The letter read, according to Louella, "I have separated from my wife, Sari E. Sanders, also known as Zsa Zsa Gabor. On and after this date I am not responsible for any of her debts."

This action infuriated Zsa Zsa. "I paid for everything," she told Louella.

The day of Sanders' divorce suit, Louella ran one of those preachy columns that were her trademark. "If matrimony were not such a sacred institution—not to be treated lightly—then you would have to say that the antics of Zsa Zsa and George are exactly a three-ring circus. They love each other; they hate each other; they love each other; they hate each other. And all this depends on their moods."

Zsa Zsa sobbed so loudly during the court action that a legal court reporter had to be moved so that he could hear the words of both attorneys and the judge.

"Zsa Zsa Gabor—somber in a black dress and thick veil—gave the greatest performance of her career today in divorce proceedings against the suave British actor George Sanders," Dorothy Kilgallen wrote. "She ran the gamut of emotions from anguish to anger as she described her marriage to the actor. She broke down completely three times during the testimony. In fact," wrote Kilgallen, "Zsa Zsa was only able to pull herself together whenever a cameraman suggested a picture."

George's private apartment was the focus of Zsa Zsa's complaint. "He lived there at the very least sixty percent of the time," Zsa Zsa claimed.

Asked by attorney Jerry Giesler (handling the case for Zsa Zsa) how many times "George went off to his apartment," Zsa Zsa answered, "I don't know, but many, many times. He told me that he had to have his independence."

While both divorce actions were on the docket (George's and Zsa Zsa's), the actress told a reporter, " 'I certainly will have a nervous breakdown after I divorce you,' I told George. And he said he would have one if I didn't. He sent me to his own psychologist to talk the whole thing over. The man told me that George would have a complete collapse if I ever left him. So what was I supposed to believe?"

"Did George's decision to file first come as a shock?" a reporter asked. "Nothing that George did would ever surprise me," she answered.

The day George's suit was filed, Zsa Zsa was back in Las Vegas with her sisters. She quickly called still another press conference "I'm very worried about my six-year-old daughter Francesca. George just walked out of the house and left the child with a new maid—with a stranger. That's George for you; he never did like kids or animals."

In the end, Zsa Zsa's petition for divorce was granted the day testimony ended.

But both George and Zsa Zsa continued to maintain that each was the other's greatest love.

17

❋ The Final Folly

"Hey, I got my cowboy outfit!" Rubi kicked open the dressing-room door with a cordovan cowboy boot, and, as usual, the outfit became him. He looked very much like Bret Maverick in a western cutaway and buff pants. Toy guns were strapped to his thighs. An immaculate ruffled shirt covered his big chest, and a Stetson sat rakishly upon his head. Rubi looked very good in tight pants—that was one thing everybody agreed upon. And his face, at forty-five, had the craggy quality of Gary Cooper and Randolph Scott. But was this enough to sell tickets at the box office?

Zsa Zsa was convinced of it, desperately committed to it, to such an extent that she was willing to put some of her own precious money into a film that would co-star her with the Latin lover who had pursued her around the world.

Desperate may be the best way to describe the movie venture they conceived at the end of their blazing love affair. Rubi needed the money a movie career would provide, if only to finance a somewhat more permanent relationship with Zsa Zsa. As for Zsa Zsa, she needed the film because the blacklist of which she had been warned was finally closing in on her.

Rubi had already spent the million or so dollars' settlement he had received from Barbara Hutton. And this put him in a dangerous position with Zsa Zsa. No matter how much money she had hidden away, no matter about her future earning power, she was not about to support *any* man, not even one as treasured as Rubirosa.

But he refused to work. He had tried it a couple of times. When he was married to tobacco heiress Doris Duke, for instance, she talked him into taking a seat with a stock brokerage house where he could work, more or less, at buying and selling from the big board. And the profit was to be all his.

He was provided with a secretary, an assistant, and telecommunications equipment to keep him in touch with the major capitals of the world. This lasted about a month, and ended the day he went to lunch with a platinum blond client and never returned. Even earlier, when he was still the son-in-law of Dominican dictator Rafael Trujillo, he was despatched as special envoy to France, Italy, and Spain. He decked himself out in Savile Row suits, Italian shoes, and drove a cream-colored Rolls-Royce. And while it's true that Rubi dallied about the foreign offices of those countries, he had a great deal more to do with secretaries than with the diplomats. That's it, his father-in-law decided, giving Rubi the nebulous title of chargé d'affaires at various embassies and sending real diplomats over to back him up— and to do the *real* work. His job mostly consisted of wining and dining the big wheels of other nations—such as Eva Peron of Argentina. "But what he did best," said Elsa Maxwell, "was to show off formal clothes to the best advantage. He didn't wear them; he inhabited them."

Zsa Zsa inherited this fatal malaise when she decided to make her affair more permanent. Permanent, to her, meant that it cost *her* money.

She decided that if Rubi wouldn't go to work she would bring work to him. She was unable to see that it was a ridiculous idea. She proposed to cast Rubi, essentially playing himself, in a film to be called *The Western Affair*.

"Within an hour from the time I thought of it, I had Bundy Solt [a screenwriter and an old family friend] on the phone from Hollywood. He had just finished a screenplay for Paramount. Would he be interested in turning out an original script for Rubi and me?" Zsa Zsa said.

Supposedly Bundy replied to Zsa Zsa, "What an idea! What an incredible idea. I will start on it immediately." This is a bit hard to swallow, since Bundy knew the movie business inside out. More than likely, he did it for Zsa Zsa, whom he had pampered and spoiled more than once.

In any case, a script was completed. Zsa Zsa described it this way: "It was to be a true *Western Affair,* a hilarious takeoff on all westerns. Our picture would begin with Buffalo Bill's triumphant tour of Europe, when he and his cowboys were feted by the crowned heads of Europe."

Rubi was set to play a rogue called Dusty who falls in love with a French countess (Zsa Zsa). She was to be named Françoise, a blond, delicate girl who daydreamed about the West while drifting languidly about the gardens of her château learning to use the lasso. To quote Zsa Zsa, "Her pride would be her western grandfather, a man who had moved to Arizona and wore chaps like everybody else out there."

Years later, Françoise goes back West and finds that her inheritance consists of a broken-down saloon, the Deadwood Gulch, owned by a handsome Spaniard, Don Castillo, a reincarnation of Dusty.

Republic Pictures, a poverty-row company that was owned by Howard Hughes at one time and produced B-grade Westerns, had agreed to partially finance the film and distribute it nationally if Zsa Zsa could get the project off the ground.

When the script arrived, according to Zsa Zsa, Rubi immediately changed character. "I had never seen him so enthusiastic," she said. "Somewhere inside him was a man who desperately wanted to achieve something for himself. It was struggling to get out."

Rubi gave up gambling, gave up polo, and even swore off nightclubs. "When he visited me, we walked about twirling guns and practicing our western drawls. We even recorded our dialogue and played it back in order to perfect it," Zsa Zsa told Hedda Hopper. "Rubi strummed his guitar and rehearsed the Spanish love songs he was to serenade me with in the picture."

But Rubi needed a work permit. His morals and outrageous behavior with American heiresses Doris Duke and Barbara Hutton placed him in a difficult position when he applied for the permit from the U.S. Immigration and Naturalization Service. On the application he described his role in the film as that of a "big-time gambler in the Old West." Fine and dandy, said the U.S., but first show us proof that you have acted professionally before.

Ah, if Rubi could only have traded on the performances he had given to capture Barbara and Doris, but those, of course, were for a very select bedroom audience.

They tried to slip Rubi in using a little-known clause in the federal law that allows aliens to qualify for artistic work if they are persons of unusual ability. "Well he *is* a person of unusual abilities," said Elsa Maxwell. "But, darling, we cannot describe those abilities in public, can we?"

So Rubi and Zsa Zsa failed. Then they tried to gain a federal exemption under a clause that allowed a permit to be issued if a person is paid an unusually large salary for his services. The contract with Republic Pictures would have paid him $1,500 per week.

"Not enough," ruled the federal officials.

"The denial was a terrible blow for Rubi, to his hopes, and it was back to the old grind for me," Zsa Zsa told a friend.

And Rubi? He was furious. "The American press has been after me ever since I met you," he told Zsa Zsa. "Now the government is directly insulting me by refusing to approve such a small common courtesy."

Zsa Zsa became defensive. "How dare he attack my country. We fought, and Rubi packed his bags. We made up and flew to Paris. I went back with him to his old life, his old house in Paris."

But it wouldn't work. It was over. "One night I adored him . . . the next I left him."

"It's funny how such a great love as this can just wind down, trickle out until there is no feeling left."

Once on the *Tonight* show Zsa Zsa was asked, "Was Rubirosa the love of your life?" "No," she answered, "but I was certainly the love of his."

Full Blown. Zsa Zsa, wrapped in ermine, diamonds, and a Dior gown, was snapped at Ciro's on a Saturday night in 1952.

Notorious. Zsa Zsa and the eye patch that supposedly hid the black eye given her by the battling lover Rubirosa. The date was December 29, 1953. Rubi married heiress Barbara Hutton six days later.

Always an Actress. Zsa Zsa woos the judge with tears at the 1954 trial that separated her from George Sanders. "He was a beast," she claimed.

Beleaguered Lovers. Zsa Zsa and Porfirio Rubirosa caught by the press as they walk away from Rubi's flying love nest in a Burbank airfield, 1954.

Jet Setters. Zsa Zsa and Rubi about to board an airplane in Paris at a private airfield in 1954, their scandalous affair still under way.

Idyllic. Zsa Zsa, daughter Francesca, and Jolie after an Easter celebration in the early 1950s. The trio had been the guests of Conrad Hilton at a swank party.

The Parents. Zsa Zsa converses with ex-husband Conrad Hilton about a decade after their bitter divorce. They become old friends. The year was 1955, and the party was for their daughter, Francesca. *AP/Wide World Photos*

Celebrities. Zsa Zsa and Magda face an ever-present press as they arrive from Paris in 1955. Their comings and goings became world news.

Hostess. Zsa Zsa's skill as a party giver is shown by these guests at a 1955 bash: from left, actor Laurence Harvey, actress Marion Davies, and her husband, Captain Horace Brown.

All Four. Eva, Mama Jolie, Zsa Zsa, and Magda at Sardi's sometime in the mid-1950s. Lunch was on Mama, as usual.

The Right Man. Magda found happiness and very great wealth after wedding plumbing mogul Tony Gallucci in 1956.
AP/Wide World Photos

Cleaned Out! Magda with her empty jewel chest after an $80,000 robbery in New York, 1960.

Mama the Bride! Zsa Zsa is on the left, hugging Jolie's bridegroom Edmund de Szigethy after the wedding ceremony in 1957. Madga smiles at the camera as Jolie looks on. *Phototeque*

Happy at Last. Eva Gabor weds the love of her life, Richard Brown, in 1959—a match that would dissolve in bitterness ten years later.
AP/Wide World Photos

Those Lips, Those Eyes.
The "new look" Zsa Zsa in
1957 as she tried valiantly
to salvage a scarred career.

Mama. Zsa Zsa, Francesca,
and a prized Yorkshire terrier
photographed in Rome. 1959.

In Vegas. Zsa Zsa, fiancé Hal Hays, Mama Jolie, and Liberace in Las
Vegas, 1959.

The Big Diamond. In 1960 Zsa Zsa displayed her twenty-five-carat
diamond from millionaire contractor Hal Hays, shown at her side.
When the engagement crumbled, Zsa Zsa gave back the diamond.
AP/Wide World Photos

Again a Bride. Zsa Zsa and new husband Herbert Hutner prepare to cut the wedding cake following their 1962 wedding. *AP/Wide World Photos*

Number Five. Zsa Zsa and billionaire Texas oilman Joshua Cosden greet reporters after their 1966 wedding. The honeymoon was at her mansion. *AP/Wide World Photos*

George II. Magda and George Sanders after their wedding in 1970.
The match lasted only six weeks. *AP/Wide World Photos*

Green Acres. Eva and Eddie
Albert in a publicity shot
from the top-rated series
that made them millionaires.
The year was 1967. *CBS*

❋ BOOK FIVE

The Wages of Fame

In America, my little Eva, you will live your life
in a fishbowl surrounded by hungry-eyed people
waiting for a peek at your private life.
    —GRANDFATHER TILLEMAN, 1938

18

❊ The Fan

*I*t was just one letter—a bit more cheeky, to be sure —from another ardent fan, full of praise and adoration for "the lovely and ethereal Eva Gabor."

Perhaps it was the bizarre slanting of the handwriting; perhaps it was the practiced flair of the signature; perhaps the emotion of the letter struck a familiar chord. In any case, Eva read the letter and made a vague mental note about it.

"It was much too familiar, that letter," Eva told friends. "That boy made a play for me, in so many words, but I wrote a brief reply anyway. Fans, after all, are an actor's life blood."

In the late 1940's and early 1950's, Eva was particularly dependent on—but also highly successful with—her quickly multiplying fans. Unsuccessful in Hollywood and only a temporary star on Broadway, Eva was one of those actresses who build an entire career on the road. Play-by-play, city-by-city, and theater-by-theater, she assembled box-office power in places such as East Hampton, New York, and Phoenix, Arizona.

In just a few years her weekly salary skyrocketed to as much as $5,000, greatly exceeding the take-home pay of many Hollywood stars. During the same era, for instance, Marilyn Monroe was still earning $900 per week, and Rock Hudson was pulling in $1,200.

But the fans—they were the key to it all. This explains how the troubled young man from California got his foot in the door.

She had all but forgotten about him when the second letter arrived, although she recognized the handwriting instantly. This time the prose was effusive, gallant, gracious. It was the sort of verbiage that might have been penned by an aristocratic gentleman to his lady during the era of Elizabeth Barrett Browning.

Eva was his madonna, his sweetheart, a chaste lover who was saving herself just for him. "Someday, Eva darling, we'll be together forever," he wrote. A slight flush of fear passed through her, leaving a sense of uneasiness. She had already thrown the envelope away, and she searched frantically through the small wastebasket near her desk. When she pulled it from a crumpled pile, she saw the postmark. San Diego! Was he moving toward her? Or was it just a coincidence? That was it—a coincidence. The young man probably popped down to San Diego for a vacation, an afternoon on the bay, but nothing to worry about.

This time, she tucked the letter in a small desk drawer. Something warned her to keep it. The slim young man with the cold eyes had made it to second base; his lady love could no longer forget him. He began searching the papers, papers from all over the country, in order to follow her every move. He had to know where she was and what she was doing.

For Eva, there was another plane to catch, another play, another theater waiting. "Even though the letters became more and more familiar, I treated them as a joke. Fans can be very, very peculiar," the actress said. In her autobiography, *Orchids and Salami,* she wrote, "He had stopped calling me 'My dear Miss Eva' and shifted to 'Eva honey,' not such a transgression."

The next letter took her by surprise. She had worked all day rehearsing a new play and got back to her Manhattan town house well after dark. She collapsed onto her bed with the day's mail. Flipping through an orderly pile, her heart flew to her throat when she recognized the now unmistakable handwriting.

This time the message wasn't merely familiar, it veered into craziness. "You will find that I am irresistible," the young man wrote. "Even cops clear a path for me." Eva was almost afraid to turn over the envelope and was hoping for the distant security of a California postmark. It was postmarked Milwaukee! He was moving east.

Eva immediately called her agent. "I'm becoming frightened," she said. "What can I do?" The agent replied, "I wouldn't worry too much about it. Why worry about a fan? He will simply worship you from afar and then drift out of your life, out of your mail."

The actress wasn't so sure, but she was working nonstop. The growing alarm was momentarily pushed aside. Meanwhile, the money from her suburban theater tours was pouring in. By limiting her reportory of plays to a handful—particularly *Her Cardboard Lover* and *Blithe Spirit*—Eva was able to attract packed houses. However, it was rough going at first. She wrote in her autobiography, "The tag 'glamour girl' implied that being glamorous was the limit of my accomplishments. When my agent asked for a plump salary, some directors and managers were polite, others giggled, and most of them turned me down."

Imbued with the indestructible Gabor confidence, she headed out to make it on her own terms. Finally, the East Hampton Theater took a chance. "Come," they said. "We'll try *Her Cardboard Lover* and see how it goes."

And it worked. God how it worked! A steady stream of press photos featuring an alluring Eva began enlivening the pages of Long Island community newspapers, culminating in a glorious color rehearsal shot that graced the front page of a Sunday magazine. East Hampton was able to hang up a "sold out" sign after only ten days of ticket sales.

More importantly, "Starring Eva Gabor" was splashed in neon across the front of the picturesque theater entrance. "East Hampton happens to have been the first place in the world where I was a star, a real star with a star pasted above my name on the dressing-room door. When I first drove past the theater and saw my name up there, I burst into tears," she told an interviewer in the 1950s.

The same summer, another theater turned her down cold because "she wasn't a big enough star." Then an important actor, also represented by Eva's agent, had a fit of temperament and reneged on a contract with a Rhode Island producer. The frantic theater director called the agent. "Get me another star, quick!"

"How about Eva Gabor?"

The manager groaned. "I said I wanted a *star!*"

"Eva Gabor is a star, and if you don't believe me, call East Hampton and find out what happened there," the agent said. The director made the call, and an hour later the Rhode Island theater signed Eva.

Ironically, this flush of success made her slightly vulnerable to fans. Since newspapers printed Eva's coast-to-coast schedule, they knew exactly where to find her. Eva's obsessive young man was particularly assiduous. Before long, he had the addresses of Eva's homes, her unlisted telephone number, and even the number of the phone on the set of her television show. He was closing in.

Eva was unprepared for the next letter. It was hidden in a stack of bills beneath a jewelry statement and on top of the phone bill. Her hands shook so violently that she tore the letter as she ripped at the envelope.

"Get ready! I'm Coming!" was the blunt message. "WAIT FOR ME."

By now the fan was calling her "My best little baby."

Eva described some of her growing hysteria in her 1954 autobiography: "Not only did his letters grow crazier and crazier, but he was coming closer and closer. When a letter came from Los Angeles, it was faintly amusing. When one came from San Diego, I was curious. When another came from Milwaukee, I started to study the map. The letter from Chicago caused me to fall apart. The man was actually closing in on me—all because of one short note I had written, 'Thank you for your kind words.'

"Soon I knew exactly how the fox feels when he hears the baying of the hound. Each morning I opened the mail fearfully."

Eva was back in Manhattan for an extended stay. One happy morning she woke up and realized that the letters had stopped! She should have been relieved. It was over, wasn't it? It was all going to end.

Then, while Eva was nursing a glass of wine, a chill ran down her spine. "He's quit writing. That means he's coming here in person." Her cozy town house seemed full of shadows. "My heart was in my mouth whenever I opened a closet." Then the letters started coming again.

The manager of a scientific bookstore was amazed to see Eva Gabor, dressed to the nines, browsing through the store and asking for help in buying a large military map of the United States. "It must be so intricate," she told that man, "that even surburban density will show up."

In a way, she was declaring war on the terror stalking her life. The map was mounted above her desk, allowing Eva to stick large red pins in the cities where the young man's letters originated. Blood red marked the spots—Los Angeles, San Diego, Milwaukee, Chicago, Springfield, Illinois, Detroit, and finally Cleveland. The one-man armada was sailing steadily toward her.

The breaking point came on a gray, damp winter afternoon in Manhattan. A stiff wind blew in from the east and tossed scraps of waste paper and leaves through the near-deserted weekend streets. Eva rattled around her murky town house, contemplated a walk in Central Park, and then went back inside after trying to face down the heavy winds.

Thick shadows darkend her normally cheerful den, so she lighted a fire, donned a thick sweater, and sank back into a sofa to read a mountain of mail. Light from the flickering fire cast burnt-orange shadows onto the letters.

"I shuffled through the mail, and there it was! It was postmarked Newark, New Jersey. . . . I actually trembled," she remembered later. Then I started talking to myself. Around me was a protective layer of eight or nine million people. I was not alone; I could handle it."

Eva, by far the strongest emotionally of the sisters, grilled a filet mignon, tossed a salad, and dressed in a tangerine hostess dress to greet guests who were to arrive later. She had decided to dine on the best bone china and crystal before the fire. Dammit, this was her life, and no cheap punk out on the street was going to terrorize her or continually slither into her dreams.

As her knife slid into the superb cut of meat, the telephone shattered her reverie. "Oh, why not just let it ring?" she asked herself. Impossible! It was undoubtedly Jolie calling, as she did every day.

"Hello," Eva trilled.

"Eva?" The voice scraped up both sides of her forehead. She knew who it was the minute she heard the voice, knew who it had to be, but her mind couldn't accept it.

"Listen, baby, I can't get into the city until nine. I know waiting's going to be hard for you, but you'll have to do it. I'm out in Jersey and I would have come in earlier but there's a little matter I have to take care of first."

Eva, in her autobiography, indicated that she had never been so frightened or traumatized, not even during the days when Jolie and Magda were fleeing the Nazis. She couldn't find the strength. Then she whispered, "Ted?"*

"Of course," he answered jubilantly. The young man began to spew words into the receiver: "It's been a long, long time, baby. But I'll make it up to you. This'll be a night neither of us will ever forget. And I'm gonna let you write your own ticket. I know you probably won't want to go out so . . ."

A knot formed in Eva's stomach. Suddenly her warm, friendly, secure town house felt ice-cold and hopelessly empty. She could hear her heart pounding. Concentrate! Concentrate! she thought to herself over and over. Your only chance with this man is to outbluff him.

She forced her voice to assume the authoritative tone she used so effectively on the stage. If ever she needed all her acting techniques, this was the time. "Ted, are you the man who has been writing me all these letters?"

"Naturally." It was the voice of a lover who was enormously sure of himself.

"Now listen to me," she said with as much bravado as she could muster. "I don't want to see you—not tonight or any other night. I don't want you to write me. And don't you dare ring my bell! If you do any one of these things, I promise you, I'll call the police and show them *all* your crazy letters." She slammed down the phone.

Luckily, the weekend houseguests arrived soon after. "How were you able to carry it off?" asked one of them. "I would have run away as fast as possible."

A hard glint showed in Eva's eyes. "Nobody, and I mean nobody, is going to force their way into my life."

Much later, a police psychologist reasoned that Eva had done with her own voice what corps of police could never have accomplished.

*"Ted" isn't the man's real name but is used for dramatic purposes.

"She burst his psychotic, erratic fantasies, and the neurotic man had no choice. To protect his own twisted thinking, his own fantasy, he had to retreat back into the nightmare world which he had carefully constructed in his brain."

Ted was apparently gone from her life.

But three months later, Eva received a beautiful thank-you note. It was in Ted's fine style. At first, Eva thought it was sarcastic. But the tone was dead serious. He thanked Eva for a wonderful evening in Manhattan, complimented her on the gown she wore, and concluded, "You will always have a very special place in my heart."

She noticed something else in the envelope—an exquisite handkerchief. Eva's fingers moved over the beautifully woven cloth. But she wondered, "How close did I come to danger?"

But Ted never wrote her again. He disappeared into the faceless mass of fans that surround every star.

19

✳ Zsa Zsa vs. Congress

A gigantic color banner of the lusty Zsa Zsa Gabor striking a seductive pose from the film *Lili* was unfurled before the men in the U.S. House of Representatives. "If this scarlet woman continues her tricks with this Latin American playboy of hers, foreign aid as we know it today may come tumbling down around our feet."

Congressman Wayne L. Hays, a big man with a thundering voice, looked around the house to see if his words were having the proper effect. It was better than he expected. A silence had settled over his peers.

A longtime proponent of tighter controls on foreign aid, Hays had finally found an example of wild spending so outrageous that most American taxpayers would be shocked. He let the hush play its course before he pulled out his ace in the hole.

"And here," said Hays, unfurling still another photo of Zsa Zsa, "is the most expensive courtesan since Madame de Pompadour. And I have seen evidence that direct American aid to the Dominican Republic is being sent right back to our own shores in the form of expensive gifts to Miss Zsa Zsa Gabor and her friends. . . . If we want to give foreign aid to movie stars, let's pass a special bill and get rid of the middleman. Hell, let's pass a bill and send the money straight to Zsa Zsa out there in Beverly Hills."

There was a strong reaction. The congressmen rose to their feet, clapped, whistled, and cheered. But they all got the message: If foreign aid was ending up in the lap of a Zsa Zsa Gabor, then something had better be done or there would eventually be big trouble on Capitol Hill.

Back in Beverly Hills once again and on her front lawn with the press, Zsa Zsa came out swinging. "If Mr. Hays, and I use that term loosely, ever comes from behind his Congressional wall of immunity and repeats those statements, then I will sue. *And I will win.*"

Most of the country at first couldn't figure out why a Democratic congressman from Ohio and a big-mouthed movie star were fighting it out over foreign aid. But the tabloids soon made it clear.

The New York *Daily News* offered its readers all the inside dirt in a little piece called "Zsa Zsa Gabor, the Tin Soldier, and His Honor from Ohio." It seemed that a young and very handsome Lieutenant General from the Dominican Republic had visited intimately with Zsa Zsa and Kim Novak (a close friend of Zsa Zsa's) and then rewarded them with expensive cars, furs, and jewels.

It also seemed that the handsome young man's father was the head of the Dominican Republic, where 52 percent of the population lived at the starvation level. In this same banana republic, the United States was gleefully spreading around almost $2 million in foreign aid.

"Horrors!," said the Affiliated Women's Clubs of American.

"Dastardly!" echoed the American Legion.

"Plug up this hole," said the leadership of the Republican Party.

And there, right in the middle of a national hurricane, was Zsa Zsa Gabor, pleased as punch with her new $11,500 Mercedes and $17,500 sable coat. "Well," said Mama Jolie, "what else would you give a pampered woman like Zsa Zsa Gabor? A box of Whitman's candy?"

Besides, Zsa Zsa purred to reporters on her lawn, Kim got a $14,000 car.

None of this helped the public understand what had happened. Who took who and for what? became prime questions.

The mystery man behind it all was Lieutenant General Rafael Trujillo, Jr., twenty-two, who looked quite a bit like Tyrone Power and was pure devastation to the ladies.

That June of 1958 he was a student at the U.S. Army's Command and General Staff College. He was lonely there, and everybody seemed to have trouble figuring out how a cocky young man of twenty-two was a lieutenant colonel in a country so closely affiliated with the United States. They might have been even more shocked had they known that Rafael received his generalship at the advanced age of four.

Worse, the big boys at the military command center didn't like Rafael's uniforms; they even made fun of them—to his face! How could he explain that twelve ounces of gold braid were de rigueur in the Dominican Republic, or that his pants had to be skintight to measure up to military fashions in Latin America? Rafael even had two sets of trousers for each ceremonial coat—one pair that allowed him to sit (for meetings and dinners), and a second that prevented him from sitting (for state balls and ribbon cuttings).

Fellow students often laughed out loud when Rafael (whose nickname was Ramfis) stumbled around in his dandified uniforms. It was even funnier when he had to run, tripping over his sword, back to the barracks to change for dinner. And his military evening dress was made of a stretch material that showed off his strong legs. All in all, he looked like a captain in a comic operetta.

So he was lonely—fashionably as well as socially. He finally called up the only celebrity known to him, Zsa Zsa Gabor, introduced to him by Rubi.

In so many words, he told her that he was lonely. Daddy's little boy was used to the jet set, to weekends in the South of France and summers in Switzerland. He did manage to take several weeks' leave to head for Hollywood after Zsa Zsa said, "Why don't you come on out, darling? I'll see that you have a really grand time."

"Will I meet some movie stars?"

"Tons of movie stars," Zsa Zsa replied.

"Kim Novak?" he asked, embarrassed to reveal his little-boy's crush on the blond bombshell.

"Especially Kim Novak," Zsa Zsa answered. "She's one of my closest friends." Finally she used his pet name: "Ramfis, trust me, we'll have a ball."

"Right away, I developed a fantastic telephone relationship with Ramfis," Zsa Zsa remembered. "He would call up to ask about the weather in Los Angeles, to report on his studies, or just to tell me how well he had done on a particular test."

When Ramfis finally sailed into Long Beach on his yacht *Angelita,* the press was waiting for him—and he would never escape them as long as he partied around Beverly Hills.

First he tried to host an introductory reception on the yacht. The night was June 21, 1958, and the *Angelita* was berthed next to a particularly nasty guard dog at the gate and further protected by an electrified fence blocking the slip.

Dominican soldiers in red and blue dress were posted around Ramfis' yacht during a samba party that lasted through the night. Out in a light drizzle where the press waited, there was little to see except for occasional shadows on the boat's stained-glass windows, which had once graced a thirteenth-century Italian church.

There was one little speck of action, but the dozing reporters missed it. At about 4:45 A.M., just before sunrise, two lovely women—one with a lavender-blond mane of hair (Kim's was that shade)—ran out the gate and into a waiting limousine.

They'd lost their scoop, but the reporters stayed on anyway, until eight A.M., when the samba music finally ended. As if to add further insult, the flag of the Dominican Republic was hoisted just as the reporters departed.

The next night, the *Angelita* was taken out to sea, around the point at Palos Verdes, and into the small yacht slip in Santa Monica harbor, supposedly for reasons of privacy. But it should be noted that the new berth was much closer to the homes of Kim and Zsa Zsa.

Zsa Zsa's own party honoring Ramifs several nights later allowed him to mingle with 200 guests, who included many of the big names in Hollywood. "He left my house starry-eyed," Zsa Zsa said later.

And before he left the party he had a firm date with Kim Novak set for the next evening.

One afternoon a few days later Ramfis' social attaché and guardian in American called Zsa Zsa: "Ramfis has a little surprise for you."

"Oh, how nice."

She expected a small diamond, silver jewelry, or perhaps a case of champagne. Then, on December 5, when Zsa Zsa was rehearsing for the George Gobel show at NBC-Burbank, a man came over to her. "Please come with me," he said. She followed and was startled to see a new red Mercedes convertible. "It was perhaps the prettiest car I had ever seen," Zsa Zsa said. "It was so delightful."

The delivery man told Zsa Zsa that the Mercedes had been flown in a chartered plan from Kansas (the location of the war college) to Los Angeles so the actress would receive it before she flew to New York several days later.

"Oh, Ramfis," she gushed, "this is such a beautiful gift. You shouldn't have. How can I ever thank you?"

"Your friendship is thanks enough," he answered. "But if you really want to express your gratitude, never mention it again."

Zsa Zsa jetted off to New York and a filming schedule.

Ramfis had already sent flowers by the time she arrived, filling her rooms with tiger lilies, 500 pots of daffodils, and a blanket of roses. He called a dozen times, like a schoolboy with a first crush. "Zsa Zsa," he asked, "why don't you come down to New Orleans and be my guest. I have the Consul General of the Dominican Republic on board so you will be well chaperoned."

Again, Zsa Zsa followed her heart and not her head. "New Orleans, the parties he gave—all of it was perfect. *Wonderful!*" she later said.

The idyll was all over within a month. Zsa Zsa kept her coat and her car, Kim gave hers back (at the insistence of her bosses at Columbia Pictures), and Ramfis sailed for home to explain how he had gotten his father involved in the international crisis that surfaced on the floor of Congress.

"And to top it off," the elder Trujillo stormed, "you flunked out of the military college as well."

But in Congress, the debate over the scandal was just heating up. More than a few representatives were convinced that the current debate over the 1959 foreign aid package of $3,603,000,000 (earmarked for 230 countries) should be held up until there was a complete investigation of the funds being paid to the Dominican Republic.

Representative Charles O. Porter, a Democrat from Oregon, charged that money from American taxpayers financed equipment and services. Since Big Daddy Trujillo didn't have to pay for these items, money was freed up for his personal use and to pay for Ramfis' "spending allowance."

"The fact that Trujillo Sr. gave his boy a million dollars a year to play with while attending the U.S. Army Command and General Staff College is not only ridiculous; it is downright humiliating to America," Porter thundered on the Congressional floor.

Every once in a while during the debate, flunkies from the Dominican Republic would rush over to Congress with fresh batches of explanatory statements. One of these pointed out that the aid was not in cash but merely in goods and services. Then it was announced in another that Ramfis' allowance was, after all, only $60,000 a month, "which he gets directly from his father," the statement concluded.

Zsa Zsa luxuriated in it all, often driving about in the red Mercedes and wearing the gorgeous fur. This put another brick into the growing edifice of the Gabor legend.

20

❋ Temper

Princess Grace rarely became angry, but this morning was an exception. She paced back and forth twisting a lace handkerchief until its filigree was shredded. Outside the curving windows of her study, winds had teased the sea into a carpet of waves. Sunlight played across them, creating bright blue ridges across the water, as if shards of sapphire were hidden beneath the water.

Normally, this view and its impressionistic colors calmed her, but not today.

Signs of festive activity were evident throughout the principality. Wheel barrows of pink tulips came through the palace gates, followed by refrigerated truckloads of tiny cerise roses from Guatemala, sunset-colored orchids picked the day before on Mexico's Yucatán Peninsula, and hothouse hyacinths from a nursery atop one of Rome's seven hills.

Six dozen chefs, far below her office, were icing a sixteen-foot-high cake inch by inch while assistants decorated it with glazed pears, cherries, and pineapple circlets.

The great and the beautiful—Sophia Loren, Audrey Hepburn, even Princess Margaret of England—had jetted in only hours earlier, filling the sunny streets with spectators.

It promised to be the most dazzling benefit that Prince Rainier and Princess Grace had ever hosted. Then, without warning, a tempestuous one-woman hurricane erupted, attracting a social thundercloud that eventually settled over Grace's head.

Pacing angrily she clutched a bunch of newspaper clippings in her left hand. "Social Battle Erupts on Eve of Monaco Benefit," claimed one of the papers. Another simply stated, "Slam! Bam! Bad Manners in Monaco!"

The Princess ran her long pale fingers through her blond hair. A headache began to threaten her well-being.

What were her choices? She could order one of her old friends out of Monaco and thereby avoid a nasty scandal. Or she could stand by this woman and perhaps lose hundreds of thousands of dollars destined for charity. She knew what must be done. The incident itself was well chronicled.

Of the 200-odd fights Zsa Zsa had waged in public, none had more world impact than the knock-down, drag-out tiff with a British aristocrat that occurred when she and the lady, Mrs. Hannah Marcow, were disembarking from the plane that carried them to Monaco, both of them invited to Princess Grace's extravaganza for the International Red Cross.

There is no one who can say for certain what occurred between the movie star and Mrs. Marcow, since all printed versions varied widely.

Mrs. Marcow matter-of-factly told reporters that Zsa Zsa "virtually created a physical incident while we were deplaning. She wanted to get off the plane before me, and she pushed and pushed until she got her way."

Zsa Zsa said it was "the rude, ridiculous Mrs. Marcow who did the shoving. She pushed me and my daughter Francesca. Then I shoved her back, telling her that nobody pushes me or my daughter around."

Then, Zsa Zsa told gleeful reporters, "she called me a 'dirty Hungarian' and 'a Hollywood tart.' "

Naturally, the excitement spread from the plane, down the long ramp, and into the airport, where reporters were ready and waiting for the horde of celebrities arriving for Grace's "Shower of Stars."

Before Zsa Zsa or Mrs. Marcow had time to reach their respective hotel rooms, "the Zsa Zsa Tiff" was already burning up the French radio airwaves.

A message from Princess Grace awaited Zsa Zsa at the hotel. "She finally phoned and, after listening to my story, suggested that I not appear at the show Friday night," Zsa Zsa remembered. "She told me that the incident had gotten out of hand and was an embarrassment to her personally," Zsa Zsa told the press.

Grace, of course, described it in a more genteel manner: "I just don't want *you* to be embarrassed, Zsa Zsa. So I think it would be better if you don't appear on the show tomorrow night—that's what I told her, adding that it was unfortunate and hadn't changed my affection for her [Zsa Zsa]."

"But all of Monte Carlo and Monaco was divided," Zsa Zsa explained, referring to her own ability to bring down even the strongest walls in a matter of minutes. "I was suddenly being called 'the Nazi of Monte Carlo.' "

"Imagine! Me! A lady whose own grandmother was shot by the Nazis in Budapest."

As the publicity began to wear thin, Zsa Zsa turned her venom on Princess Grace. "I still count her as a close friend, but the one-time actress is sure no princess—not yet!"

Zsa Zsa told the New York *Times* that she advised the Princess, "If you ever *do* become a princess, then behave like one." Further, Zsa Zsa said, "She wasn't even a good hostess. We sat there in the gloomy castle for hours and only got a handful of potato chips, champagne of a dubious variety, and some stale anchovies."

She looked down at the reporters surrounding her and moaned. "I went to Monte Carlo specifically at the invitation of the Princess. . . . I was giving for free a performance for which I would have been paid at least $10,000."

The French Riviera was the scene of another famous Gabor feud, this time with the ageless and kindly Marlene Dietrich.

Marlene, headlining a show that featured her $20,000 transparent dress with diamonds scattered here and there, had asked Zsa Zsa to the Cannes Casino once for a Wednesday-night opening.

Characteristically, Zsa Zsa arrived late to be sure that the paparazzi photographers were out in droves. "Hello, darlings, hello. I'm here to see my dear, dear friend Marlene." On her arm was a personal photographer she had brought with her.

Inside, and right in the middle of Marlene's first number, the audience heard a raucous commotion at the double entry doors. Hundreds of heads turned in time to witness Zsa Zsa plunging in and out of the doors again and again to the tune of flash pops from the photographers.

Marlene, in the middle of her classic "Falling in Love Again," made a slight hand motion to Zsa Zsa, indicating politely that she sit down immediately.

Zsa Zsa was not to be deterred. Weaving back and forth and blowing kisses, she continued to mug for the cameras until she was finally enthroned in a ringside seat. The personal photographer, maneuvering double-jointedly, even managed to get a shot that portrayed both Zsa Zsa and Marlene.

At concert's end, Marlene sent a messenger to demand the film. "Absolutely not, darling," Zsa Zsa told him. "If she wants it let her come out here and personally ask me for it."

Slowly Marlene entered the club from a side door and faced down the photographer. "I would like the film, please," she said icily.

The photographer looked quizically at his boss. "Oh, all right," said Zsa Zsa. "Give her the damned film."

Marlene shrugged the ermine pelts draped across her shoulders and pocketed the forbidden roll.

Zsa Zsa rose slowly and, waiting until the club's audience was hushed, said, "What do you think he could do with it anyhow? He couldn't sell it for a penny."

By this time she was talking to Marlene's back. (Marlene's long and warm friendship with Eva Gabor, however, has survived the decades.)

Perhaps Zsa Zsa's most damaging blowup happened in the autumn of 1969 right out in Burbank at the sprawling NBC TV studio complex. She had signed with the network to appear in *Here Come the Stars*, hosted by fellow show business hothead George Jessel.

Two shows were set to tape that same day—the one involving Zsa Zsa and the other honoring Art Linkletter. An acreful of personalities were therefore stashed in the long line of dressing rooms that encircle the network's largest soundstage.

All makeup and costume fittings were to be finished by one P.M., with the first show to start taping a half hour later.

Typically, Zsa Zsa's Rolls-Royce limousine pulled up at the stage entrance at two-thirty P.M. "Oh, darling?" She beckoned a page boy. "Could you please get me, in this order, a manicurist, a dresser, and a cream cheese sandwich on dark pumpernickel?" She grandly dismissed him with a gesture of immense pomposity. The boy was flustered. "Uh, ma'am, I'll check," he said politely.

Jessel, angry but keeping it in, knocked on the Hungarian star's dressing-room door and opened it a few inches. "Zsa Zsa, I know you aren't aware of it, but you are already holding up the show. How about getting ready and coming on out here as soon as possible."

The door was slammed in his face. "I will be out as soon as I get my manicure and a sandwich."

The page boy had been deterred by Jessel but was close enough to hear Zsa Zsa and then George burst into lengthy strings of expletives. "It was the sort of language which cannot be printed in a family newspaper," said a Los Angeles *Times* reporter covering the all-star show.

An NBC producer who could hear the shouting match from the stage rushed back and banged on Zsa Zsa's door. "Look, honey, this is all costing us about $10,000 a half hour. Let's get the show on the road."

So the melee continued, reaching its apex just as California Attorney General Evelle Younger was guided in to have his makeup adjusted. Jessel took one look at the Attorney General and dropped his voice to a whisper. "Shut Zsa Zsa up," he told a costume assistant.

Angered beyond reason, Zsa Zsa called the Burbank Police Department from the private phone in her dressing room. "Please come over and escort me out of here," she cooed to a male dispatcher. "First I was insulted, then threatened. I'm afraid to leave alone."

By this time a crowd had gathered around the dressing-room door. It opened a crack. "I will be leaving in a few minutes," she said to nobody in particular."

This bulletin was relayed to George. "What the hell, let her go."

The show's production assistant, a nervous young man in a pinstripe suit, wilted. He grabbed the nearest stage phone and called the NBC head office. "Georgie and Zsa Zsa are pulling this entire show down around our feet," he said. "I think its a 'no go.' "

Minutes later a phalanx of executives were bearing down on the studio. One of them, apparently the one with the most clout, called the others into a football huddle. "This show was to have honored Zsa Zsa, anyway. So let's scrap it." Done!

There were, however, two sides to the story. Zsa Zsa said she arrived at the time called for on the personal invitation sent her by the network. "I was only late because NBC neglected to send the car for me."

"In any case," Zsa Zsa later told reporters, "the contract was breached when the studio makeup artists and hairdressers failed to appear."

She smiled that dazzling Hungarian smile and put a hand on the shoulder of a handsome blond reporter. "I have to look like Zsa Zsa Gabor, don't I?" she purred. "That's what they want, isn't it?"

No answer was needed. "When I got here I sent my hairpiece over to be curled and combed out. It was supposed to be in elegant Grecian curls. It came back looking like a reject from Phyllis Diller. I sent it back again. Several minutes later, while I was still dressing for my appearance, George Jessel and some other dreadful man burst into the room and saw me nude—saw everything. Well, naturally, darling, I screamed bloody murder."

Coincidentally, an NBC page, Christian Johnson, nineteen, approached the door with Zsa Zsa's sandwich at the precise moment that George was accentuating a four-letter word. Christian slipped onto the floor, splitting his bellhop pants and sending the sandwich flying.

"That's it!" she screamed. "That is finally it. Out, all of you." The full crew leaped out into the hall and left the actress moaning wildly.

To the press she said, "Then, darling, I called these wonderful police." She linked arms with a burly uniformed policeman, was surrounded by two others, slid into her car, and drove off the lot.

An NBC associate producer, Tom Grant, watched her leave, saying, "I don't know what hit us."

Hollywood memories being blissfully short, it was possible for Zsa

Zsa to sign for four more NBC appearances later that year. "Why, darling, they need me," she told Rona Barrett. "Have you looked at their ratings lately?"

A Waterloo of the social kind, and after the shootout at NBC, pitted the Hungarian bombshell against the notoriously serious and stuffy Merle Oberon, and it all occurred at a bash loaded with jewels, swimming in gardenias, and smothered with 1,000 pots of blooming jonquils.

The showdown came at ten paces, in the reception line. Merle, ever the glittering Hollywood princess, was welcoming very select guests to a Beverly Hills party, honoring the crème de la crème, so to speak.

She was in mid-smile when she glanced downwind and caught sight of Zsa Zsa with her own former fiancé, the flamboyant Hal Hays, a builder and multimillionaire.

Merle's neck stiffened for a second, and she whispered something to a butler. Then her frozen smile reappeared as Zsa Zsa, Hal, and the other guests proceeded past Merle's dais and into the formal living room for cocktails.

As soon as she could, Merle sidled up to Zsa Zsa and whispered, "Mr. Hays may stay for cocktails, darling, but *you* and only you were invited for dinner. There will be no place for Mr. Hays."

Zsa Zsa's eyes turned dark. "I just naturally expected, darling—"

Zsa Zsa was allowed not a single syllable more before Merle answered with a chilly "I'm terribly, terribly sorry, darling."

Moving cleverly through the cocktail crowd, Zsa Zsa managed, slowly but effectively, to divide the guests into armed camps.

To one lady, Zsa Zsa protested: "The invitation came so late, don't you know. It came while I was in New York. Since Merle demanded an immediate acceptance, my secretary handled that very routinely. When I learned it was in honor of Mr. and Mrs. Henry Ford II, you can just imagine how thrilled I was."

Zsa Zsa explained that Hal Hays had been personally invited to escort her. "I never, never go to parties alone and just naturally assumed that I was to bring my own escort."

Perhaps it was mere coincidence that the party was held on Halloween night and in view of five society reporters. There was never a ruling as to who had been riding the broom.

And Zsa Zsa made sure that the other Los Angeles reporters on the party beat were fully apprised of the affair at Merle's. "It was such a shock to me," she sobbed to one reporter. "I needed time to even figure out what to do and say. Then I realized that I was so personally hurt and protective of Hal that I simply couldn't stay to dinner without him."

Another recipient of Zsa Zsa's misguided anger was the French film star Corinne Calvet, who for some unknown reason had drawn the Gabor ire. The deluded Zsa Zsa decided that to get even she would unmask the film star, would reveal her as an impostor.

It started on a chatty girl-talk telephone show: "That Corinne Calvet is not a French girl as she represents herself," said Zsa Zsa for no apparent reason. "She is *really* a cockney English girl who until a very few years ago couldn't even speak French. When my former husband, George Sanders, knew her in England, she spoke with a thick cockney accent."

This salacious cat call soon appeared in print and jolted the beauteous blond Corinne.

"I'm amazed that such a silly, untrue, and peculiar statement from a lady I don't even know could have generated so much publicity," the French star said to reporters before calling her agent. "Sue," she said, "this is precisely the sort of thing that can ruin a career." A lawyer was at work that very day.

Suit was filed forty-eight hours later, followed by a press conference. "I am French and nothing else," Corinne said, visibly shaken. Then she proudly announced that she was filing a million-dollar lawsuit in Santa Monica Municipal Court.

Her attorney, Stanley Fox, told reporters, "Corinne actually possessed the attributes that are denied by Zsa Zsa. She was born in Paris —far, far from the sound of Big Ben. Her petite maman and père were Pierre and Juliette Munier Dibos."

Twenty-four hours later, Zsa Zsa, in one of her girlish little tête-à-têtes with a select corps of reporters, announced that "Corinne should put up or shut up. If she keeps silent herself, that means I'm right." Two hours after that, the busy little Gabor filed a countersuit.

The Gabor attorneys asked for proof that Corinne was French. Keeping these documents for use in her own case, Corinne called reporters to her house to announce that "Zsa Zsa Gabor is trying to ruin me."

In court, Corinne, easily as beautiful as Zsa Zsa, told the judge that "Miss Zsa Zsa Gabor went after me maliciously and with intent to do great harm." To the press she said, "I think Zsa Zsa's mouth should be washed out to the tune of $500,000 for damage to my career and $500,000 to punish her."

It's anybody's guess whether Corinne or Zsa Zsa ever tangled face to face, since the case was settled out of court in Corinne's favor. But the episode was typical of the Zsa Zsa–instigated verbal battles that have erupted, at the very least, once a year.

"I don't know how she does it," Louella Parsons once said, "but she can make more fuss about nothing than anyone in the history of Hollywood—and, believe me, I've known them all."

Over the years Zsa Zsa has aimed verbal barbs at politicians, comedians, fellow actresses, and every once in a while private citizens who step into her invisible twilight zone of ire.

Broadway columnist Earl Wilson, a Gabor watcher since the beginning, believes that Zsa Zsa often gets wrong ideas into her head and after a while begins to believe them, to accept them as truth. Earl likes to tell a story that Zsa Zsa concocted about him from a single sliver of truth.

The telling and retelling by Zsa Zsa of this story finally angered Wilson to the point that he printed the following slogan: "She's the unbelievable Zsa Zsa Gabor. You cannot believe a damn thing she says."

Wilson was bitten by the Zsa Zsa stinger during a tour to Europe in the early 1950s. At the time, she was involved in the on-again, off-again romance with Rubi. Rubi was playing polo one afternoon, and Zsa Zsa, then living with her lover in his exquisite town house, insisted that the Wilsons come with her to the polo grounds and then back to the house for tea and drinks.

"We had time for one glass of champagne, and I took pictures of Rubi and Zsa Zsa with the polo prize he had just won. Then I had to dash off for another appointment," Earl said. He'd enjoyed it and thought Zsa Zsa looked particularly radiant.

But sometime later a friend phoned him with questions about "those awful things Zsa Zsa is saying about you." Earl was stunned. "What awful things? I just saw her in Paris, where we had a delightful afternoon."

"That's just it," said the friend. "She says you, your wife, and your son were broke, stranded in Paris, and needed a place to stay. She further said that she and Rubi put you all up at his château."

"Oh, that couldn't be true," Earl said. "She wouldn't have said such a thing. Somebody obviously misunderstood her."

But the story, in one form or another, kept coming back to the columnist. He still didn't believe she had said it. Then Earl went to a party at Prince Mike Romanoff's Beverly Hills restaurant. "I noticed publicist Warren Cowan, an old friend, circulating through the room with Zsa Zsa," Earl remembered. "Warren gave me a handshake and turned to Zsa Zsa. 'You know Earl Wilson, of course?'"

"Of course, darling," said Zsa Zsa without batting an eye. "He, his wife, and their little boy had to stay with Rubi and me in Paris."

Earl was stunned. "What was that, Zsa Zsa? I've been hearing that you spread this ugly rumor, but I thought I was just getting mistaken information."

Zsa Zsa strongly denied Wilson's claims. "Well, why shouldn't I tell it, darling?" she said. "It's true."

The columnist shrugged his shoulders resignedly. "She truly believes it, and nothing I say will change that," he said. "Bizarre, it's just bizarre."

Several years later, the tabloids offered up a story about Zsa Zsa and her violent anger when the actor Franchot Tone refused to defend her honor. The story goes that Zsa Zsa was in a nightclub in New York when a burly man—a private detective—began making loud remarks about her age and her figure. "You are just an aging star who knows how to build up your figure and to make the most of it," the man supposedly said.

Zsa Zsa allegedly turned to the debonair Franchot and demanded that he do something about it. "You should defend my honor."

Franchot eyed the man making the remarks—a man generally known as a tough guy—and said, "Darling, I really see no point."

The Gabor hand gracefully reached out and poured champagne down the front of Franchot's dinner clothes.

21

❋ The Family Jewels

*M*iami's North Bay Village Racquet Club is one of those swank hideouts for the rich and famous, so luxurious that the door handles on some suites are formed from rare hand-blown glass and the towels are woven by hand in Cairo. Delicious breezes play across hibiscus bushes with flowers the size of dinner plates. The winds carry heavy aphrodisiac perfume of countless hedges of night-blooming jasmine.

Life there is hushed, bathed in perpetual sunlight, and protected by a security system that averages one guard for every fifteen guests. Heiress Barbara Hutton, silent star Gloria Swanson, and Italian Countess Vivalda Rappini once thought nothing of displaying ropes of pearls, great cuffs of diamonds, and enormous rings—not to mention the rubies and sapphires that cascade down summer-weight gowns.

Decades passed before a single major gem was stolen from its owner. Then, on January 4, 1964, a spectacular, daring heist was carried off in such a swashbuckling manner that dowagers instantly switched to paste copies of their magnificent jewelry.

Eva's fourth husband, the handsome Richard Brown, had already changed from a Palm Beach suit into white pants and one of those silk shirts designed for the poolsides of the rich.

Some seductive Hawaiian music permeated the room and attracted Eva's attention. "Darling, let's go down, for coffee at least," she said.

But when they got down to the party it was quite dull: a lot of Texans drinking too much bourbon; some matrons in ghastly Kansas City dresses; and a groaning, starchy buffet table.

"You were right," she said, taking Dick's arm. "Let's go back up."

Dick, a Wall Street stockbroker with little taste for large parties, agreed. It was about ten minutes to midnight. Eva remembered that precisely, having glanced at the lobby clock just before the elevator door closed. Dick, already unbuttoning his shirt, strode through the living room of the suite and into the bedroom. As he bent over the bed, he saw the closet door open inch by inch, revealing a blond giant of a man leveling a nickel-plated revolver directly at his rugged face.

Dick's stomach pitched, but he was smart enough to control his response, to mask any trace of fear: "This isn't very funny, buddy. I'd get out of here if I were you. Do you know who we are?"

Until then, the bandit's face had been hidden by a western bandana. Dick reached out to pull down the mask, but before his fingers touched the cloth a terrified scream rang out. "Dick, Dick!" It was Eva, apparently in great pain. Then silence. Oh God, he thought, they're going to kill her. He started to run back into the living room, but was tripped by the man with the shiny gun. His shoulder cracked against the floor, his head hit a wooden table leg, and he felt the kick of a boot in his stomach.

"Get up, you dumb ass," the man ordered. "Walk slowly, very slowly, into the living room."

By then he could see Eva through the door. The vision enraged him. Trembling, ashen, and with blood running down her face, she was in the grip of a beefy brown-haired man, a surfer type. She had obviously been slapped with a pistol.

The sobs from her stage-trained voice echoed off the walls and traveled through the air to the party still in progress below on the terrace. The blond man tightened his hand in Dick's hair and pulled back his head. The barrel of the gun slipped inside the broker's mouth and was pointed upward toward his brain.

"You'd better shut up, or I'll blow his brains out," the man growled. The voice was peculiar, as if an adolescent was playing tough guy. "He had obviously seen too many James Cagney movies," Eva laughed later.

The sun-bronzed giant of a man shook Eva and whispered, "Where the hell is your ring, the big diamond, the one they always write about?" Through great gasps, she said, "In the club safe downstairs."

Dick's shirt was jerked down over his shoulders to form a makeshift strait jacket. Then he was shoved up against a large window. Thick fingers grabbed his head and turned it away from that of his wife. But, and even in the face of danger, the ardent husband kept turning back toward Eva. The hand then grabbed the stockbroker's belt and cata-pulted him onto the bed next to his wife. Still he fought the two men and tried to memorize the two faces of the obviously amateur hood-lums. Tired of Dick's maneuvering, the dark-haired robber placed the revolver against his temple—this time pulling back the hammer with a terrible click. Although Dick still didn't sense the scent of death, Eva did. She pushed a pillow over his face and held it, blinding his view and muffling his voice.

The time slid by in slow motion, forming a shadow play as the robbers, after binding Dick's hands, ransacked the suite, ripping apart Paris gowns, dismantling the luggage, and crushing a heavy jewel box. Perspiration poured down Eva's face, fogging her vision.

A tangle of pearls and an expensive wristwatch were dangled over her face. "This ain't all," said one of the men. "Where's the rest?"

"I told you before, the safe," she sobbed. "Everything's down in the safe."

Grabbing Dick by his bound hands, they jerked him to his feet and worked frantically to untie him. Eva whispered, "The dopes can't even untie their own knots." Finally, they found a pair of sewing scissors and accomplished the task.

On his feet, his eyes flashing with fury, Dick took out the key to Eva's compartment in the huge hotel safe. One of the men ordered, "Go down and get the ring. You've got three minutes to get it back here." The face of a watch was poked up against his face. "One slip —she goes," said the blond man.

Dick raced downstairs, through the lobby, extracted the twenty-carat ring, and sprinted back to the room. A man in dinner dress tried to greet him: "Dick—" But Dick shoved him aside and stuck his leg in an already closing elevator door.

Thoughts raced through his mind. "This is the kind of thing that happens to other people. Other people die like this. But now it's me and it's hell." For the first time he was uneasy being a rich man.

With only fifteen seconds to spare, his key was in the door of the suite. A fist crashed into his groin. "You like that, pretty boy?" said one of the men. "Your looks and your money don't count for very much, after all, do they?" Dick lowered his eyes in anger while tears cascaded down Eva's cheeks.

While Dick was gone, one of the men had jeered at her: "Pretty boy won't be back, doll. He'll save his own ass." Eva had spat at him before saying softly, "He'll come back. He loves me. But you wouldn't know the meaning of *that* word." Rough hands had shoved her back onto the bed.

Now the tall man pointed the gun at Brown's head and let his finger caress the trigger. He took one step closer, again lightly fondling the gun. There was a look of triumphant power on his face, a portrait as ugly as it was fascinating. But when he saw no fear on either face, he swore and said, "We got the ring. Let's get out of here."

They were gone as quickly as they had come.

Thirty seconds later, Dick and Eva broke free, and she ran down into the lobby yelling frantically, "Help! Help! We've been robbed."

Finally she collapsed into the arms of a security guard and was rushed to Miami's Francis Hospital, blood trickling down from the wounds on her face.

The next morning, she awakened to a roomful of flowers and a phalanx of reporters outside. "I never want to see a real diamond again," she lamented. "The ring they took was worth *only* $10,500. But that didn't matter. When you're fighting for your life, you quit thinking about your possessions. Those men were so terribly rough, I didn't expect to get out of it alive."

Back in New York City, Eva identified two famous diamond thieves of the era—Jack (Murph the Surf) and Alan Dale Kuhn—as her attackers. They were the same men who had earlier that year stolen the fabulous Star of India sapphire. Later, both confessed to the Star of India heist and the robbery of Eva Gabor in addition to other crimes.

At one point, Zsa Zsa vowed to swear off gems as well. But eventually, both sisters came to view the dozen or so robberies they suffered as occupational hazards. They would rather live with the danger than forsake the gems that add to their beauty and fame. "You can't be alluring by wearing plastic pearls and glass rings," Zsa Zsa once said.

The nag of fear produced by the crimes is simply one more price of being a Gabor. "Really, darling, it reads up so exciting in the paper," said Zsa Zsa. "But when it's happening to you, there is only sheer terror."

Zsa Zsa entered that privileged circle of robbable ladies in 1949, when she was held up by a suave, elusive diamond thief known to New York police as Raffles, so named because he fit the pattern set by the fictional diamond thief of that name, played on screen by David Niven.

The 1949 robbery happened at about ten-thirty P.M. in the penthouse apartment occupied by Zsa Zsa, her daughter Francesca Hilton, and the maid Lulu Barth.

Lulu was still up and ironing clothes when she heard the front bell ring. She hesitated for about ten seconds. Should she answer it? There hadn't been any call from the security station downstairs. They always, *always* call, she thought to herself.

But the ringing continued insistently. So Lulu opened the door a crack. The man out in the hall forced his calf through the small opening, preventing the maid from shutting the door. She could see that he was about thirty and that his face was rendered unrecognizable by a pair of oversized sunglasses.

"I'm here to fix the wiring," he said bluntly.

Lulu looked at him dubiously and refused to free the door chain.

He sure as hell didn't look like an electrician. And he had a British accent. "There isn't any wiring to fix," Lulu answered him.

Then—and the action was so quick Lulu almost missed it—he pulled a gun and pointed it through the crack. It was aimed directly at her forehead. Slowly she opened the door.

"Where is your mistress?" he asked. Lulu nodded toward the bedroom.

Holding Lulu roughly by one arm, the man jerked her along to the bedroom door and opened it. Zsa Zsa had been reclining on the bed with a book when the quite sinister apparition moved into view. "Get up," he ordered. Zsa Zsa remained huddled in her satin quilt.

"I told you to get up!" he barked.

"But I have nothing to put on," Zsa Zsa answered.

"Jesus Christ!" said the burglar, rushing around the room until he found a black night robe. He tossed it over Zsa Zsa's shoulders and turned his back while she put it on.

Frightened as she was, Zsa Zsa straightened her tousled hair and adjusted her nightgown into decorous folds. Shyly she raised her eyes to gaze at the invader. She couldn't help thinking it—the man was dazzling, even though his dashing face was hidden by the glasses. As she drew the robe over her head, Zsa Zsa dallied, watching the man through the gauze.

The man's jaw was firm, the nose was Roman, and the shoulders broad. His dark bandit suit was well tailored from Scotch worsted. "He looked as if he might have walked off the set of an Alfred Hitchcock film," Zsa Zsa said later. The robber walked about the suite in great swashbuckling strides, as if he were Errol Flynn, as if he were only playing a part. Later, when he was finally nabbed by police, reporters called him "the poetic thief."

"Maybe so," sniffed Zsa Zsa. "But this was no gentleman. He left his manners at home."

The bandit moved the gun barrel from Lulu's forehead and levelled it at Zsa Zsa's heart. "Where are your jewels?"

She responded by pouting and gazing at him vaguely.

"So, you want to be that way about it," he said. "Look at it this way. If you don't produce those jewels, I'll kill your baby and then you."

She handed him the box from the top drawer of a white bureau. Inside were some twenty-five pieces of jewelry, a collection that had taken years to amass.

Like a crazed pirate he ran his fingers through huge baroque pearls, lapis and jade beads from her years in Turkey, scatters of diamonds from Connie, and wonderfully crafted pieces from her grandmother's shops in Hungary. "Junk, most of it," the robber said angrily as he continued to shuffle through the box, keeping an occasional piece and tossing the rest on the floor.

"Darling, forgive me for saying this," said Zsa Zsa acidly, "but you have abominable taste."

"Where's the good stuff?" he said. "I've seen it in the pictures and read about it in the society columns. Where is it?"

There was only a second of hesitation before she directed him toward a chair that had a slipcover reaching to the floor. "There's a tin box under there," she said. "And that's where you'll find 'the good stuff,' as you so crudely call it."

Moving slowly toward the table a step at a time, the bandit kept the pistol aimed at the furious Zsa Zsa and the trembling Lulu. The tin box was easily pried open. "My God," said the invader. "It's wonderful. Never have I seen so many jewels in one place before."

The sparkling treasure spilled out onto the rug in wave after wave of diamonds, rubies, emeralds, and a rare semi-precious trove of lapis, jade, turquoise, and sapphires. The owner of the jewelry couldn't help wincing as the best pieces were picked from the pile and stuffed into the robber's pockets.

There was a sleepy whimper from Francesca in the next room. Zsa Zsa leapt to her feet. "Get back down," the robber ordered. "Go ahead, shoot me!" she said. "But I'm going to my daughter and get her settled." As it happened, the baby was hungry, and the robber let the mother feed her. "Hurry up," he said gruffly. "I want to get this over with."

"And you think I don't," Zsa Zsa snapped back.

At Zsa Zsa's insistence, Francesca was allowed to remain in her small bed.

After ransacking the living room, the robber herded them to a wrought-iron love seat and produced some heavy waterproof rope. Zsa Zsa could see the long edge of her diamond necklace streaming from one of his pockets. "It was all I could do to keep from snatching it back," she said.

As the robber began systematically going through the closets, the as yet ungagged Zsa Zsa continued to lecture him. "Really, now, why do you do this? There is so much opportunity in America today. You could even become President of the United States, but if you keep this up—"

Too much! He ran over and stuffed a cotton handkerchief in her mouth, then grabbed his loot and disappeared. After she struggled free, Zsa Zsa said to Lulu, "You know, dear, I'm beginning to find out that buying beautiful jewels is one thing. Hanging on to them is another."

When Zsa Zsa's losses were totaled, it was learned that the gentleman known as Raffles had absconded with $600,000 in gems, making it the largest single jewel heist in the 1940s.

Almost ten years later, Raffles (finally identified as Ian Anthony Memensley) was tripped up and caught by police in West Los Angeles. He was from Rhodesia and told police he was in the robbery racket to furnish a honeymoon apartment for his fiancée. Police also learned that he had spent almost four years in medical school, was a paratrooper in World War II, and could speak eleven languages.

"All this was an adventure, a lark," he told police. "There was something romantic about it."

Zsa Zsa continued to have nightmares about the incident for several years after. "It's a terrible thing to wake up out of a dead sleep and find a man standing over you with a gun," she recalled. "You never get over something like that."

All the melodrama resulting from stolen Gabor gems perhaps reached its apex when Zsa Zsa sued the Waldorf-Astoria Hotel for $253,000 after baubles worth that much were stolen during one of her lengthy stays at the hotel.

The gems were worth a quarter of a million, but Zsa Zsa's performance was worth much more.

During the trial, dressed in a black velvet dress slit to the thigh and topped with a waterfall of sable, she burst into tears when the hotel's chief attorney made slightly salacious remarks about Zsa Zsa's relationship with Conrad Hilton and her "scandalous conduct with Porfirio Rubirosa."

She sprung up from her seat and leaned toward the judge. "Did you hear what he said about me?" she asked with a toss of her furs. "I did," the judge answered sternly. Then *he* faced the corporate attorney: "Now, you stop that right this instant."

On the stand, Zsa Zsa played it to the hilt. "I'm just a poor little actress coming home from work when I get robbed in *that* hotel. There wasn't even a bellhop on duty to hear my cries."

The judge nodded gently in sympathy, but nonetheless ruled that the hotel was not responsible for a girl's best friend: her diamonds.

22

❋ Eva the Enigmatic

*O*n a first-class flight to Australia recently two teenage girls came up the aisle and approached Eva Gabor deferentially. They held out autograph books. "Zsa Zsa, would you please sign?"

A slight look of consternation passed over Eva's face. "I'm not Zsa Zsa, darlings, I'm Eva, but I'd be delighted to sign for you."

The girls accepted graciously. It might be the "number-two Gabor," but it *was* a Gabor.

Eva has a great sense of humor about this continual mistaken identity, as well she should. It's been going on since the 1950s.

To the general public, for the most part, Zsa Zsa is the Hertz and Eva the Avis in the celebrity pecking order. Zsa Zsa has been so much bigger than life and so flamboyant that her long shadow has often been thrown across Eva's path.

But exactly the opposite occurs when the entertainment business is involved. Eva, the longtime workman TV and stage actress, is likely to be first choice for a commercial or a series simply because she is largely without temperament, and she does not incur the frivolous expenses so often associated with her sister.

Joyce Haber, former gossip columnist for the Los Angeles *Times,* called Eva "the least boring Gabor."

"Somebody once said," wrote Haber, "that survival in Hollywood means being able to tell one Gabor from another. And there's something to this. Eva's the least tiresome—and also the youngest. . . . Although she's still older than a breadbox. The Gabors, you see, burned their birth certificates at the age most women burn toast. . . . Anyone who has known them for any length of time can tell immediately which is which. Their whole demeanors are different."

Perhaps, but Eva has on occasion considered herself a victim of the very glamorous image that has made her fortune. The landslide of fame brought down upon her by the public whirlwind surrounding Zsa Zsa has trapped her like a butterfly with glue on its wings. The wages of fame for Eva Gabor have cost her a precious chunk of her own identity.

Her dilemma has often shown up in the in-depth newspaper articles about her. For instance, one interview by a Los Angeles *Times* reporter went like this:

Eva's voice wavered a bit as she sat across the table from the society reporter. She looked, for a moment or two, particularly vulnerable as if she were trapped in an invisible net. The reporter chose her words carefully: "Are you ever past worrying about your looks—ever?"

A look of anguish crossed Eva's face. "Never, not while I'm alive, darling." She shook her head. "The whole process I must go through before going out makes it a terror just to go out to dinner."

Frank Gard Jameson, the aerospace mogul who was her husband at the time, took Eva's hand in his. "We have dinner out less and less frequently because it's such an immense production. The average housewife goes to the restaurant to relax and enjoy the food. But when Eva walks in, she becomes the center of attention, as if a battery of searchlights were aimed directly at her face."

Eva thought about the dilemma and said somewhat wistfully, "I love it, however, darling. I love the fast lane."

"Of course you do," said Jameson. "But think of the hours spent in arriving at the total perfection before you make your entrance."

The youngest Gabor was speaking specifically, but her analysis applies to the entire family. It costs dearly—in money, energy, and emotional erosion—to be a Gabor, whether it's Eva, Zsa Zsa, Magda, or even Jolie.

Interestingly, while Zsa Zsa does all the talking about remaining young and beautiful, it is Eva who made remaining young into a science so precise that even her mansion is designed to serve this image. For more than ten years Eva has lived in a baronial Beverly Hills home that is draped with silks, satins, and antique furniture. And while the immense greenhouse for orchids served Frank's hobby, the olympic-sized swimming pool, the tennis court, and a gleaming gymnasium are there to serve the goddess of beauty.

"Sometimes I will play tennis for three hours at a time, then swim, and finally will work out in the gym for several hours. All of this is very, very hard work."

The gymnasium is a temple, a homage to the glamour brought from the Old World by the sisters and which finds its most perfect expression in Eva. Chrome barbells, huge mirrors, and stationary exercycles sit in a wing just off her boudoir as if to remind her hourly that being a Gabor is a full-time job.

Recently, when she allowed the cameras of *The Merv Griffin Show* to invade this shrine, she was quite blunt about the gritty job of remaining young. Speaking in a tone you might expect from a navy captain, she waved an arm toward the gym: "It's sheer torture. I have to be up with the chickens every day and go to work on my body. First there's stretching, then the weights. I hate it, but I do it." There's a faint hint of masochism in her tone.

Discipline is the key to Eva's nature. "I made up my mind to become an actress when I was four years old," she said. "I've been in training ever since. I learned early that you only have so much energy to give. You have to spend it correctly."

Somewhere beneath the "giddy Hungarian" facade is a real, warm-hearted lady. But this is well concealed. She approaches life as if it were one huge dramatic role.

"I'm acting when I serve as a hostess, acting when I run my wig business. I was born to act, and life itself is the greatest part. Acting to me isn't just a TV series, a talk show, or a play. And, fortunately or unfortunately, I'm a workaholic. Most people don't need to work as hard as I do. I've been trying to find out from my psychologist why I have this need."

A look of confusion crossed her face as she continued. "I'll go off on a tour to promote my wigs and dresses, and before long I'm traveling just on nervous energy alone. As you can imagine, this is incredibly exhausting."

Hidden behind the mansion walls, the Waterford silks, and the million-dollar wardrobe is a lady apparently still insecure about her place on the ladder of success.

Trying to fathom this ever-present insecurity, columnist Dorothy Manners once asked her, "Eva, were you ever poor, really poor? I don't mean just a little pressure due to bank loans, but low-down, no-good poor."

Unhappy memories showed in Eva's eyes, followed by an uncharacteristic silence. The diamond-studded hands ceased waving and the pink lips turned down. When she answered, it was as though she were recalling something she hadn't thought of in quite some time.

"Was I poor? *Was* I poor, Dorothy? I can remember having only thirty cents in my pocketbook and a husband to support. Yes, my first husband. I had eloped with him from Hungary against my mother's advice, and Eric Drimmer, a new osteopath, was just starting and had no patients.

"We lived behind a store in Hollywood. It was just one little room. I had a little car with no top to get me to the Paramount studio, and my $75 weekly salary disappeared the day I got my paycheck.

"I'll never forget that topless car. When it rained, and it rained a lot here during that dismal year, I held an umbrella over my head with one hand and drove with the other. I washed clothes, ironed, and bought the cheapest cuts of meat. To top it off, Eric had to cook, because I could barely make a three-minute egg."

Like Scarlett O'Hara or Becky Sharp, the heroine of *Vanity Fair,* both of whom she resembles, Eva looked out of the single small window in that apartment and vowed to herself that she would never be poor again, that she would never again be a little nobody window-shopping at the rich life that swirled about her in Hollywood.

To escape, Eva, just like her older sister Zsa Zsa, cashed in on her great beauty and the spun-sugar Hungarian image. But in the 1980s, Eva speaks out in the hope of correcting the image people have of the Gabors.

"I don't just sit around taking bubble baths," she said recently, "and I'm not the frivolous playgirl the public expects. I work all the harder at being an actress because this 'Gabor image' is so very difficult to live down. Since my co-workers expect me to be late and temperamental, I always try to get to work earliest and display no hint of temper. People think my sisters and I just sit about on couches and never work."

The image problem was particularly acute after she married Frank Gard Jameson and, almost automatically, became a part of his world of aerospace hierachy and high society. She not only adapted but became a major hostess to politicians and the great of Los Angeles. She became a close friend of the Nixons, the Reagans, and an even closer friend of Spiro Agnew. She has retained all these relationships.

Several of her parties even assumed legendary proportions and ranked her among this country's top hostesses. In the late 1960s, for instance, she hosted a Democrats for Nixon bash that required two catering services and five florists. A Los Angeles *Times* reporter who spent the day of the party with Eva noticed that she handled the Secret Service men with as much aplomb as the pastry chefs back in the kitchen. "The Secret Service had been all over the house, burrowing into closets and measuring the bluffs outside in order to establish command posts."

Specifically for the occasion she rented the mansion in Malibu belonging to the former Mrs. Paul Getty. Eva confessed to Dorothy Manners, "I'm crazy to lease this place for $30,000 for only three months. But I love it so—the place is so elegant and lovely."

Her role as a political hostess continued to accelerate as the Reagans came to power, causing her to preside at parties in Beverly Hills, Washington, D.C., New York City, and Palm Beach.

"A woman could make a full-time career just being the wife of Frank Gard Jameson," Eva once said. (The marriage collapsed in 1983.) "It's a major accomplishment just following him around meeting and entertaining business executives, not to mention the admirals and generals who are his close friends."

"Sometimes Frank will call up and say, 'We're having 250 to a buffet dinner next week. Is that okay?' Of course it's okay, but it adds a whole dimension to my life."

Eva rarely talks about her wig and dress businesses, which she pursues with a dog-eat-dog intensity. But Frank has occasionally discussed it: "Eva, almost single-handedly, started a wig business and revolutionized the design of wigs at the same time. Traditionally, wigs were hot and as heavy as football helmets," Frank told newsmen. "Working for several years, Eva developed a wig that weighs only an ounce and a quarter and costs but $25. It lets a woman have a dozen or more wigs of different styles and colors and it has brought a total change to the wig marketplace."

In several financial articles, business reporters speculated that Eva makes, after expenses, several hundred thousand dollars from her lucrative side venture. Indeed, many suggest that she makes $500,-000. Only her wig dresser knows for sure.

Jolie bluntly claims that Eva is "very, very rich. But she pays for it, darling. She pays for it in a hundred ways."

23

✳ The Zsa Zsa Mystique

*B*el Air Road, a main line for the super rich, is as immaculate as if it were washed hourly. The cars that drive up and down it have expensive muffled engines belonging to Rolls-Royces, Mercedes, and all varieties of Porsche. There is no litter —no carelessly tossed beer cans or cigarette butts. Thirty-year-old hedges that look as if they're trimmed by manicure scissors have grown up to guard the privacy of millionaires, movie stars, and not a few sheiks from Arabia.

The road has been the focus of Beverly Hills society for so long that adjectives like chic, posh, and fashionable seem trite and unnecessary. Bel Air Road's winding pattern starts down on the flatland and soars quickly upward over seven ridges, the topmost of which are wrapped in ocean fog in the morning. In the winter, fingers of dark storm clouds wrap cozily around the mansions. At the crest of the highest hill, a sweep of iron gates protects the palace of Zsa Zsa Gabor, a sprawling estate that is also a temple to beauty and an altar to fashion. More than that, it's a monument to one woman's personal style and opulence.

Built for the eccentric Howard Hughes, the mansion stood vacant for years until Zsa Zsa bought it for several million. She faced a formidable task of redecoration. The house mirrored Howard's bizarre persona with light gray interior walls, murky paneling, and awesome red velvet drapes that had been used in the Hughes film *Vendetta*.

Typically, Zsa Zsa all but pulled the house down in order to refashion it in her own image. Today it is washed in pastels. The outside is in subtle shades of cream, offset by charcoal trim and a French mansard roof. Inside, paneling of jonquil yellow, New Mexico morning blue, and salmon has transformed the walls into a glowing backdrop for the lady who dominates the house. There is that vague feeling that it's all a stage setting.

While most of the Hollywood rich are coy about the money it takes to support their glittering facades, Zsa Zsa states matter-of-factly, "The maintenance of all this costs about $500,000 a year. The money flows out in an endless fountain."

Los Angeles writer Burt Prelutsky, who once spent several days with Zsa Zsa to capture her elusive nature in a magazine article, wrote, "I believe that she is frightfully misunderstood. Somehow I know that beneath the jeweled facade there is a homespun Hungarian girl who likes the simple things."

If this is the case, Zsa Zsa hides all traces of it successfully. For instance, her wardrobe is spread through a temperature-controlled chamber the size of a small studio apartment. Just the sight of it is staggering, housed as it is in a three-tiered dressing room thirty feet long, twelve feet wide, and fourteen feet high.

The door opens on an Arabian Nights tableau of a million sequins, yards of rich velvets, silks, chiffons, and heavy rococo brocades. The colors range from beige to royal purple, from metallic green to rainbow stripes woven into flowing organza. Organized by type, the clothes are further protected by hand-crafted Louis Vuitton bags.

Along one wall the parade of fashion begins with hundreds of nightgowns, robes, and three-piece negligees. The colors are eclectic —tangerine, blood red, avocado green, and dark bedroom blue. Feathered and unfeathered, elaborate and simple, they're the stuff of which romance is made.

Next in line is a king's ransom of evening gowns. Dozens of designers—predominantly Christian Dior and Yves St. Laurent—are represented, as are all styles, from simple Empire shifts to full-skirted ball gowns.

Hanging above the formal wear are evening coats and jackets organized by type: sequined, embroidered, satin, silk, velvet, and feathered. So carefully are they positioned that the coats in many cases hang precisely above the dresses they match.

Then there are caftans, theatrical costumes, long coats, afternoon dresses, and pants and matching blouses. ("I hate them, darling, but one must have them, I suppose.")

When Edith Head, the Academy Award–winning film designer, toured the wing, she commented, quite seriously, "This is larger than the entire women's costume collection at Paramount. Each shoe, beaded handbag, or designer scarf can be located in a matter of seconds. . . . If plans are suddenly cancelled for a barbecue and Zsa Zsa is invited instead to a formal dinner, I've seen her change clothes, jewels, and shoes—and all in less than fifteen minutes."

In part, this fabulously organized wardrobe was provided by the various men in her life. "I was wasting so much time getting dressed that three of my former husbands were infuriated—especially George Sanders. George used to say that he had no place for even his shirts because my trappings were everywhere," Zsa Zsa said.

"Houses, even the best of them, aren't created for women," Zsa Zsa lamented. "And they certainly aren't created to house wardrobes such as mine. Luckily, I bought this house when I was single and was able to add the mammoth dressing room."

It takes an enormous amount of work and organization to be Zsa Zsa Gabor, and she makes that quite clear. "Being glamorous, especially when you make your living off that quality, is a full-time, all-consuming, and very, very hard task," she said.

"A woman who is constantly in the public eye can't afford to look boring. So I buy, buy, buy." Because of this turnover, Zsa Zsa replaces most of her clothes every two years. "I rarely keep anything longer than that, darling, except for the Christian Diors, the St. Laurents, and other classically designed gowns."

For the past eleven years Zsa Zsa has given $30,000 annually in high fashion clothes to various charities. "And this, of course, is more than the ordinary woman will buy in a lifetime."

When she moved into the former Howard Hughes mansion she immediately started an addition to her bedroom wing—including a totally mirrored dressing room, a bath that is almost thirty feet wide and forty feet long, as well as the three-tiered wardrobe.

With each passing year, Zsa Zsa's preoccupation with these trappings of glamour has increased. She gets high on jewels, furs, and clothes to such an extent that it has been perceived by some as an addiction. And this seems to be but a symptom of the quiet hysteria Zsa Zsa has experienced as old age bears down on her.

"Oh, God, I get sick, physically sick, at the thought of growing old," Zsa Zsa told a journalist several years ago. "No woman likes it, but it terrifies me."

The result of this has been a vain attempt to push back the clock. Three years ago, Zsa Zsa dispatched messengers to the downtown offices of the Associated Press and the Los Angeles *Times* to hand-deliver Xeroxed copies of a birth certificate that she claimed had been recently smuggled out of Hungary. A copy of her baptismal record was produced as well—perhaps to lend divine credence to her claims. The documents list her birth date as February 6, 1928.

Even though the Los Angeles *Times* and newspapers across the country accepted these documents at face value, there's no doubt that Zsa Zsa was born quite a few years earlier than 1928. Many Gabor experts believe that Zsa Zsa was born in 1920, as this would have made her about sixteen when she married her first husband.

To accept the "1928 theory" creates laughable circumstances. It would mean that she was married for the first time at about eight and that she was about fourteen when she wed Conrad Hilton. Further, since the members of her family have always maintained that Zsa Zsa was second runner-up in the 1936 Miss Hungary Pageant, she would, at eight years old, have been the youngest bathing beauty and certainly the most precocious.

"All the lies about my age are driving me crazy," she told the UPI bureau in Los Angeles when she offered the birth certificate. "Every time I read about myself in the paper, I see that I am a different age —usually far older than I am. And God knows I'm old enough without adding any years."

Since all three of the Gabor sisters in person look as if they are in their early fifties, it must be galling to have the real birth dates thrown in their faces.

Even Eva becomes offended when asked about her age. In Australia, while doing a live television show, she dodged several questions about age and then snapped, "Ordinarily I don't answer that question, but since it seems so important to all of you, I'll tell. I am 102, Zsa Zsa is 104, Magda is 106, and mother, of course, is somewhat older."

Some reference guides have cleverly sidestepped the Gabor birthdates. For instance, the *World Almanac,* which lists ages for most prominent celebrities, leaves a blank in its entry on Zsa Zsa. When confronted by one reporter about marrying Connie at age fourteen, she said, "Conrad made me promise to never, never reveal my true age. And I haven't."

24

✿ One Dreadful Autumn

Z sa Zsa clutched the hand of newspaper reporter Judy Barden, gripping it so hard that Judy's natural reaction was to pull it away. But Zsa Zsa continued to grasp it as if she were seeking a life buoy. The journalist's desire to back off was overcome by her news sense. If she hung on, if she won the confidence of this woman, she might have a hell of a story.

She'd been called to the London hotel suite overlooking Hyde Park by a secretary whose voice wavered with fear. "Miss Zsa Zsa Gabor is giving a press conference," pleaded the voice. "Please come. Please!"

But Judy was the only one there. Zsa Zsa was seeing the press one at a time, as if she were a psychic about to announce great impending doom.

The reporter looked at the famous woman before her and wondered what could have caused such disarray, both mental and physical. Zsa Zsa's gray jersey dress seemed to have been twisted again and again by hands searching for something to hold. The famous halo of blond hair appeared windblown, and there was a noticeable lack of jewelry.

Tea was served, and Zsa Zsa learned close to the reporter: "I go constantly in fear, not only in America but here in Britain also. You don't know how terrible it is."

The year was 1968, and the winds of protest were blowing strong.

"Somebody is out to kill me," Zsa Zsa lamented. "And not just me but my mother also. Never have so many things happened to me as in the past year. Even my sister Eva talks about me as if I were insane. And there are those who would like to put me away *for good!* That includes Conrad Hilton, who says, after all these years, that my daughter Francesca Hilton is not his."

To another reporter, she said, "Every day they watch me, follow me, even trace me with special sound equipment. Someday I'll be found dead, mysteriously, maybe in this very hotel room."

Zsa Zsa's eyes opened widely; her fingers trembled so badly they couldn't hold a cup of coffee. This Zsa Zsa bore little resemblance to the cool, chic, funny lady who had charmed half the world.

During one fairly normal interview with a radio reporter in London, Zsa Zsa suddenly blurted out, "And they are going to kill me before this month is over." Tears started forming. "And I don't even know why they're going to kill me. Can you tell me why?"

The reporter shook his head sadly. "No, Miss Gabor, I don't know. Why don't you call Scotland Yard."

"I will do that," she said thankfully. "I'll do that tomorrow." She grasped the young man's hand. "You may have saved my life."

The next morning a rested, beautiful Zsa Zsa met with a detective from Scotland Yard. Dressed in a sedate suit, with hair groomed perfectly, the actress calmly described the widespread plot that allegedly was destined to end in her death.

"Do you have any idea who would want to do this?" the detective asked.

"No," said Zsa Zsa. "Absolutely not." She walked over to a bedside table and returned with a pile of news clippings about her financial troubles in London and Spain. "Maybe some of these people," she said, indicating the growing trail of angered shopkeepers, hotel managers, and boutique owners who were chasing her across Europe with satchels of unpaid bills.

Zsa Zsa then walked over to the hotel window with its view of London. She gazed out, and a frightened, lonely look haunted her face. "It could be an international plot. It could be anybody."

The man from Scotland Yard promised to help.

Reporters besieged the detective as he tried to exit the hotel unseen. "What's up?" asked one of them. "It's a death threat and from an anonymous source," the man replied tersely.

"Is she just imagining things?" asked a reporter from the London *Times*.

The detective flicked through his notebook and then looked up at the reporter angrily. "No, I think there's some basis to her fear. We wouldn't be here otherwise. But more than that, I can tell you nothing."

Upstairs, Zsa Zsa's mind was obviously still in turmoil as she tried to sort out the ugliness that had come to dog her steps in that dreadful autumn of 1968. There had been escapades before, some of them quite outrageous. But the world had always indulged her, forgiven her, and swept all traces of scandal under a rug of glamour. This time, however, the ugliness refused to vanish.

Still, she must have wondered how a little tiff in sunny Mallorca had become a raging worldwide incident. She had gone to the resort in early December to rest a bit in the sun and to buy Christmas presents. Then her activities veered out of control. Her reputation had preceded her to the island, throwing up social storm clouds.

In September at the Ritz Hotel in London, she had slapped the face of a young bellboy during an argument over hotel towels being carried off in one of the many Gabor suitcases.

After Zsa Zsa had a second hysterical spat with employees at the Palacio Hotel in Lisbon who had refused to take her check in payment, several reporters began following her trail.

"Zsa Zsa Gabor vs. Libson," read one headline on a Reuters dispatch. The reporter also discovered an alleged Gabor ploy when Zsa Zsa tried to slip off one international airliner and onto another to keep from paying excess baggage charges.

"Can you imagine?" Zsa Zsa said to reporter Blane Stevenson. "The hotel manager wanted to hold my jewelry worth a million dollars as bond in case my check for the $500 hotel bill was returned. They opened my suitcases and found several hotel towels which had been used to wrap up my chinchilla coats. But the maid had given me permission to use them."

The fight between the Palacio Hotel and Zsa Zsa became a standoff. She would not turn over her jewels, and the hotel refused her check, telling police they had evidence that Zsa Zsa left hotels time and time again without paying. "We will just wait until she pays," said the manager. "Her luggage will be held until cash is produced."

Zsa Zsa held court in the lounge across from the hotel registration desk. To most reporters, she appeared to be a lady in great distress. And the sobs that occasionally wavered into her speech didn't hurt her case.

Into this fracas walked a cool man from the U.S. embassy. He listened to the hotel version and then went across the lobby to hear the Gabor version. It was a job for a Henry Kissinger, but the young man, Bill Stevens, would have to do. Within two hours he was successful. A détente was reached. Zsa Zsa turned over the towels, paid $200 of her bill, and left a check for the rest.

Bill was sweating as he escorted Zsa Zsa from the hotel and waved goodbye with a jaunty "Have a smashing time in Mallorca."

Mallorca was unprepared for the one-woman hurricane about to hit. Zsa Zsa stayed in the best hotel suite, ordered thousands of dollars' worth of custom-made clothing, and treated the hotel staff members as if they were Russian serfs.

Typically, Zsa Zsa shunned the island's bright sun as if it were the plague, appearing outside in full dress and wearing sunscreen to protect her famous complexion. In that garb, she made a royal progress through the exclusive boutiques. In one of them, Zsa Zsa eyed the expensive array and called salesmen and seamstresses to her hotel. She chose twenty-five dresses from the line—including several costly evening gowns, fifteen hats, and a king's ransom in accessories. "She took the very best items we had—almost all of them," said the owner of the boutique. "That lady sure knew her clothes."

But Zsa Zsa advanced not one cent for alterations, promising to pay on completion of the work. She did, however, persuade her hotel to advance her $2,000 for a deposit on the $3,500 order. Early the next morning, she bolted. She had packed all the expensive clothes in a large suitcase, put her small dog in a special carrying pack, and settled down in first class for a flight to London.

The engines were revved up and the plane was about to taxi when several stern-looking Mallorcan police came down the aisle. "Miss Gabor," said one of them in flawless English, "will you please come with us?"

"I will not," answered Zsa Zsa with a hard edge to her voice.

"Very well," said the officer. "We'll take you off by force."

"Once they got me outside the plane, they started beating me up," Zsa Zsa told New York columnist Earl Wilson after she returned to the United States. "I was treated like a hardened criminal."

Zsa Zsa matched the police charges with loud, hysterical denials as the officers continued to escort her to the unpleasant little jail in the center of town. Zsa Zsa's bellows could be heard for blocks. "I demand to see a judge, then a lawyer, right now."

A uniformed police commissioner took Zsa Zsa's arm. "Madame, you will get your chance before a magistrate tomorrow. Until then you stay here," he said, waving a hand toward the squalid jail. So for almost seventeen hours one of the world's greatest beauties sat in the jail awaiting the workings of a medieval justice system. Later, Zsa Zsa's ex-husband George Sanders, a man quite familiar with Mallorca from many vacations, decried her treatment as barbaric. "They are still a bit uncivilized," he said.

The next morning, Zsa Zsa was ordered to pay her hotel bill and the $3,500 she had spent on clothes. Careful negotiations were under way while Zsa Zsa was held in court. Hour by hour, attorneys in both Mallorca and London worked out an arrangement with a London bank, which finally guaranteed the purchases.

After the incident, both reporters and customs officials in London were shocked to see Zsa Zsa arrive wearing bandages and visibly limping, It had been but forty-eight hours since she was taken to jail, and now, with a captive audience, she gloried in the attention. "I was beaten horribly," she told reporters who gathered about her. "I didn't think this kind of thing went on outside of Communist countries." She daintily lifted the hem of her suit to show that her legs were swathed in bandages. "I will never even spit on Spanish soil from now on," she said. "And I will never, never go back to Mallorca."

Her entry to England was free of scandal. And the customs men of the United Kingdom must have heaved a sigh of relief, remembering the dreadful experience they had with her earlier in the year. Several months before, the actress had been jetting in from Chicago with her usual load of suitcases and, peculiarly, a small green bag with a grille at one end. The sniffing and moaning of a small dog could be clearly heard by the officials.

"May we examine that case?" asked one of the customs men.

"Only if you can tell me why you need to."

"Miss Gabor," said the man warily, "we believe that there is an animal in there, and you know we have a six-month quarantine here. Please don't be difficult."

The men finally eased the satchel from her hands and freed a white ball of a dog, which pranced merrily about the table.

Zsa Zsa scooped up the dog and partially hid it in a fur coat. "This is a very high-strung terrier," she said. "And it has only been out of London for ten weeks. How can you quarantine such a darling little animal?"

Then, according to British customs officers, Zsa Zsa became abusive and belligerent. According to court records filed in London, Zsa Zsa said, "Wait? Wait? You want *me* to wait? I don't have to f—— wait for anyone."

"But, Miss Gabor, you'll have to wait," a customs man answered.

Then Zsa Zsa moved over until she was facing him. She bellowed, "Take off your f—— hat when you f—— talk to a lady."

Zsa Zsa was then immediately hauled into magistrates' court and fined $24 for using profane language. Asked to describe the Gabor outburst, an official said gallantly, "I can only say that it was not the language one would expect from a truck driver, much less a lady."

An additional fine of $96 was levied against Zsa Zsa for trying to sneak an animal through British quarantine.

In great style, she was driven to court in a Silver Cloud Rolls Royce, decked out in furs and a Parisian suit. For once, Zsa Zsa publicly apologized for both her language and conduct.

Several days later Jolie jetted in from America to help extract Zsa Zsa from the economic and social quicksand. "I don't know why Zsa Zsa's doing these silly things," she told reporters. "I do know that I'm tired of all this fuss. I'm sure that somebody my age should not have to run about looking after her full-grown daughter. It's really quite debasing."

On December 27, 1968, a phone call from a news source (perhaps Jolie) to Abe Greenberg's "Voice of Hollywood" disclosed that Zsa Zsa had committed herself to the Priory Nursing Home on Upper Richmond Road in London. The source said Zsa Zsa would be there for one month to undergo a regimen of psychological treatment and complete rest.

A week earlier, Greenberg had said in a story that "Zsa Zsa Gabor is more to be pitied than scorned. This girl needs air."

Zsa Zsa has refused to talk of the bizarre episodes in Spain, Portugal, and London. But Jolie has, several times. "It's true that Zsa Zsa has had a very mixed-up time," she said during a 1968 radio interview. "It all began in London with a buying spree to end all buying sprees."

According to Jolie, Zsa Zsa cut a great swath through London's finest stores. "She bought things that not even she could afford," Jolie said. "She bought a house in five minutes, a truckload of antiques in even less time, and, to top it, a ridiculously overpriced $22,000 mirror."

One afternoon, Jolie remembered, Zsa Zsa appeared in central London in full hunting dress and riding one of her Arabian horses. Since it was a busy weekday, and since Zsa Zsa always attracts crowds anyway, throngs of people flocked to see the show.

After the dust settled, Jolie said she was able to negotiate a deal wherein the stores took back all the expensive trappings. "We paid them ten percent on the dollar to compensate for their lost sales."

"It was just a brief, unfortunate spell," said Mama Gabor. "One afternoon she gave away a million-dollar necklace, and the next day she ordered the entire contents of her Beverly Hills home shipped to London."

"I settled this quickly," Jolie continued. "We got the necklace back, and the furniture was returned to Beverly Hills."

Jolie and a great many others close to Zsa Zsa are bitter about the way Zsa Zsa's spells are dealt with so nastily by the press. "I think we all go through confused times like Zsa Zsa's, don't you?"

Husband number six, the multimillionaire inventor Jack Ryan, has often lashed out at such vindictive publicity about his ex-wife. "Think of what she has achieved, the world image she is always expected to fulfill. She lives in such a public glare that some side effects are bound to show up. It would be impossible for her to get off the merry-go-round of glamour which has entrapped her. It's very, very hard to be Zsa Zsa Gabor."

George Sanders, the husband Zsa Zsa loved most, said bursts of temperament are bound to erupt. "Zsa Zsa is perhaps the most misunderstood woman of our times," he told Edward R. Murrow. "She allows her vitality and instincts to spring from her without distortion. Not for her is the conventional mask of studied behavior. Looking at the whole picture, you find that Zsa Zsa is intrinsically quite wonderful and doesn't deserve the somewhat contemptuous treatment to which she is all too frequently exposed simply because she doesn't fit any pattern. . . . All in all, she gets a bum rap," he concluded.

BOOK SIX

Bedtime Stories

*"As I got ready for bed one night,
I looked at the glorious vision before me
and thought, My God, I'm going to bed
with* Zsa Zsa Gabor.
—JACK RYAN, 1983

25

❋ Woman of Mystery

*M*agda, her face transformed by distress, clutched at the silk draperies and parted them to look down at the street—for the tenth time. The concrete canyons of Manhattan had already assumed their twilight gloom, which only served to feed her growing alarm.

The wailing of an ambulance pierced the silence of the town house. This was a signal of danger. He must have been in an accident, must be lying right now in some hospital emergency room.

She looked uneasily at the mute telephone, reached out for it but thought better of it, and settled into the deep recesses of a sofa. As her hand clasped the stem of a martini glass, her eyes again focused on the glittering new engagement ring, and she felt a warm glow.

It had been only four hours since Tony gave it to her, less than two days since he proposed; but for the first time, the love seemed so real and so permanent. After three thoroughly disappointing husbands and five romantically barren years in New York cafe society, Magda was swept off her feet by a brusque Italian.

Tony Gallucci was the sort of man all the Gabors dreamed about. Amorous, tempestuous, and darkly handsome, he approached life as if it were one lusty adventure. And he was rich, an industrial baron with a widespread empire of factories that produced plumbing components.

Magda's reverie was interrupted when she realized that the room had darkened. Her heart raced as the events of the afternoon replayed in her mind. There had been an early lunch, then midafternoon cocktails, a congratulatory call from Jolie, followed by more cocktails—maybe too many.

During the last round of drinks, Magda's poodle Coco suddenly interrupted the celebration, begging excitedly for its regular evening walk. Tony volunteered. "I'll take her, you get ready for dinner, back in a sec."

That had been hours earlier, and Tony hadn't even telephoned. In a perverse way, Magda actually hoped for some quite minor accident, some negligible emergency. Anything was preferable to the suspicion that she had been deserted again.

Emotionally and physically, Magda had the presence of a doomed heroine, with her windswept Titian-red hair and wide vulnerable eyes. Now, waiting for Tony in her white evening gown with the long black gloves, she could have stepped out of a painting by Edouard Manet.

"To understand Magda you must fully understand the flower that closes its petals to the sun," Jolie once described her. "She blooms in private with an alluring timidity."

According to Jolie, that night in Manhattan Magda's worst nightmares were verified the moment she heard Coco, finally back and whimpering pitifully at the door. Magda jerked it open, revealing the frightened poodle—minus her leash, her rhinestone collar, and Tony.

At first it made Magda lightheaded. The bereavement was instant and consuming. She stumbled into her dressing room and, typically, repaired her makeup to perfection, changed into a thousand-dollar hostess gown, and ran a brush through her hair. Then she fell backwards into a gilt chair, opened her small desk, extracted notepaper scented with Chanel No. 5, and wrote, "I love Tony. There is no way that I can bear life without him. . . . Goodbye."

The missive was placed near a Tiffany lamp, so that soft amber light was aimed directly at the heartbreaking message.

A vial of strong narcotics was already on the bedside table, and she placed a glass of white wine next to it. Then Magda defiantly threw back her head, swallowed the pills, and placed one alabaster hand on her forehead. There was time for her to arrange her hair into a spill across a satin pillow and to adjust the folds of her dress into a chic splash. She reclined backwards to accept the welcome darkness.

Only minutes later the phone at her bedside began ringing. She stared at it for a second and ignored it, drowsiness having engulfed her.

Jolie had been preparing to go out for dinner when "a great fear" passed through her. "It was vague, but I knew instantly that it had to do with Magda," Jolie said. "Maybe it was a sixth sense," she said in her 1975 autobiography, *Jolie.* "But I knew something was dreadfully wrong when she didn't answer the phone."

She threw on a fur coat and rushed to her daughter. The tragically beautiful tableau caused her to gasp. Then she realized that *she* had given Magda the pills for sleeping, and that there had been only four of them. The worst thing Magda could expect was a painful barbiturate hangover.

In *Jolie* she indicated that her own indefatigable love of life was outraged by her daughter's suicide attempt. Using all her strength, Jolie jerked Magda up off the bed and doused her face with ice water.

Magda whimpered awake, sobbed, and heaved her shoulders. "Oh, my dear, it was a fine performance," Jolie remembered. "But, for the moment, this was a great tragedy for her. She had a great, great love for Tony."

Finally, she helped her eldest daughter into her mink and pulled her through the New York streets toward Broadway, with its brilliant lights and sidewalks teeming with gay theatergoers.

"Look at all this," she said, waving a hand toward the vivacity. "Life is always worth living, even without that certain man."

Further on, they came to a pair of full-length mirrors in a store window. She grasped Magda's chin with one hand and forced her to face the alluring face reflected back at her. "You're young, beautiful, talented, and clever. In many ways, your life is just beginning. I wish I was as young as you again. And besides, after what we went through in Hungary, are you ready to give up your life for a man who didn't come back from a walk?"

Magda nodded her head in agreement, and they walked back to the town house arm in arm.

The next morning Jolie was dying to know what had really happened to Tony, and she called his house. "Tony had a rich, charming lady friend who had married an Italian marquis," Jolie recalled. "She had just returned from Italy minus her aristocratic husband. I had felt for several weeks that the love between them might be rekindled," said Jolie. "And that is exactly what happened."

Tony encountered the lady on his fated walk with Coco, they started talking, he suggested a quick one in a cocktail lounge, she accepted. Coco and Magda faded temporarily from his mind. As he opened the door to the lounge, he discovered the leash and empty collar in his hand. Coco had wriggled out of it long before.

This entire surrealistic experience was typical of Magda's luck since she had arrived in America (the long affair with Dr. Garrido, the Portuguese diplomat, having ended). Even her arrival in the late 1940s was shrouded in a peculiar mystery. Newspapers had been alerted to Magda's arrival; reporters waited, waited, and waited.

By the time the cabin boys disembarked, it was obvious that the third Gabor sister had slipped past them. There was a persistent rumor at the time (which still surfaces today) that the beauteous Eva and Zsa Zsa, horrified by Magda's thick Hungarian nose, smuggled her off the boat through a cargo door, bundled her into a private ambulance, and spirited her to a Long Island clinic. "Only when her nose was compatible with those of her sisters was she allowed to emerge and breathe the free air of Manhattan," a Hearst gossip columnist claimed.

She had shed her Polish Count, the first husband, long before leaving Europe, but was still introduced by Eva and Zsa Zsa as "Her Excellency, the Countess Bichovsky." After a moderate flurry of interviews and photo sessions, Magda disappeared from public view, surfacing only occasionally to act in summer stock or to appear in club acts with her sisters.

But in high society she often sailed higher than Eva or Zsa Zsa, and she became a regular guest at the weekend parties of the superich. It was at a formal hunt in the Virginia countryside that she met her second husband, a Hollywood writer, William Rankin. According to Jolie, William and Magda became engaged that very weekend and eloped only a few days later.

On the telephone to her mother, Magda described him as an intimate friend. Jolie answered, "You've never mentioned him before." Magda was defensive: "Well, Nuci, William Rankin is a man you will get to know well, because I'm going to marry him."

When she next called home to Mom it was as Mrs. William Rankin. "Ah, Nuci, he's bought me a beautiful mink coat and an expensive red car. He's so terribly generous." In her memoirs, Jolie claims that she paid for both the coat and the car, having been billed for these and other expenses of her eldest daughter.

"This marriage was certainly not one of the best," Jolie concluded. Thus the Rankin marriage ended with a whimper, but the next of Magda's consorts was to create such a stir that it peppered the gossip columns from coast to coast.

Sidney Warren was a dynamic, intense lawyer to whom Magda turned for help in untangling her troubled legal and financial affairs. He offered a strong, experienced shoulder, and she took it.

Soon, much too soon according to Jolie, Magda rushed to the altar a third time. "Nuci, you know I'm the quiet, serious one in the family. Well, Sidney also likes the simple things of life. We will be married, buy a farm, and settle down. This is it, Nuci, this is it."

"I was horrified at first," Jolie told the London *Daily Mirror*. "I looked across the table at her and said sternly, 'But I can see you're not in love with this man. Don't do this.' "

Magda would not be deterred: "I know, but this love will grow."

The Warrens moved into one floor of Jolie's brownstone and turned it into a marital battleground. One afternoon not long after, Jolie returned home to her lovely house and found that her own butler, Harry, had been mobilized by Magda to help throw all of Sidney's belongings out in the street, literally. Of course they had all been neatly packed by Harry before being set outside above the gutter.

Jolie confronted a raging Magda, her face a mask of fury.

"How can you do this? How can you throw a man out on the street?"

Magda passed her by without a word. "Harry," Magda ordered, "now, change the locks."

Later Jolie pulled aside her drapes and saw the wretched lawyer packing up and down in front of the house. "I felt so dreadfully sorry for him," Jolie said. "He finally called me from a pay telephone, and my heart went out to him."

"I promised to reason with Magda," she told him. But, according to Jolie's memoirs, Magda told her things that "caused me to agree with her. It was a terrible marriage and had to be ended immediately."

Then came Tony Gallucci. "He was the sweetest, nicest man I had ever met," Jolie said. "He seemed to match my lovely eldest daughter."

After the leash-and-collar affair, Tony married the Italian woman. This lasted less than a year, and apparently he sorely missed the Gabor charm.

A reunion came at a New York garden party at which Magda arrived fashionably late. Tony looked up from his place at the bar and smiled timid recognition. He began pushing through the packed crowd to reach her side. Magda's eyes misted. They were still very much in love.

Jolie urged caution. "He's afraid of marriage, Magda. He'll never ask you to marry him."

"Nuci, you don't know how much Tony loves me."

Over the veto of Jolie, Magda and Tony Gallucci were married on a sunny spring afternoon in 1956. That very night they moved into his seven-bedroom mansion in Southampton, Long Island. The couple would also share a Manhattan penthouse.

Magda became very much the glittering hostess, but Tony, unhappily, continued his erratic pattern of boozing and wenching. "It hurt her very much," Eva once told a columnist. "But it was typical of Magda to smile and pretend the bad things didn't exist."

Jolie and Zsa Zsa were amazed when Magda paddled so adroitly in the Southampton social swim that not only was she fully accepted but she became a trend setter with her parties. "But trouble was always right around the corner," said Jolie. "Because of Tony's constant drinking habit."

At the time of Magda's reunion with Tony, Jolie was applying her iron will to push Magda into an acting career. "Magda wasn't happy," Jolie said on a Los Angeles talk show. "She was restless and jealous of the other girls. She didn't know it, but I was pressuring my theater friends to give her a job. Then she met Tony."

After Tony walked out with the poodle and before the reconciliation, Magda had her agent, Jeffrey Jones, bring Tony to her apartment. This was apparently after the cocktail party reunion.

The next night Magda was back in Tony's arms.

Magda had several lucrative theater contracts to fulfill after the marriage, much to the outrage of Tony, an old-fashioned Italian male chauvinist.

She was touring summer theaters in a little bit of hokum called *This Thing Called Love.* One of the stops was a noisy theater in Coney Island. Tony wriggled in his seat every time the young and handsome leading man came within a foot of Magda. Finally, at the climax of a love scene, the actor began kissing Magda passionately.

There was a crash from the back of the theater. Tony, raging, had caught his foot in a folding chair, flung it away, and hurtled down the aisle to sock his wife.

When it came to money, Tony lavished it on her to the point of overindulgence. When Magda wished for a swimming pool, Tony bought ten acres adjoining the mansion (at $20,000 an acre) to house the pool and a sprawling compound of dressing rooms.

According to Jolie, Tony's drinking was the only thing that marred the marriage. "In all other ways, it was happy, perhaps the most blissful marriage any of my daughters would ever make.

"Magda learned to live with the drinking. She became the aggressor. She even beat him up because of it. One time Tony called me and asked for help," Jolie said. " 'Magda is beating me up. She slapped my face! What can I do?' "

Jolie thought for a minute: "So hit her back."

26

✳ Till Death Us Do Part

*N*ew York's newspapers had a juicy story that warm afternoon, and they made the best of it. "Fabulous Eva Gabor called 'love pirate'! Jilted model takes her life."

Across the Manhattan street another news barker yelled, "Get the full story over here. Eva Gabor, Dick Brown, and the 'Case of the Heartbroken Model.' "

It was much the same in Chicago, St. Louis, Boston, and San Francisco as the story came over the wires into the newsrooms and out to rush-hour readers filling the late-afternoon streets.

It was April 10, 1959, and a fresh wave of scandal broke over the Gabors, this time implicating Eva.

To be fair, Eva was little more than an innocent bystander, but fame swept her into the headlines and kept her there for almost a month.

It had all started at eight A.M. that morning when police were called to the apartment of a New York City model, Venita Ratcliffe. They found her wrapped in a silk robe in the center of her bed. The bottle that had contained a lethal dose of sleeping pills was still clutched in one hand.

Across the room on a dresser police found a pitiful note, addressed to handsome stockbroker Richard Brown, who was engaged to Eva. The note said, among other things, "I understand, now that I would only continue to be a pest in your life. But, Dick, I love you more than life itself. Without you, there is no meaning for me."

The note indicated that Venita had talked to Dick earlier on the night she killed herself, and that she was already resigned to suicide. Perhaps the phone call was just the straw that did it.

But there was such heartbreak to the note, so much drama centering on Dick and Venita as star-crossed lovers, and so much glamour surrounding Eva's unknowing part in the scandal that tabloid editors gobbled it up.

In Hollywood, Eva was on the set of *It Started with a Kiss* when the story broke in Los Angeles. Eva gasped when she heard about it and was escorted to her dressing room. With the help of an MGM publicity man she issued a statement: "I'm very, very sorry that this beautiful girl took her life. But I am only an innocent bystander in all this. The romance between Richard and me began long after he left Venita."

Several hours later, the nation's scrappy tabloids dug their claws into the scandal, coining the description of Eva as a "love pirate." It spread like wildfire, as such stories do. Soon it was on radio, then television, where oversized photos of Eva, Dick, and Venita were shown.

Louella Parsons immediately called MGM's publicity office and warned that some quite nasty things were being said about Eva by friends of the late model. "You and I know there is nothing to it," Louella said. "But you better defuse the bomb as quickly as you can."

When the description "love pirate" reached her on the set, Eva blew up. "A love pirate?" she yelled. "What do they mean by that?"

According to the Associated Press, Eva began screaming, "I *do not* go around taking anyone's man. I am much too spoiled, for one thing, and there are so many attractive men around these days. *I am no love pirate.* Remember, if a man is truly in love, the most beautiful woman in the world couldn't take him away. Maybe for a few days, but not forever."

Dick, then thirty-seven, was a dress manufacturing magnate and a prestigious stockbroker when the scandal broke. In her tragic note to her former love, Venita, twenty-six, called him "Daddie" and referred to herself as "Mommie."

There was no doubt that Richard and Venita were not even seeing each other when Eva met the stockbroker on a film set in Spain. It must have been quite a shock when Eva found herself being trumpeted about as if she were a jet set love queen. She had been through three divorces and a torrid affair with Tyrone Power without ever attracting the media to any extent. Now they came at her from all directions, dredging up old lovers and ex-husbands; and they manufactured juicy gossip if they had to.

After six bitter weeks the scandal was over, and Eva immersed herself in theater and television work.

For the most part, Eva's husbands haven't been the stuff of which headlines are made. Right from the beginning she went for pretty faces and well-muscled bodies. But her men were all quiet and shunned the glare of publicity.

Her first, Eric Drimmer, disappeared without a whisper. Charles

Isaacs, husband number two, was dynamic and well established when she met him. He had Old World class and catered to Eva shamelessly.

There was only minor friction in the Isaacs household, and it was over Eva's all-encompassing career. "Everyone laughed at me and said, 'Why do you want to work, because now you could buy the studio.'"

"Nobody seemed to understand the depth of my commitment to acting," Eva told Louella Parsons. "People wanted me to give up all that I had achieved. They just didn't understand."

On the other hand, Eva was the most important thing in Charles's life. "She was the light of his life," remembered one of Charles's friends. "There was nothing he would not do for her. He knew he had found the one girl for him—for life!"

It was a cruel irony that Charles was stricken by cancer the very month Eva decided to leave him. "I wanted to be an actress more than anything in the world. Not even Charles understood. I wanted it so desperately that I had to prove it by leaving him to stand on my own two feet."

The day she moved out of the Isaacs mansion both she and Charles knew that he had only several months to live. "He was literally dying when I left him," she told a newspaper interviewer. "That was the worst thing I ever did. And I have paid for it bitterly."

It broke his heart. "The cancer didn't kill his spirit," said a friend. "He had the kind of philosophy that took everything in stride. But losing Eva—that crushed him completely."

Jolie was present at the last meeting between Eva and Charles and was haunted by it for years. The disease had so ravaged his body that he displayed only a mournful hint of his former panache. The limousine pulled up to the front of Eva's house. A strong chauffeur reached into the car, lifted Charles out, and carried him across the grass to an outdoor chaise. Even talk was painful for him, but he tried to answer all of Eva's questions, gazing at her adoringly. Then he seemed to cave in, and the chauffeur carried him off. Just as the car turned out of the drive, Charles glanced back at Eva—one last time.

"Eva would have inherited more than $6 million if she had waited several months longer. But that's not important," Jolie recalled. "I was hurt myself when Eva told me she wanted that divorce. It crushed me, because I knew how much he worshipped her and that he had only a few months to live."

When the divorce was granted on April 5, 1949, court records noted that a financial settlement had been made privately. The exact amount Charles gave Eva was up for debate. Louella Parsons thought it was around a million. "I have my reasons for thinking that," she said. "I do know that he would have given her anything."

Explaining her decision to leave Charles, Eva said, "I should have been smart enough to stay happy. But my ambition at that time ruled my life."

She tried to prepare her husband a year before she finally left him. "One night I sat down to have a long talk with Charles. "It is no use. I can't take being artistically inactive. I have to pack up and try my luck on Broadway." Charles shrugged his approval.

Her next marriage—to plastic surgeon Dr. John Williams—resulted from a whim. "Or was I just insane for a few weeks?" Eva said later. She was starring in *The Happy Time* on Broadway when she first met John. "I wasn't even in love with him. I didn't even like him," she told a columnist in the 1950s. "And after we were married for one minute, I wanted to leave him."

Eva consulted Mama. "Do you love him?" Jolie asked. Eva shook her head no. She looked warily at her mother. "But, Nuci, I don't entirely dislike him."

In her memoirs, Jolie said that after so much disastrous advice she refused to say another word.

Eva pleaded: "But you have to tell me."

Cornered, Jolie said, "A plastic surgeon has a very good future. If you help him now, he'll repay you in the future."

Then she flew to Beverly Hills for an appointment with her future son-in-law. Dr. Williams took her to dinner, to the theater, and even held her hand warmly in fancy restaurants. "This is a wonderful man," Jolie gushed. "When I held his hand, it was warm and dry. If it had been cold and sweaty, I would have recommended against the marriage."

The wedding was on April 6, 1956, in Beverly Hills, and the marriage lasted until October. Eva obtained a legal separation from the handsome physician on November 28, after moving out some weeks earlier.

Several unkind columnists noted that the marriage lasted long enough to outfit the three sisters, and perhaps Jolie, with expensive face-lifts. But those were only rumors—weren't they?

Eva explained it this way in *Orchids and Salami:* "I had a flop on Broadway [*The Little Glass Clock*] so I decided to marry as a balm for my hurt feelings. I had already met John, and he kept pestering me, so I married him. And here I was going with Tyrone Power at the same time."

Her alliance with Dr. Williams occurred during the most romantically complicated time of her life, when she was dating four or five men in Hollywood and New York. So hectic was it, in fact, that she apparently forgot what he looked like. Seven or eight years ago, Dr. Williams stepped into a Century City elevator and after the door closed noticed that he was standing near Eva. "Eva," he said, "how are you?" She glanced at him with a distant and confused expression on her face. "Do I know you?" she finally asked. "Yes"—he laughed —"I was your third husband."

In a similar instance, the physician entered a swank restaurant at the same time as Zsa Zsa. She took the offensive. "You look so familiar to me," she said. "We have met before, haven't we?" Again the physician laughed. "I was married to Eva." "Ah, yes," Zsa Zsa said, "Dr. Williams."

27

✳ Tyrone and Eva, Eva and Richard

*T*he love affair between Tyrone Power and Eva Gabor
failed to earn a permanent place in the annals of Hollywood gossip—mainly because the two principals were discreet but
also because most of the time they spent together was while Ty was
filming in London.

But a blazing affair it certainly was. Zsa Zsa was asked recently if
Eva had a serious, consummated affair with Ty. "Most certainly, darling," she answered. "It was a far deeper relationship than anyone
knew."

The first public notice of the affair occurred on May 26, 1955, when
Ty slipped into Eva's NBC dressing room as she was preparing to
appear in a live segment of the network's *Justice* series. A New York
Post photographer captured a shot of Eva in Ty's arms—both of them
reclining on a dressing-room sofa.

On October 26, 1955, columnist Earl Wilson literally stumbled
over the affair. When he entered the chic Metro Club, there was the
usual bustle created by celebrities trying to attract his attention. Earl
glanced about the room in boredom. Nobody unusual here tonight,
he thought and turned to leave. Then he noticed Eva and the vacant
chair beside her. "She's always good for a hoot," he said, signaling
the hostess to guide him over.

Eva was instantly icy and distant, even a little defensive. There was
no way Earl could have known that Ty had only temporarily vacated
the chair. When he walked back toward the table, Earl noticed anguish
written on his handsome face. But saying nothing, he sat in the only
other available chair—three seats down from Eva.

Several sips of a drink later, Eva jumped up. "Why don't we all change seats, darlings?" Ty's face reddened, causing Earl to realize his mistake. The columnist cleared his throat. "Uh, I've got to mingle. Let Ty take my seat." Eva accepted with great relief. Eva and Ty were officially an item.

In January of 1956, Jolie took Eva on a winter vacation to St. Moritz, with a brief stopover in London. Over breakfast, Eva said coyly, "Nuci, why don't we spend more time in London?"

"Suddenly I realized that *someone* special, someone I didn't know about, was keeping Eva there. I quickly found out that it was Ty, that they were in love," Jolie said.

"Don't lose your heart to this man completely," Jolie advised. "You could be hurt, and hurt badly."

Several months later, Ty and Eva mutually called it off. On the rebound from Ty, Eva drew closer to John, only to find out, in her opinion, that he was a crank. "I asked him once for a vitamin shot for exhaustion," Eva recalled, "and he said, 'All day I take care of my patients, and now I come home and have to take care of my wife. Well, I won't do it.' "

After the November divorce Eva told a press conference, "Now I'm alone and a lot better off. He even wanted me to sell my five-story building on Fifth Avenue in New York and reinvest in California real estate. And, fellas, that, as you know, would have meant plenty of community property."

Jolie wasn't particularly impressed by Eva's public explanations of the failed marriage. "What *really* happened?" she asked. "He complained that I was always on the road, Nuci, and I told him, 'Somebody has to pay the rent. You don't make enough!' "

Jolie gasped. "You humiliated him—do you realize that?"

Eva met Richard Brown a year after the divorce. On her wedding day she said, "I got lucky this time." They had dated for a year before staging the ceremony in 1959, after which Eva inherited an instant family—Richard's two sons, aged eighteen and twenty. The ceremony was hardly romantic, held before a justice of the peace in Las Vegas, with Red Buttons giving Eva away. "But they were obviously in love," Red said later.

It was an ideal relationship for Eva the actress. When she went on location, Richard packed up and followed. When it came time for her to move back to Hollywood for the *Green Acres* TV series, he moved to California as soon as a position opened up there for him.

Eva cagily talked Filmways, the producers of her long-running show, into giving Brown a vice president's title and the work to go with it. His salary was commensurate with Eva's, and he was a producer in the film division. (Dick is now a producer in London.)

Jolie claimed in her memoirs that Dick was flat broke when he took the Filmways position. "He had tried many different things, and none of them seemed to succeed. The Filmways job wasn't just convenient; it was necessary."

When the marriage had lasted eleven years—unheard of for a Gabor and a great rarity in Hollywood—the Hearst newspapers did a profile of the couple. "He is my anchor," said Eva, letting her hand grasp his. "He is a lover as well as a friend."

Coyly—too coyly—Eva admitted that she was "so dependent on Dick that I don't even have a key to my own house. Richard has it. Luckily Richard is always with me. We are never apart if we can help it, but his work with Filmways occasionally takes him to New York for a few days. While he is gone I fall apart completely. The last time he put me in my car with my secretary and sent us to Palm Springs. I just sat in the house and never went out."

"I don't even put on a dress without his approval," Eva said in a 1970 interview. "He is a *real man.*"

Apparently he was also such a real man that he needed to date other women. "Eva truly didn't look at another man during the thirteen years they were married," Jolie said. "Ah, but *he* did. I knew about it, but decided not to tell Eva. . . . When Eva finally found out, she immediately went to a psychiatrist. She was crushed completely. She found that he had a lively, regular affair going on right under her nose."

Eva kicked him out.

Richard tried several times to reconcile with Eva, according to Jolie. "That was the one thing she couldn't handle—infidelity," said Jolie. "It had never happened to her before. In fact, she didn't think it could happen to her."

After a divorce action in the early 1970s, Eva was again husband-shopping. And along came Frank Gard Jameson. He was handsome, lean, a captain of industry (president of North American Rockwell), and athletic (a former football player and a tennis champion).

He swept Eva off her feet and into a world she really hadn't experienced before: the old guard society enclaves of Beverly Hills and Palm Beach. On his arm she also flew into the jet set, where her sister Zsa Zsa had long been a favorite.

The courtship filled society columns on both coasts. The engagement ring alone merited five stories, and wedding publicity was immense.

On the afternoon of September 27, 1973, all the Gabors, a good part of Los Angeles' elite, and many leaders of California business gathered for the outdoor ceremony. A thousand orchids filled the pool of Frank's home, and 5,000 sprays of flowers and potted plants decorated the garden in which they were married.

At first it seemed that Eva and Frank lived a charmed life. They maintained residences in Portugal, Palm Beach, Palm Springs, Manhattan, and Beverly Hills. Their decorous rooms graced the pages of *Architectural Digest, Home* magazine, and *Vogue.* Their parties were famous in Washington, D.C., and Paris; and for almost ten years the adjectives poured out of journalistic typewriters as reporters described their bliss. But ten years to the summer that they wed, Eva Gabor filed for divorce in Santa Monica Superior Court. And she did it quietly—no newspaper statements.

28

❊ The Consorts

*T*he man was deliberately cold and calculatedly distant. There was a sandpaper edge to his voice as he told her to roll up the delicate silk that encased her left arm. "You can sit there," he said impassively, indicating an uncomfortable metal chair. As she sat, five blinding lights were aimed at her. The heat from them was intense; the terrible white light was debasing.

The man with the gruff voice took a wide band with sensors inside it and tightened it around the exposed left arm, creating a discomfort not unlike a tourniquet. To the lady's left was a buzzing, clicking contraption connected to the tourniquet by an electronic umbilical cord so sensitive that it could measure the slightest sign of distress.

To make it even more harrowing, three video cameras were trained on the tense tableau. After what seemed an interminable length of time, the man leaned toward his trapped quarry and inquired, "What is your name?"

"Zsa Zsa Gabor," came the answer in a clear but slightly annoyed voice.

"And where do you live?"

"Ten thousand and one . . . " The voice was gaining assurance, even though the questions became more and more intimate.

The inquisition occurred on a drizzly December day in 1982, when Zsa Zsa submitted to a grueling five-hour session with the most sophisticated polygraph equipment in the world. And the inquisitor was the formidible Edward Gelb, president of the American Polygraph Association.

For Zsa Zsa, it was a question of honor.

Superattorney F. Lee Bailey, planning a TV series of celebrity polygraph challenges, saw Zsa Zsa on a late-night talk show and decided to call her on her eternal claim that she *always* married for love, never for money.

"Bring on the machine," she told F. Lee Bailey. Still, as she was chauffeured through the streets, there was a vague but gnawing fear that the machine, an emotionless bundle of steel and wires, would mock her much as talk-show audiences had done through the years. She paused outside the studio for a few minutes, hesitating, then glided toward a rendezvous with the truth.

Guided by Edward Gelb, Zsa Zsa lied several times to provide a comparison for the infernal machine, and then sailed right into the juicy questions.

"Did you marry Conrad Hilton for his money?"

"No," Zsa Zsa answered defiantly.

"Were you in love with Mr. Hilton?"

"Yes, I loved Connie," she said as her eyes filled.

Gelb countered, "Just answer the question yes or no."

"Yes."

Out of her sight, the needle traced a record of her truthfulness.

The questions bored on through the private cavities of her heart for the rest of the afternoon. Someone described lie detector tests as emotional rape, and this was certainly the truth here. It was a wilted, overtaxed, and uncertain Zsa Zsa who drove away from the studio. How had she done? What sort of risk had she taken? Should she have bared her soul so publicly?

While Zsa Zsa was driving home, Edward Gelb and a panel of experts finished verifying the marathon session and were surprised at the startling results. She had been telling the truth when she made the following claims: Six of her seven husbands were married for love; only her fourth, Herbert Hutner, was wed for his fortune; she accepted alimony only from Conrad Hilton and from no other husband; and, with the exception of Connie, *all* of her husbands cost *her* money.

F. Lee Bailey looked at the results in astonishment. "Anything less than a polygraph administered this way, and I wouldn't have believed it," the lawyer told Zsa Zsa by telephone. "You were telling the truth." Edward Gelb concurred: "Question-by-question, she was honest with us—completely honest."

Back in her Bel Air mansion, Zsa Zsa was snappish. "They were all sitting there hoping to catch me in a lie. I turned the tables on all of them." (Unfortunately, the Gabor segment of *F. Lee Bailey's Lie Detector* was never shown publicly because of contractual differences.)

"I marry for love and only for love," Zsa Zsa yelled. Perhaps, but all her husbands except George Sanders served some practical or emotional purpose. Burhan Belge was her ticket out of war-torn

Europe; Connie served as an emotional and financial father figure to a still adolescent girl; Joshua Cosden, Jr., an oil baron, helped her climb higher on the rungs of high society; Herbert Hutner, chairman of the board at Struthers Wells Corporation, lent dignity and old-line money to her name; Jack Ryan, a millionaire inventor, helped revamp her career; and attorney Mike O'Hara engineered her divorce from Ryan and lent his legal expertise for a brief time.

All these shared another peculiar circumstance. They were all wooed and proposed to by Zsa Zsa, and according to her, not all of them said yes the first time.

George Sanders, husband number three, told an interviewer from *Photoplay* magazine that she ardently pursued him, employing candlelight suppers, romantic evenings at the seashore, and even rudimentary home cooking. "Before the marriage, Zsa Zsa was quite the loving, dutiful sweetheart. It was only after the marriage that things began to change."

"She courted me in an old-fashioned way," said husband number six, Jack Ryan. "She invited me night after night to have dinner in her home. She was so lovely and so irresistible that I began cancelling all other plans, even important business engagements."

He continued: "Her cook, an elderly servant from Hungary, made a variety of delicious Hungarian dishes. Then the old lady retreated to the kitchen, leaving Zsa Zsa and me alone in the darkened living room. We sat on the floor and ate at the coffee table under lamps which had been turned down low. It was amazingly seductive."

Some nights Zsa Zsa pressed a button that opened an enormous television screen. With the press of another button, excerpts from her films flickered onto the screen. "The scenes were all romantic, sensual, and showed her from the most flattering angles."

So they sat holding hands and watching Zsa Zsa's legend drift by in a montage of shadows. "It was quite an aphrodisiac," recalled Jack. "She always knows how to make you feel wonderful about her. . . . The total effect was stunning."

Like all her husbands, Jack found the transition from lover to husband a bumpy one. "Zsa Zsa's life is like a business," he said. "She fit me into several little compartments—the compartments in which she most wanted me—and then raced pell-mell through her life. Sometimes I was asked to come along for the ride; sometimes I was left at home."

She is, unfortunately, less a woman now than an institution, Jack discovered; and her rituals and conduct hark directly back to her girlhood in Hungary, where she was spoiled shamelessly.

"She could raise such a ruckus if cold toast was delivered to her breakfast in bed that a sensitive man could get ulcers after the second day. . . . You need regular tours of rest and relaxation in order to take it," Jack said. "She's rather like lemonade—not all sweet, not all acid, and the overall experience is very nice indeed."

Jack was in a unique position to know the full-time Zsa Zsa, since he lived in an adjoining mansion for ten years before their relationship developed into a romance.

The fact that Zsa Zsa ignored such obvious bait over the back fence is interesting. Jack, who invented the Barbie Doll, the Sparrow III missile, a machine to test radio crystals, and fifty other discoveries, was a socially oriented multimillionaire. Announcing her engagement sometime later, Zsa Zsa purred about Jack, "Darlings, I've never married an Ivy Leaguer before."

In addition to his financial status, his extravagent lifestyle was on display for Zsa Zsa daily on the Beverly Hills estate—a perfect view of which could be had from Zsa Zsa's study.

The forty-room Tudor mansion was built on two acres that included, among other peculiar things, 140 telephones, a tree house large enough to accommodate a dinner party, and an electronic system taken from a surplus navy destroyer. The machine, hand-tailored by Jack, controlled hundreds of lights and gadgets spread through the grounds. It could even light the tennis court and lock the front gates.

Zsa Zsa and Jack had an impassive back-fence relationship for some time. "Whenever I was giving a party—particularly the large ones with a tent and orchestra—she would call on the phone: 'Jack, darling, what's happening?' " An invitation inevitably followed, and Zsa Zsa would often slip in the back entrance to join the party. "The other guests were always delighted," said Jack. "I've never seen anyone light up a party the way she does. When she comes in, magic follows."

The conversations became soulful talks, which in turn became whispers of love. "Sure, I fell in love—no doubt about that," Jack said. "Who could resist her?"

They were married on October 6, 1976, in the bridal suite of Caesar's Palace in Las Vegas. On the license, Zsa Zsa said she was fifty-five, Ryan was forty-eight. And the bride wore white—what outrageous spunk!

"He wanted us to get married in that tree house of his," Zsa Zsa told reporters. "But I felt mother would have been a bit shocked."

It wasn't long before major conflicts developed. "Yelling at a party, that's what I hated most," Jack remembered. "She would try to insult me so that she got her own way no matter what." Frequently Zsa Zsa would shriek, "You are no gentleman, because you don't give enough. What did they teach you at Yale—*restraint?*"

Less than a year later, the marriage was in serious trouble, and Jack said he was trying to get out. "But she's so charming it's hard to confront her." So he devised another solution. On a sparkling August morning in 1977, Jack sat behind his office desk to plan a civilized getaway from Zsa Zsa's indifferent but somehow possessive clutches.

He grabbed a sheet of linen bond, wrote a few sentences, then crumpled it up angrily and tossed it into a wastebasket. He tried again and again, but the words he wrote sounded cruel and cold. Jack wanted to be courtly and chivalrous, like a white knight who dips his lance in salute to a fair lady and then rides off into the mist.

It was an almost impossible task, since Zsa Zsa has an elegant manner of weaving herself into the fabric of a man's life so that she seems an inseparable part of it. Of course, Jack could have simply called up his lawyer and told him to start divorce proceedings, leaving Zsa Zsa with a summons that would undoubtedly have been delivered by some rude county marshal in an ill-fitting uniform.

Jack's lawyer advised that course. It would be so much easier, so much less emotional, he told his client. Jack refused to consider it. He explained his action to a friend: "What we had has burned out, but it must be concluded with style. I don't want to plunge a knife into her heart with an impersonal summons."

As he sat in his corporate office hour by hour, Jack found himself remembering the lyrical humor of his life with Zsa Zsa. He could close his eyes and hear that sparkling laughter echo from his past. "I've got it," he decided. "I'll make it satirical. I'll write a letter of resignation." Within an hour the letter was completed, typed by his secretary, and placed in the slim briefcase that was rarely out of his sight. The letter was subsequently revised on a flight from New York to Los Angeles.

Jack cagily understood that his marriage to such a famous woman had put him into the semilegal status of a public consort, much like a figurehead prince married to a queen who holds all the real power.

During his tenure, Jack was always there to lend a tuxedoed arm as his wife made her royal progress through the jet set society of Palm Beach, the nouveau riche ambience of Beverly Hills, and the old-moneyed splendor of Palm Springs.

During the first year of the marriage, Jack was drawn into the luxurious quicksand surrounding the Gabors. He moved, so to speak, into the eye of a social hurricane to such an extent that he established an office in Zsa Zsa's house from which to manage his multimillion-dollar empire.

It was heady stuff at first—racing across the top of the world with a woman who accepted no limitations. Then it became just the slightest bit annoying, then boring, and finally self-destructive. To quote George Sanders on life with Zsa Zsa: "One can't drink the nectar of the gods for very long. It becomes too sweet and sickens the stomach."

Jack's marriage to Zsa Zsa didn't cave in suddenly. It was chipped away slowly by a sort of emotional erosion. "Will a man ever come who can capture me completely?" Zsa Zsa mournfully asked a friend. "When a marriage fails I always assume a mantle of guilt even though it's not my fault."

So the Ryan-Gabor alliance slowly wound down. Jack felt helpless against the incompatibility that separated them. She felt growing regrets and not just a little anger. Long months elapsed before the marriage legally ended. For one thing, Jack didn't have the heart to deliver his terse resignation. He stuck it deep in the briefcase and carried it in and out of the Gabor mansion for almost sixty days. It was his secret, and it tugged at his heart every time he saw it among his business documents.

Zsa Zsa, however, seemed to have a frightening clairvoyance about the impending domestic crisis. It seemed as if she could read Jack's mind to the extent that he had to dodge her increasingly probing questions with dexterity.

"Darling," said Zsa Zsa one evening, "Do you have something to tell me that you are keeping back?" Jack's face flushed and he stammered, "Of course not."

They were seated at a low table on the Aubusson rug in Zsa Zsa's living room, eating an impromptu buffet by candlelight. Undeterred by her husband's denial, Zsa Zsa pouted and shook her head. "It's just that you seem to have some little secret, Jack. Why not just tell me now?"

Jack's mind raced. Had he somehow left a copy of the rough draft lying around in his home office? Had he talked about it to mutual friends? He was certain he hadn't.

Zsa Zsa refused to let it rest. She pestered him over morning coffee, bombarded him with dozens of phone calls, and even mentioned it in bed. Jack suddenly felt like naked prey. He had learned that the Gabors love nothing so much as a game of cat and mouse, particularly when they are firmly installed in the role of cat. Jack had no doubt, therefore, that he was the helpless mouse, all set up to be emotionally toyed with by expert claws.

Zsa Zsa's inquisition continued and became a bit sharp. She told Jack that she *knew* he was hiding something from her, that she knew his mind was obsessed with things that would affect her personally.

Finally, on one particularly stormy evening, Jack ended it all by handing over the letter with fumbling hands. She took the envelope, showing considerable distaste, letting it drop onto the satin comforter covering her bed. A sly smile spread across her face. "Oh, Jack, darling, I've known about this for weeks. You ought to know better than to try and keep a secret from me. After all, we're two intelligent and sophisticated people.''

He was caught off guard. Then it dawned on him. Zsa Zsa's round-the-clock private detective, who lived permanently in the mansion's basement, had pirated the letter, shown it to Zsa Zsa, probably copied it, and then slipped it back into Jack's briefcase.

"I never thought that guy rummaged through *my* things," Jack said later. "But looking back, it makes sense. Why should I have been exempt from her permanent fears? She probably knew about it the first day I carried it home, the very day I wrote it."

Jack declines to produce the crucial letter, preferring to reveal that it centered about this sentence: "I feel that I'm unqualified to continue in the role of consort—and even if I had all the qualities in the world, I cannot continue."

Several days later, Jack slipped out of the Gabor mansion for good, carrying a small overnight case full of possessions and leaving the lady of the house to break the news to a waiting world.

"Darlings," Zsa Zsa told the Associated Press, "he was far more interested in his Barbie Dolls than me. And who wants to play second fiddle to a roomful of plastic dolls?"

Jack was left with the feeling that no other woman in the world could ever replace Zsa Zsa's stylish sense of romance or her electric excitement in bed.

She was left with the forlorn sense that still another marriage had turned to dust in her hands, leaving regrets that could only multiply with age.

It would have all ended on that bittersweet note if Zsa Zsa's indomitable will hadn't asserted itself and fashioned a finale of comic opera proportions. Gossip dubbed it the "Battle of Bel Air Hill," a private shootout that pitted Zsa Zsa's persuasiveness against Jack Ryan's private security force, a handful of burly UCLA students wearing tan policelike uniforms.

At stake was a lavish Queen Anne desk willed to Jack by his father, an ornate brocade chair, and a few other private possessions that Zsa Zsa had reluctantly allowed her bunkmate to install in the Gabor castle. For Jack, the lavish house was little more than an exclusive hotel room. With the exception of his private desk and its accouterments, the house had been untouched by the Ryan hand.

On October 6, when the resignation was finally accepted, Jack thought nothing of calling for his eight uniformed students and a van to collect his belongings. He let them in the electric gate and directed them toward the study. Then he drove off.

Zsa Zsa, dressed elaborately for a dinner party, took one look at the uniformed men, screamed, and then pressed the button to alert the Bel Air patrol. She then grabbed the train of her gown and retreated to the boudoir.

The Gabor mansion, at the top of Bel Air, is just above police headquarters on the flatland. In minutes the Bel Air officers, with tires squealing and lights flashing, stormed through the gates and confronted the Ryan's deputies. But instead of the toy pistols carried by Ryan's men, the police levelled real guns at the moving party. Jack's men dropped the desk, put down the cartons, and shrank against the van.

Zsa Zsa, waving her diamond-cuffed wrists, ran to the front door and grabbed the arm of a Bel Air patrol sergeant. "Darlings, they're stealing my furniture. They have invaded my house."

The Ryanites were allowed to gracefully retreat. And Jack's desk, surrounded by his personal paraphernalia, is still in Zsa Zsa's den and is used by the endless parade of personal secretaries who troop through the mansion. "Lovely desk, isn't it?" she often tells visitors. "My husband, Jack Ryan, gave it to me.

"This marriage was the worst mistake of my life," Zsa Zsa told friends. "Even my daughter warned me against it. We were married only a year, but it was the strangest experience of my life."

The Ryan collection of Barbie Dolls in his own mansion raised the hackles of jealousy in Zsa Zsa. "Believe me, those dolls were much more important than me."

"I'm a real woman, not a toy," she said during divorce proceedings. In the suit, she complained, among other things, that Jack had taken her Rolls-Royce apart and then refused to put it back together.

Long before the Battle of Bel Air Hill, Zsa Zsa went shopping for her sixth divorce lawyer and found a great romance. Several friends told her to try the unassuming Michael O'Hara, an attorney with a low profile, a quality she desperately needed this time.

Michael, a tall, dark man with James Garner looks, decided to take the case, and Zsa Zsa roared into his life before he knew what hit him. He was wearing a $500 pinstripe suit and a haircut by Jon Peters, Inc., which made him, according to Zsa Zsa, "one of the most breathtaking men I'd ever seen."

And he was a diplomat, promising to take the weight of the divorce from her shoulders and then gallantly ushering Zsa Zsa to her car. "It was my understanding that they fell into each other's arms soon after," said Jack, who was pointedly not asked to pay alimony. "Love at first sight is not a new emotion for Zsa Zsa."

The marriage that soon followed was to last five battle-scarred years and ended with Zsa Zsa publicly calling O'Hara every name in the book. One thing, however, was certain. They were starry-eyed lovers at the beginning. "I remember watching Zsa Zsa and Michael at a fur show here in Palm Springs," remembered Allene Arthur, society editor of the Palm Springs *Desert Sun.* "He was obviously in love, and she was enraptured by him and the furs."

In a series of bold stories in the *National Enquirer,* money was named as the major cause of incompatibility. Zsa Zsa was quoted as saying, "I thought I was marrying some big-shot successful lawyer, but I wound up footing all the bills."

A former secretary to Zsa Zsa said that daily battles over money were not that uncommon in the Gabor mansion anyway. "Mike just added another dimension to it," the secretary said. According to the *Enquirer,* one battle in particular was the straw that broke the marriage's back. In taped interviews with one of the tabloid's reporters, friends said that Zsa Zsa had been on a three-month cosmetics promotion tour and found a stack of unpaid bills on her desk. Grabbing them, she threw them across the room at her husband, spewing invective.

Michael refuses to discuss his wife except to say that it is a "closed book." "He just doesn't talk about her," a colleague said.

Perhaps the most interesting of all Zsa Zsa's men was an ardent suitor she never married, a millionaire contractor named Hal Hays, a man almost as flamboyant as she. In the late 1950s there was a long courtship between the two, to such an extent that rumors of a secret marriage circulated. Although the entire relationship was wild, it was their breakup that caused the most excitement.

Early in 1960, Hal gave Zsa Zsa a massive platinum and diamond ring, with the stone weighing twenty-five carats, which reportedly cost the contractor $250,000. Adding to the ring's rarity was the rare blue-white color that shone from the center of the bauble. Gossip columnists called it the Zsa Zsa Diamond.

It was to be the only engagement ring (or perhaps any kind of ring) that Zsa Zsa returned. She reluctantly gave it up when it became obvious that, as compatible as they were on the surface, the relationship could not stand the closeness of marriage in the "big" little town of Beverly Hills.

The diamond, however, seemed to take on a life of its own. When Hal sued the Continental Casualty Company for $4.1 million in a construction dispute, both defense and plaintiff's attorneys had the ring brought into court as an official exhibit.

Hal started it—there was no way for him to deny that. He introduced the diamond while he was on the stand as proof of his care and thrift with money. "I got that ring back from Zsa Zsa Gabor," Hal told the judge. "And that in itself makes history."

The Continental Casualty attorney, Eldon V. McPharlin, did some legal gem cutting of his own. "It's true, isn't it, Mr. Hays, that while the Capehart Project was going on, newspapers carried reports about you giving Zsa Zsa a fabulous diamond ring of some twenty carats and worth a small fortune?"

Hal appeared confused for a second.

The attorney pressed, raising his voice: "Did you give Zsa Zsa Gabor such a ring?"

"Yes," Hal answered jauntily, reminding the judge that it had been returned.

McPharlin asked, "Did you know that Zsa Zsa said on a television show that she returned the ring when your engagement was broken?"

"Sure," answered Hal. "And the ring was never even paid for. It was a kind of trial purchase. After all, these things do not last forever."

Several days after the testimony, Zsa Zsa became even more crucial to the case when Hal admitted that she had, in a semiofficial capacity, participated in the delicate negotiations between Hal's company and Continental Casualty.

"How closely did she participate in the negotiations?" Continental's lawyer continued.

"Well," Hal answered, "she sure could influence men!"

Hal was merely being flippant. According to court records, Zsa Zsa had been given the title of vice president and became a voting member of Hal's company as soon as the engagement was announced.

One thing is certain, Zsa Zsa was Hal's official hostess at a series of posh galas he tossed for the Washington honchos who saw to it that his empire received lucrative housing contracts.

In 1959, guests at a Washington cocktail party were surprised when Hal greeted them alone. "Where's Zsa Zsa?" one of them whispered. "Later, later," Hal answered. About an hour later, when the men were mellow with alcohol, Hal boomed loudly, "I want you to meet the new senior vice president of my company." A swinging door opened and Zsa Zsa, covered with furs and jewels, swept into the room.

As for the rest of Zsa Zsa's husbands, she has discussed them only in brief generalities. "Mr. Hutner was very, very sweet, darling. And he gave me the freedom to marry Joshua Cosden. But Joshua was so handsome and so sexy that our marriage could not have lasted. We broke up, however, because of geography. I wouldn't change my values, and the Deep South, where Joshua lived, would not accept me as I was."

When Zsa Zsa claimed that all her husbands, except Hilton, beat her, she said, "And I think that's good, darling. I prefer it that way."

Talk-show host Mike Douglas was at a loss for words, then blurted out, "But wasn't that beastly?"

Zsa Zsa shook her head. "But I love it. I like to know that a man has the upper hand, and that I can make a man mad enough so he beats me. Some of my husbands hit me a little bit more and some a little bit less."

29

✳ Goddess of Love

*T*he scent of rare perfume wafted through the room. Somewhere far off in another room a Mahler symphony played softly on a stereo. Jack Ryan, in white tie, leaned tentatively against the doorjamb wondering what part he was to enact in the romantic scenario playing out before his eyes. The only light was a bright shaft from an adjacent dressing room that gave the boudoir a soft quality. Jack was sipping at champagne as his fingers hesitantly untangled the white silk of his bow tie.

Suddenly Zsa Zsa's shadow fell across the deep carpet. She had changed into a black negligee so filmy that the curves of her body were silhouetted in the amber glow.

He could just barely see her face, but her eyes were luminous. He walked slowly up to her, still fumbling with the stubborn knot in his tie. When he shyly stopped several feet from her, Zsa Zsa grasped the front of his shirt and pulled him toward her.

The sensual explosion made Jack dizzy. He thought fleetingly before he fell onto the bed, My God, this is Zsa Zsa Gabor!

"Zsa Zsa is quite simply the most romantic woman I have ever seen —like the heroine of a great popular novel come to life before your eyes," Jack said. "She has carefully built up the amorous aura to such an extent that when it crashes in on you in bed, it's an avalanche of eroticism."

As their bodies melded, Zsa Zsa whispered urgent words in the dark. "They were wonderful words," Jack said. "She created an entire world by whispering in the dark. And she makes you feel as if you are the most important man in the world, and even more than that, you realize that she is, also, the most important woman in the world. . . . Those words are plotted carefully for effect, because, after all, it happens in the dark," he said.

The glorious nights continued for several months before marriage was even mentioned. Then one day when the dalliance continued through the morning and ended with a romantic brunch at noon, Zsa Zsa proposed.

As the clock struck twelve, Zsa Zsa's face became a mask of mortification. She had heard the gardener's truck plow up the hill. "Oh, Jack," she said. "He will know that you spent the night here. We must get married, darling."

"That touch of dated morality—just a hint of it—was quite dazzling, and we fell headlong into marriage," Ryan remembered.

Zsa Zsa's astonishing sexual aura is an exhausting full-time job for her—from her infallible sense of fashion to the musical modulation of her voice. Bed is but the final scene of a great performance.

Once when Jack took her on a business trip to Japan, she staged a remarkable show. Several Japanese millionaries hosted the Ryans at a lavish traditional dinner complete with eleven courses and lovely geisha girls. When the women glided from behind a rice paper curtain, Zsa Zsa was mesmerized. They deftly maneuvered their silk robes and created great swirls of gold, silver, blue, and orange. Then they drifted out of sight, but the Oriental music continued. In an almost hypnotic trance, Zsa Zsa slowly stood up and moved onto the recently vacated stage. She spread her arms seductively, tilted her chin upwards, and began swaying with the music's rhythm.

"The dance was impromptu and only faintly reminiscent of the geisha performance," Jack said. "The Japanese men were thunderstruck."

One of them leaned over toward Jack. "She must surely be the sexiest woman in the world."

Of all Zsa Zsa's many talents, her sexual mystique is perhaps the hardest to define. When she was seeing John F. Kennedy, Walter Winchell asked him off the record, "What is so irresistible about her?"

Kennedy reportedly told the columnist, "It is hard to put her excitement into words. Just taking her to dinner is sensually fulfilling." Winchell, discussing his coverage of the Kennedys at a guest lecture seminar at the University of California at San Diego, denied that Zsa Zsa's relationship with the President ever went beyond a few casual dinners. Zsa Zsa adds little to this assessment. "I was very, very friendly with President John Kennedy," she told one reporter. "Naturally, Jackie hated me."

George Sanders believed that it was her narcissistic adoration of her own physical glory that was the wellspring for her sexuality. One night early in their relationship, he lolled back on a bed while she prepared for the night's conquest. With a simple satin shift clinging to her body, Zsa Zsa ran a silver-handled brush through her cascade of hair. As the great locks tumbled over her eyes, she first looked admiringly at her own face, then looked savagely at George. She ran her fingers through the hair and caressed her swanlike neck. She walked slowly to the edge of the bed, then plunged on top of him.

Though George often shied away from discussing his ex-wife, he reminisced about her to a reporter from *Paris Match:* "No matter how annoying she was emotionally, her physical presence overcame it."

Apparently, no single lover was enough for Zsa Zsa. She was most fulfilled when she had two sensually different men at the same time —the lusty Rubi and the urbane George. "Ah, that was the perfect setup for any woman. I had Rubi in Paris and George in Hollywood. Rubi was insanely jealous, but George wasn't jealous of Rubi for the first several years," Zsa Zsa recalled. "George always said that Freud was right when he said that any physical attraction only lasted for two years. But when Rubi and I continued our alliance into the third or fourth year, George finally began to worry a little."

In the end, of course, she couldn't resist Rubi's bedside manner. So George drifted away. "Rubi was *so good* in bed," Zsa Zsa told reporter John Hiscock. "He was so wonderful that he was addictive."

It's possible that much of Zsa Zsa's considerable sexual prowess was learned from Rubi, whose erotic knowledge was staggering. Adrienna Margeaux, a Parisienne beauty who dallied with him in the 1940s, described him as a "walking encyclopedia of sex." One thing is sure, Rubi heightened Zsa Zsa's physical aura. One late afternoon in Paris, a Rubirosa valet watched them making love in the living room of Rubi's two-hundred-year-old town house.

At five P.M., just as the Paris streets took on the salmon glow of sunset, there was a clanking in the entrance hall, followed by the scent of sweat and oiled leather. Rubi, fresh from the polo fields of the Bois de Boulogne, strode through the dusky room calling Zsa Zsa's name. His hair had been whipped up by the wind; his red shirt was torn open, revealing his angular shoulders; the white polo pants slanted across his hips; and the thick leather boots were scuffed.

When she didn't answer, he threw himself into a leather chair and draped one leg over the side, sipping brandy directly from a crystal decanter. "Zsa Zsa," he said, "where are you?"

The front door opened again and in came a breathless Zsa Zsa. Having rushed back from the set of a film, she was still in costume, encased from her neck to just above the knee in clouds of pink chiffon. "Rubi?" she called. "In here," he said.

He leapt up, jerking the red shirt off with one hand. They met together in the middle of the room. With one smooth maneuver of his left hand the costume was unzipped and slid onto the floor.

The scene was beautifully sexual, making the valet ashamed of his voyeurism. He turned away. In Alice Leone-Moats's 1977 book *The Million Dollar Studs,* she described the reaction of a tailor who had been summoned to the Paris town house to fit Rubi and Zsa Zsa with his-and-hers outfits. "The cutter from Hilditch and Key still looks dazed at the memory of the first time he saw Zsa Zsa," Miss Leone-Moats wrote. "There she stood," he told the author, "wearing a filmy brassiere and the tiniest panties embroidered with sequins. She was a staggering sight."

He concluded: "She had an allure which was ageless."

Grand Entrance. Eva, Zsa Zsa, and Jolie make their way through a 1968 Palm Springs party. *Ron Galella*

The Gabor Look. Eva and Jolie take a break from Eva's 1973 fashion show. *Ron Galella*

Perfect Match? When Eva married Los Angeles old guard socialite and aeronautical millionaire Frank Gard Jameson in 1973, many friends said it was the perfect match. But it collapsed in 1983. *AP/Wide World Photos*

Social Butterflies. Aswim in Palm Springs society are Eva, Jolie, and Magda at one of Mama's costume balls in 1974. Eva refused to wear the Old West apparel.

All That Glitters. Zsa Zsa displays some handsome jewelry at a 1972 movie premiere.
Ron Galella

Number Six. Zsa Zsa and millionaire inventor Jack Ryan on their honeymoon in London, 1975. The match was to be Zsa Zsa's most troubled since George. *AP/Wide World Photos*

Anniversary. Jolie and her husband, Edmund de Szigethy, pose for an anniversary portrait in 1975, looking younger than ever.

Two Peas. As this photo shows, Zsa Zsa (left) and Eva have grown more alike physically as the decades have passed.

Beverly Hills Country Girl. Eva gathers eggs from the henhouse in the backyard of her lavish Holmby Hills estate. The year was 1981. *Betty Burke Galella*

Socialite. Eva hosts Judy Mazel of *Beverly Hills Diet* fame (center) and Mrs. Hubert Hutner (the current wife of Zsa Zsa's ex).

The Phony Wedding. Zsa Zsa appears blissfully happy at this press conference to introduce her seventh husband—whom she introduced as the Duke of Alba. Turns out he was a Mexican realtor and the wedding was a fake. *AP/Wide World Photos*

Old Friends. Magda with her close friend the late David Niven
photographed at her Palm Springs home in 1982.
AP/Wide World Photos

Wages of Fame. Zsa Zsa and her immense wardrobe of 5,000 garments, larger than most dry cleaning establishments. *Francesca Hilton*

Still Alluring. Zsa Zsa and Efrem Zimbalist, Jr., arrive at a 1980 party in Bel Air.

Mother and Daughter. Zsa Zsa and Francesca at
Chasens Restaurant in 1983. *Kevin Winter/Galella, Ltd.*

Sitting Pretty. Zsa Zsa rides high at a June 1984 celebrity
polo match in Los Angeles. *DeGuire/Galella, Ltd.*

✳ BOOK SEVEN

Survival

I learned a magical thing long ago,
and now my daughters have learned it.
There are no wrinkles on the heart.
— JOLIE, 1980

30

✻ *Green Acres*

*A*n elaborate Swiss clock chimed four times, lifting Eva out of an exhausted sleep to face the hushed predawn darkness. During the night, blustery desert winds swept into Los Angeles carrying clouds of dust, felling trees, and snapping power lines.

Eva slipped into a steamy shower and sighed as the powerful gush relieved the weariness of her strained body. Between sips of coffee, she pulled on a shift, tied a scarf around her hair, and left the luxury of her Westwood Village cottage.

Blasts of wind assaulted her as she ran toward the door of a waiting limousine. "Dreadfull morning, ma'am," said the chauffeur. "Isn't it," she answered before falling back into the comfort of the velvet-padded interior.

Since Los Angeles sleeps late, the hours before dawn are particularly lonely ones. Except for an occasional police car, the streets were deserted and devoid of the cacophony that usually accompanies the awakening of a great metropolis.

The limousine plowed silently through the rich, green suburban streets. In her rolling compartment, Eva switched on a tiny light that beamed onto a leather-bound script: *Green Acres,* Episode Sixty. Her musical voice, with a deliberately thickened Hungarian accent, began speaking the lines.

The transformation of the polished, sophisticated Eva Gabor into the bubble-headed, inept Lisa Douglas had begun, a transformation that was not only a great acting feat but an enormous physical task as well.

Twenty minutes later, the lighted gates of the television studio came into view. "Good morning, Miss Gabor," said a security guard as the limo pulled up in front of the open doors of a soundstage. The brilliance inside contrasted with the blackness outdoors. Eva was helped out of the car and dashed inside almost at a run. Surrounding her was the garish papier-mâché world of Hooterville, with its ramshackle houses, a general store, and a rubber cornfield that could only have been at home in *The Wizard of Oz*.

The door to Eva's dressing room was already standing open, with coffee, croissants, a hairdresser, and a makeup artist waiting. Her hair was shampooed and all traces of street makeup stripped from her face. Hair stylist Peggy Shannon worked for more than ninety minutes sculpting Eva's normally sleek hair into the teased, tormented, towering edifice favored by Lisa Douglas. Then Gene Hibbs, a magician with the makeup pots, plied his trade. It was for Eva that he perfected a technique that is now renowned. Because Lisa had to look faultlessly beautiful no matter what position she was in or from what angle she was photographed, Gene devised a system of tiny adhesive patches at the top of her forehead and above the ears. He dabbed these patches to make certain they would hold, and then slipped tiny silver hooks into holes in the tape. The hooks, in turn, were attached to elastic cords encircling her head but hidden by the elaborate hairstyle. When the cords were tightened, Eva was able to indulge in the hard slapstick routines and still look like Marlene Dietrich. This doesn't mean she needed this process to look younger or more beautiful; it was simply a device that gave her more comedic range.

Thick theatrical makeup in four shades of beige followed. Then three tints of lip gloss, eye liner, and false lashes completed the transformation. It was almost eight A.M.

Outside the dressing room, in a large alcove on the soundstage, the hum of a sewing machine and the steady snipping of dressmaker's shears broke the morning silence. An intent seamstress was hunched over a cutting table draped with patterns and surrounded by bolts of silk, chiffon, and organza. Hampers of sequins, rhinestones, and ostrich feathers were spread out around the sewing machine.

On the wall was a spill of original designs for the Lisa Douglas wardrobe executed by designer Jean Louis, hired at a dear price to clothe Eva glamorously for her tenure in Hooterville. Since the actress changed as many as seven times during each half-hour episode, most of the fittings and construction took place right on the set.

When Eva stepped into the mythical Hooterville that blustery morning in 1967, she was an important star in the television industry. Not only was *Green Acres* the number one show that week, but the ratings revealed that she was TV's most popular actress. Here finally was the great success that had eluded her for almost twenty-five years. When she was almost forty, the age when many actresses suddenly find themselves out of work, Eva stumbled into the cast of *Green Acres* with such style that it seemed as if the part had been written especially for her.

Actually, the role that made her a millionaire and brought her international fame was designed for another actress entirely, and Eva was, in many ways, the last resort. *Green Acres* was conceived by producer Paul Henning as a sort of companion piece for his superseries *The Beverly Hillbillies.* Whereas the *Hillbillies* dealt with the exploits of hicks in a wealthy, sophisticated town, *Green Acres* put a rich, chic couple in the ultimate hick town, Hooterville.

Both Henning and the CBS network had their eye on veteran Eddie Albert for the meaty part of Oliver Douglas, although several other actors were briefly considered. The part of his wife was written specifically for Martha Hyer, a beautiful blond actress who specialized in snotty rich girl roles. When the series was conceived, Martha was being paid as much as $100,000 per film, having won a best supporting actress nomination for *Some Came Running.* "If they could have gotten Martha, they would have gone with her," said a CBS executive. "We were all disappointed when the deal fell through."

As the rest of the cast was rounded out, Henning and CBS searched frantically for the right lady and tested twenty-six actresses, including stars and unknowns, fruitlessly. Eva's name was mentioned fairly late in the game. Rumor has it that Bea Benadaret, star of another Henning show, *Petticoat Junction,* and a friend of Eva's, mentioned her for the part.

"She could certainly handle it, and this would be a different way to go," Paul told CBS. "She can't be cast without a test," said an executive at the network. "Frankly, we don't feel that people will be able to understand her because of the accent."

In late May of 1965, Eva flew in from New York to try out for the role. She did her own hair and makeup for the simple test, during which she recited several lines in her singsong blend of British and Hungarian.

The next afternoon when network executives saw the film they were stunned. An hour later the role was hers.

"As excited as I was to get the part, I faced a painful dilemma," Eva recalled. "My happy marriage to Richard Brown was the most important thing in my life. Now I would have to leave him alone at least five days a week, since he couldn't leave New York."

But Richard insisted that she take the part. "We will work it out," he told her.

"I rushed back to Manhattan to make sure my town house was running smoothly for Richard, then flew back and rented a small cottage in Westwood. Richard and I began a tradition of commuting that lasted for about two years. Almost every weekend, I flew to New

York or Richard flew to Los Angeles. I refused to put anything ahead of my marriage."

A week after Eva was cast, the pilot was filmed. It was assumed that Eva was handed this success on a silver platter, that all the creativity was in the writing. The truth is, Eva took a rather flat part and made it a comedic triumph, using the Gabor wit and a flawless fashion sense.

"There were some marvelous scripts," Eva told a Los Angeles *Times* reporter. "But I established the character when I wore an elaborate chiffon negligee chasing a chicken across the barnyard. I was successful in psyching out Lisa's character because she was a lot like me. When Lisa wore jeans, she made sure she had real diamonds to compensate."

Throughout the six-year run of the series, Eva remained remarkably inventive. Once when the script called for Lisa to attempt a Thanksgiving dinner, Eva cut huge pictures of a turkey and trimmings out of a slick magazine, pasted them on cardboard, and put them in Lisa's Hooterville oven.

"I knew the show would be a hit as soon as I heard the electricians and carpenters laughing," Eva said to the pilot. "One man even fell off a ladder, he was laughing so hard."

Legend had it that Eva, using her Pidgin English, was the only one who could coax a performance out of one of the series' other stars, Arnold the Pig.

Still, after the pilot was filmed, Eva and *Green Acres* almost parted company when she insisted that they hire Gene Hibbs, Peggy Shannon, and Jean Louis—all of whom added greatly to the cost of the show.

"But it worked, didn't it?" Eva said. "Even the ratings surveys showed that Lisa's ambience fascinated the viewers. In one episode I appeared in a Jean Louis gown I had worn just a few weeks earlier. Hundreds of fans wrote me, asking, 'Can't you afford a new dress?' "

Once she was cast, Eva tore into the role with a zeal that was almost masochistic. The four-thirty A.M. to nine P.M. days never varied during the six years. In an interview with a Washington gossip columnist, Eva said, "I haven't been to a party in seven months, and I rarely have time to go out to dinner. In fact, the weekends aren't much better, since I leave the studio and go directly to the airport for the flight to New York."

As the show's ratings soared, Eva's power increased measurably. During the second season, CBS and Filmways (the company that produced the series for them) gratefully refurbished their star's dressing room in soft yellows and oranges, upgrading it to reflect Eva's taste. At the beginning of that season, she persuaded Filmways to hire Richard as a senior vice president, which allowed him to move to the

Coast. Soon Richard was able to boast, "Now my wife is actually working for me." Al Simon, executive producer of the series, said, "We actually got the best of that deal. He did a hell of a job for us." Filmways executives say Brown became a fine marketing analyst and European distributor for them.

With her regal dressing room, personal clothiers, and exclusive makeup artists, Eva became very much the queen bee of the entire lot. "She never abused her position," said co-star Tom Lester. "Eva was down to earth with everybody from the carpenters on up. She treated us like family."

One of the few things that drew her ire was *any* mention of Zsa Zsa. Fellow actors learned quickly that her sister was taboo as a topic of conversation. Once when an actor quoted Zsa Zsa's witticisms from a talk show, Eva snapped, "I don't quote President Lyndon Johnson to you, so why do you quote Zsa Zsa to me?"

On the other hand, no one was allowed to criticize her sister. One afternoon, after having seen a somewhat bloated and disheveled Zsa Zsa on a late-night talk show, another actor laughingly commented to Eva, "You know, Miss Gabor, Zsa Zsa in a certain bad light looks like movie villain Jack Palance."

Her face flushed and her eyes narrowed. "Don't you *ever* criticize my sister again—ever!"

Throughout the series, Eva realized that she faced an uphill battle to prove that she wasn't merely a temperamental, difficult glamour girl. "The first time I ever did a television show, the producers had an actress standing by in case I blew up or refused to go on," she said. "I was out to destroy that image, and this show gave me the chance to do it." After the first season Paul Henning described her as "the least temperamental actress I have ever worked with."

"It was then that Hollywood stopped linking all us Gabors together."

It hurt her, though, when critics treated her as an overnight star. "After all the work I've done, why should I suddenly be treated as a bona fide actress? Basically, I have always known I would have great success, but I was surprised at the way it came. And I was hurt because people were so shocked when I gave a good performance. Suddenly, after twenty-five years of hard work, I was 'discovered.'"

Tom Lester was amazed at the way she borrowed from her own unique character and combined it with that of the fictional Lisa. "A lot of Eva made it into the series, such as her incomparable knowledge of how to dress, her ability to always look beautiful, and her irrepressible talent to entertain everybody in sight."

Tom continued: "But Lisa Douglas displayed a degree of stupidity that Eva certainly didn't share. Now this was real acting. I mean, when such an intellectual woman appears so simple, it takes a lot of talent."

A young actor discovered by Paul Henning's daughter, Linda Kay, Tom remembers the first day he met Eva. "From the first moment I met her, she was wonderful to me. I needed a lot of encouragement because, artistically, I was insecure. She always helped and never put me down."

But there was one thing that Eva shared with Zsa Zsa and Magda —the whirling-dervish social merry-go-round so typical of them all. Working in the dressing room and often on location, a social secretary constantly manipulated a two-line telephone. It was not uncommon for Eva to be talking to Zsa Zsa in Paris while Jolie, in Palm Beach, waited on another line.

"I don't know how one person could concentrate on so many things at one time," Tom recalled.

Slowly, Eva developed a warm personal relationship with the whole *Green Acres* family. Several times a month, she hosted tennis Sundays at the sprawling estate she and Richard had bought in the swank hilltop suburb of Trousdale. "It was strictly informal. Nobody dressed," said Tom. "But she kept it a very much closed society. One time her tennis coach brought some friend over without asking, and she fired him."

Her warmest relationship, naturally, was with Eddie Albert, and he seemed to bring out the cutup in her. "They were like kids sometimes," Tom said. "They had a lot of fun during their love scenes— kissing and giggling as if nobody were watching. I think that closeness showed up on the TV screen."

Eddie, a physical-fitness buff, was always trying, unsuccessfully, to persuade Eva to take up running and, successfully, to persuade her to grow her own organic vegetables. Early one morning, after a long run on the beach, Eddie jogged onto the soundstage wearing a satin robe. Gene Hibbs was about one hour into the makeup process when Eddie strolled over, whipped open his robe, and revealed a marvelous body clad only in jockey shorts. "Eat your heart out, Eva baby," he said. "Eat your heart out."

Veteran character actor Alvy Moore, who knew Eva less intimately, remembered what an acting challenge she faced. "Coming away from a filming, she would maintain some of that air-headed quality so typical of Lisa. Eva Gabor only re-emerged bit by bit."

31

❋ Sudden Tragedy

*S*urely this ghastly nightmare was happening to some other family, not to the lucky, vivacious Gabors. Far down the road, the faint outline of an ambulance appeared in the morning mist. It rolled toward the front door of this particular house. And with each yard it traveled it brought the reality of a great tragedy to Jolie's heart. She choked back the beginnings of a great sob and drifted through the house to the bedside of her stricken daughter. With each step Jolie shrugged off a bit more of her self-pitying grief. No time for that, she thought. No time for a woman's tears—not when you have an entire life to rebuild.

First, she had to force herself to look, to take a hard, realistic look at Magda, lying near death in one of the mansion's bedrooms. "If she dies, I die also," she vowed under her breath.

She took one of Magda's limp hands. Every few minutes her eyes opened, but they merely stared blankly at the ceiling. Only ten hours earlier, this girl had been the belle of the Southampton Horse Show. The recent memory appeared in Jolie's mind. In full regalia and astride an Arabian horse, her daughter's beauty drew gasps from the society audience.

Then in the early hours of the morning, Magda and husband Tony Gallucci brought a few friends to their Southampton house. Jolie remarked to one of the guests that her daughter was finally happy. "There are problems, of course, but this is a very happy marriage."

Since Jolie was staying in a guest villa, she excused herself early and walked across the enormous grounds to her cottage and fell wearily into bed. The next thing she knew, the phone extension next to the bed began ringing. She fumbled for the phone. "Yes," she said.

"It's Tony, Jolie." His voice was frantic, quaking with fear. "It's

Magda. I don't know what happened. She's in a coma or something."
His voice broke. "It's terrible, and she can't even speak."

Jolie dropped the phone, ran out the door and across the spreading
lawn. She found that Magda was unable to speak or to move the right
side of her body. Tears rolled down Jolie's cheeks as she cradled her
eldest daughter's head in her lap.

There had been warning signs, but they seemed important only in
hindsight. Just three days earlier, Magda had tripped over her black
poodle and fallen onto the carpet, unable to stand back up. When
Tony tried to lift her, she screamed in agony. Jolie rushed to her side.
"I told the maid to put cold compresses on her head, and after several
hours she seemed fine," Jolie said later.

That had been on Thursday. On Friday, Magda's spitfire personality
had revived to the extent that she complained, "Tony knows how
badly I've been suffering, and he doesn't even bother coming up to
see how I feel." On Saturday she was well enough to attend the horse
show.

Now, on Sunday, Jolie called Zsa Zsa—in New York for a film
opening—and asked her to get Dr. Andrew Bernath, a physician
famous for treating stroke victims.

"Has she ever lost her speech before this?" Zsa Zsa asked her
mother.

"Yes," Jolie admitted. "She lost it temporarily five years ago. We
had quarreled, and Magda suffered what I can only call 'a little spell.'
It was Dr. Bernath who helped her then."

Dr. Bernath and another unnamed stroke specialist were both en-
joying long weekends when Zsa Zsa found them and miraculously
talked them into going with her to Southampton. "Only Zsa Zsa could
have achieved this," Jolie wrote in her memoirs. "The sisters may
disagree bitterly over many things, but when it comes to a crisis, they
meld together."

After examining Magda for only five minutes, one of the specialists
told Jolie, "Your daughter has suffered a massive stroke. She must be
taken immediately to Mount Sinai Hospital in New York City."

Jolie called for the fated ambulance. She was devastated and refused
to leave Magda's side, neither in the ambulance nor at the hospital.
She cradled her daughter's left hand and sat in the hospital suite until
long after sunset. At nine P.M. a rather brusque nurse tapped Jolie on
the shoulder. "You must leave now. Visiting hours are over."

"Yes, dear," she answered absently. "I'll leave in just a few minutes. Let me say goodbye."

"She can't hear you," the nurse said.

"Oh, yes she can," Jolie said. "Don't ever say that again in her
presence. Now leave me alone with my daughter."

When the nurse padded off, Jolie kissed her daughter on the cheek. "I'll be right here, darling. I won't leave your side for a second until you are well."

Then, with typical Gabor élan, she slid under the bed and, using her purse for a pillow and her mink coat as a blanket, she fell into a fitful sleep. Each time Magda moaned or moved in the bed, she sprang up and, keeping a wary eye trained on the door, held Magda's hand.

At five A.M. she left her makeshift bed and repaired her hair and her makeup before the doctors came in at six.

Jolie kept this up until her daughter was out of danger. "They had visiting hours, but I broke all the regulations," she wrote in her memoirs. "This was such a tragedy for me." In the evenings, Tony joined her at the vigil.

At first Jolie was afraid she couldn't cope with the tragedy. So many doctors told her that she could hope for nothing, that her daughter would never truly recover. It was a diagnosis she refused to accept.

For instance, therapists at the Rusk Center in Manhattan told her, "Magda will never speak. Don't even bother coming here anymore. It is a waste of time." Jolie replied, "You just wait. You're going to see a miracle."

Jolie and Tony finally brought Magda back to Southampton, vowing to rehabilitate her themselves.

Less than a week later, Jolie was amazed to see Magda sitting up in bed, trying desperately to form words. Phonetic sound by phonetic sound, and word by word, Magda lifted herself slowly out of a terrifying state of muteness. "She kept trying to tell me something—a very good sign," Jolie remembered. "But she couldn't fit the words together. I looked down at her and wished with all my might that I could trade places with her; that I could be stricken in her stead."

Six months later, and all on her own, Magda painfully crossed the communications chasm. With her beauty lighted by flames from a fireplace, she grabbed her mother's hands and pulled her closer to the hearth. "No speech," Magda said. "Die."

Tears filled Jolie's eyes and she renewed her vow: "If you give up and die, then I die also. Magda, darling, you've got to live. I'm counting on it."

Then, just as Magda was reclaiming her own life, Tony died of a heart attack, and she faced a battle for control of his mammoth estate.

In 1967, slightly more than a year after the stroke, Magda's halting vocabulary contained barely enough phrases to make her understood —about twenty-eight words.

For this reason, her lawyers advised her to stay home during the battle for control of Tony's manufacturing empire. She looked at the attorneys and shook her head. "No," she said.

"It was unbelievable the way she handled herself during this troubled time," Jolie recalled. "By reading law books, she helped build her own case and sat next to her lawyers, giving them one-word directions as the hearing progressed."

At first Tony's family offered a settlement—a modest amount compared to the vast fortune. The attorneys told her to take it and walk away from the legal battleground. Magda shook her head fiercely: "Fight . . . fight!" she said.

Her assertion that she was the major beneficiary was upheld by the judge, who complimented her on her gutsy courtroom performance. During the next several years Tony Gallucci's empire expanded massively.

Then, after studying the market, Magda cleverly figured out that an advance in technology might outdate the Gallucci manufacturing conglomerate. Again she went to court. But this time the family fought her intention to sell the industrial conglomerate. "They want you to hang on to your share," the lawyers informed her. "You should take the advice."

"No, no!" she answered. "Trouble ahead." Her share was sold.

"She was very smart to do this," Jolie said. "It was almost as if she had psychic knowledge. The factory failed, but Magda escaped with her fortune just in time. . . . From that time onward, my eldest daughter became very rich—richer even than her sisters."

In the late 1960s, Magda and Jolie both moved to Palm Springs, where Magda rebuilt a mansion and Jolie established a small winter home.

After several years in the desert, Jolie told a reporter, "Magda's mind is functioning as always—like a computer." Magda also devised her own prescription for long-term rehabilitation, which included rigorous exercise programs and three-week visits to health spas four or five times a year.

Ironically, Magda's wealth and social status and, in a bizarre way, her affliction set her up for the strangest and shortest marriage in the checkered matrimonial history of the Gabors.

32

❊ George the Second

*T*he night editor at the Los Angeles Associated Press Bureau stared at the bulletin in amazement. It had been phoned in by a reporter in sleepy little Indio on the edge of California's Mojave Desert. It said, "Academy Award–winning actor George Sanders married Magda Gabor this afternoon in a civil ceremony held at Indio City Hall." It was dated December 4, 1970.

What the hell? the editor thought. *Magda* Gabor! They must mean Zsa Zsa." He grabbed the phone and called the AP correspondent in Indio: "Don't you mean Zsa Zsa?" "No, sir. He married Magda, Zsa Zsa's older sister."

Ten minutes later, the bulletin went on the wire and was printed in newspapers around the world. Gossip reporters tripped all over each other trying to get the "real story." Many versions were printed, but in this case truth was far stranger than fiction.

Appropriately, it all started with Zsa Zsa. Several weeks after her 1954 divorce from George Sanders, Zsa Zsa told Louella Parsons, "I still love him so much. I always will."

It wasn't surprising then that she kept in close contact, at least weekly, with her ex-husband. "Some people who love each other very, very much just *can't* be married," she said. "Marriage, with its smothering closeness, often kills love."

By the late 1960s, Zsa Zsa and George began dating again on a highly informal basis. They even worked out a bizarre arrangement where George lived with Zsa Zsa part of the time. "Well, what's wrong with that?" she asked one reporter. "He's lonely, and lord knows I have the room." (Sanders' wife for seven years, Benita Hume, had died from cancer in 1967.)

"Zsa Zsa still loved George above any other man she had known, and that includes Rubi," Jolie said. "So I asked Zsa Zsa, 'Why not marry him?' She answered, 'Nuci, George has retreated into a shell and is hiding from life. It would not be good for us to be married.' "

Then one summer afternoon George confided to his ex-wife that a mild stroke had left him emotionally despondent and physically debilitated. This planted the seed, and Zsa Zsa turned matchmaker.

Several weeks later, George told Zsa Zsa at lunch that a very rich lady had proposed to him. "And I might go through with it," he said. This was like waving a red flag before her eyes. She refilled George's wineglass and leaned toward him. "George, you are lonely and so is Magda. She is also rich. So why don't you marry her?"

"His announcement of the lady's proposal shocked me, because I wanted to keep George in the family," Zsa Zsa said. "We all loved him—even Jolie. And I was doing it for him also, because he was very lonely."

Zsa Zsa convinced Jolie that the match would ease the heartache facing both George and Magda. "They will have each other to lean upon," she said.

A day or two later, George called Zsa Zsa. "I've thought about it, Cokiline, and it seems like a good idea."

"You'll see. It will be the best thing that ever happened to you. You will be comfortable, and Magda will be happy. You will be very, very good for one another."

Jolie was dispatched to ask Magda. "Magda, I believe you and George Sanders should be married." In her memoirs, Jolie depicted her daughter's reaction. "Tears came to Magda's eyes, and she said, 'Unbelievable, beautiful.' "

George soon acted very much the young suitor, dashing from Beverly Hills to Palm Springs that very day, carrying a bouquet of forty red roses. Jolie greeted him at the front door: "George, I have to be frank with you. Magda can't speak."

He shrugged. "I don't care. I want to marry her right now."

Jolie argued, fearful of Magda's feelings if the marriage didn't work out. "George, take my advice. Come and stay with me as a houseguest for a month. That will give you and Magda a chance to get to know each other. You'll find out that Magda is not Zsa Zsa. Then you can decide. After all, you haven't seen her for fifteen years."

George's eyes were bright, his enthusiasm contagious. "I know I haven't seen her for years, Jolie, but I have always loved her."

"When we drove up to Magda's, she was waiting at the front door in an elegant hostess gown. She was breathtaking," Jolie remembered.

George took Magda's hand and said gaily, "Let's have caviar and vodka and then get married—now!"

Since it was two-thirty on a Friday afternoon, Jolie tried to argue. "No, Jolie, it must be today," said George. Magda agreed. "Now," she said. "Ridiculous," Jolie muttered under her breath. "How will you even get a blood test?"

As usual, Jolie called on a family friend, Dr. George Kaplan, and Magda put her secretary to work on the license. Miraculously, all the tests and papers were in order by four-thirty P.M.

The wedding party drove to the little city of Indio, home of the nearest marrying judge. Since they had phoned ahead, the judge stood waiting in black tie, accompanied by his wife in a ball gown and furs. (It seems they were on the way to an important dinner party and had come to the city hall just for the ceremony. Reporters would confuse the facts and report that the judge and his wife had been ordered by the Gabors to dress formally.)

The reception was held at the swank Palm Springs Racquet Club. "I was as ecstatic as a young girl," said Jolie. "I think it's always nice when you recapture a son-in-law."

Also, for a few brief weeks, the tiger changed his stripes. "He was so generous," Jolie said. "He gave Magda a television set and repaired her Cadillac." Opinions on both George's mood and intentions after the wedding vary greatly. "He so desperately wanted to settle into a quiet life," Jolie said. "Excitement had become too much for him."

"The truth is, he didn't know what he wanted," said a gossip columnist who covered the wedding and its aftermath. "Personally, I think he did it just so he could be close to Zsa Zsa again. She was the light of his life, and he knew it. Zsa Zsa herself shares much of the blame for the brief, unhappy alliance between George and Magda. It's something she may never admit, but *her* love for George also grew stronger through the years. By marrying him to Magda and keeping him in the family compound, Zsa Zsa created a perilous tightrope for George to walk."

Immediately after the reception, Magda went up to her room, and George wandered out onto the veranda, where he encountered Jolie. He took her hands, saying, "Please forgive me. It's not such a bad world after all. I think this will work out."

But the marriage lasted less than six weeks. George, normally melancholy, became morose while living with Magda, and one afternoon drove off—never to return. A week after this, he applied for an annulment, which was granted by the Indio Municipal Court. Jolie explained his action: "I think marriage is for very simple people—not for great artists such as Zsa Zsa and me. We cannot love while the marriage knot is tied around us."

Magda graciously refused to contest the action.

In the long run, however, it was Magda who survived. In 1972, at a hotel on the Spanish Mediterranean, George wrote two notes, took off all his clothes, poured himself a glass of white wine, and took 300 Nembutal capsules.

"I took my life because I am bored and have lived enough," said his notes, one written in English, the other Spanish. He was sixty-five years old.

Earlier, when she found out how despondent he had become, Zsa Zsa flew to Spain to be at his side. "I only returned to Beverly Hills because he seemed fine," she later said.

Informed of the death by an Associated Press reporter, she said, "I'm heartbroken. He was the major love of my life. When I left him just two weeks ago in Spain, he seemed cheerful and was shopping for a new house."

When Jolie informed Magda of the death she turned her face away.

33

✳ Matriphony

*A*ccording to journalists who covered the affair, the bride wore blushing peach, an outlandish gown that she daintily held aloft as her high-heeled slippers stepped through rotting fish heads, puddles of garbage, and a long stretch of filthy sand.

The bridegroom? He wore white, a silly smile, and he tiptoed his way to the altar with such apparent disdain that he couldn't control the sardonic grin tugging at his mouth.

"Is this it? Is this the boat?" shrieked the bride when she confronted a ferry boat that had the distinct scent of sewage. "We'll only be on it for a few minutes," said her gallant lover just before his Italian shoes skidded on an oil slick and sent him crashing into the bridal bouquet.

The bride might have cursed if a sudden gust of wind hadn't filled the ruffled sails of her raiment, causing her to careen backwards into the arms of three wedding guests.

And what festive guests they were—a ragtag collection that included film director John Huston and United States Congressman Phil Ober. They had picked their way along the waterfront of Puerto Vallarta to pay tribute to one of the great traditions of the jet set— a Gabor wedding.

Even the invitations were bizarre: a phone call here, an informal note there, and in some cases a last-minute whisper to jet setters who drifted by.

And the only thing blushing about the bride, Zsa Zsa Gabor, was her elaborate gown. Otherwise she was shameless in gushing that at long, long last she had finally found "true love."

What a gorgeous specimen he was, this husband number eight. Tall, dark, well-muscled, and not just a bit dandified, he skittered around his love like a used car salesman.

As the last guest spilled out of a battle-scarred VW bus and tumbled into the boat, Zsa Zsa linked arms with the now disheveled groom and held his hand aloft like a referee. "Here he is, darlings, husband number eight."

By this time, it was hard for the groom to keep the grin on his face. Only the arrogant flash in his eyes indicated that he didn't appreciate being trotted out like a prize steer. He bowed at the waist and said, "Felipe de Alba, at your service."

"Ah," said a jet setter, "the Duke of Alba."

Felipe reddened. Zsa Zsa smiled. And nobody denied it. Then one of the guests addressed him as "Your Excellency," but before he could utter a syllable of protest, the ferry boat lurched forward and began bobbing up and down like a cork. Chiffon became entangled with organza, wigs and falls blew awry, and thickened makeup ran in rivulets down cheeks that could hardly bear naked scrutiny. The men were torn between being chivalrous to the ladies and preventing the seams of their tight dinner clothes from bursting.

Still, Zsa Zsa's voice bellowed hale and hearty. "What a glorious night for a wedd—" As her voice hit the second syllable, the boat hit a Pacific swell and sent a fresh wave of saltwater over the fifteen guests trapped in a romantic adventure that had veered toward the *Twilight Zone.*

There was no denying it now—this was not going to be a storybook wedding. Soon offshore blackness engulfed the party. Could group seasickness be far behind?

One of the entrapped, wiping saltwater from his forehead, grumbled, "Where the hell are we going?" "Out to Eva's boat." "And just where the hell is that?" "Hush now. We have to head to international waters or it won't be legal."

That was an understatement of the first order.

Soon, but not soon enough, the lights of the lavish boat loomed out of the blackness and fog. One by one, the guests tripped across a ramp and onto the seagoing wedding chapel.

On board, free-flowing champagne substituted for real glamour, and a groaning buffet table took the place of warm-hearted affection.

By the time everyone was well tanked up, it was certain that the star attraction was neither Zsa Zsa nor the Duke of Alba, but Eva's devastatingly handsome sea captain, Peter Moore, a deeply tanned young man in British whites.

Peter stepped out of the crowd, took the bride's arm with great style, and announced, "Ladies and gentlemen, bear with us. I'm steaming thirteen miles out to sea so all this will be in order."

Some of the guests noticed that the bride held the young captain's hand a bit more romantically than that of her intended. But no matter, Zsa Zsa is normally flirtatious, and the captain retreated quickly to the bridge—a very good thing, because fifteen minutes later the SS

Eva, as some called it, steered into the path of a tiny tropical storm.

Zsa Zsa, floating from guest to guest and vowing that this would truly be for better or worse, was about to make another speech when the floor pitched upward about twenty degrees, causing the party to slide perilously close to the wedding feast. Then the boat slid back downward, hurling the clinging guests terribly close to the boat's windows.

Giggles were replaced by groans and gaiety by an uncertain queasiness. After all, how many weddings require a tow line just so the guests can stand up? When it became apparent that the storm was no temporary annoyance, cabin boys appeared and strung rough ropes from one end of the salon to the other. Ladies gratefully grabbed them despite the ravaging effects of the ropes' rough splinters on their gloves, gowns, and furs.

Blissfully, the boat soon reached its thirteen-mile target.

Captain Moore, virtually the only unruffled human left on the boat, reappeared and bade the bride and groom approach him, since he was to double as chaplain. It was all over within minutes, when the captain, almost under his breath, muttered, "I pronounce you man and wife." It seemed that the unduly nervous Felipe de Alba, fifty-two, was now officially husband number eight and that Zsa Zsa at long last had a title, the Duchess of Alba.

Truth was, Felipe was only husband number 7½, a papier-mâché spouse who fell directly from the honeymoon bed into welcome obscurity. For this had all been a charade—the wedding, the guests, and particularly the bridegroom.

Some of the guests formed suspicions quickly when Zsa Zsa was asked why she had suddenly decided upon De Alba and she whispered, "Darlings, you know I have never lived in sin in my life. Since Felipe is so irresistible, we had to marry." Several guests laughed out loud. Others chalked it up as just another Gabor passion play. Still others thought they had seen the real thing and told reporters as much when they got back ashore.

The wedding party had sailed late on the night of April 13, 1982. The next afternoon the world was informed that Zsa Zsa Gabor Belge Hilton Sanders Cosden Hutner Ryan O'Hara was now the Duchess of Alba.

In Palm Springs, Jolie quickly contacted society reporters and dashed about the desert resort reporting on her daughter's sudden rise to the aristocracy. "It became *the* topic of conversation here for a brief but interesting time," said Allene Arthur, society editor of the Palm Springs *Desert Sun.*

Alas, the rosy bubble was soon burst, leaving even her own sisters uncertain as to what had happened. First, an intrepid Associated Press reporter in Hollywood discovered that the dashing Peter Moore possessed only a Mexican marine license, giving him no authority to perform a wedding.

Second, a television gossip columnist checked her sources and learned that Zsa Zsa was still very much Mrs. Michael O'Hara and would remain so until her divorce was final on July 4.

Finally, a diplomat at the Spanish embassy in Washington left a cocktail party to accept a telephone call from King Juan Carlos of Spain. In a few icy words, the diplomat was told to inform the press that there was *no* Duke of Alba. There was, however, a Duchess of Alba, and she was very much alive.

Before the explosion of publicity broke about their heads, Zsa Zsa and Felipe, no more married than Abbott and Costello, hosted a lavish reception at Puerto Vallarta. But by the time the Mexican press latched onto the story, the bogus Duke of Alba and his bride had disappeared into the privacy of a honeymoon.

When reporters finally found the groom in Mexico City, his gorgeous bride had apparently already flown from the nest. And Felipe wasn't even rich; he was a suburban realtor. "What were you, a private publicity stunt?" asked a reporter for the New York *Times.*

"Not exactly," Felipe explained. "Despite her desperate search for publicity, some aspects of Zsa Zsa are far from frivolous. She actually proposed to me because she was invited by President Reagan to the White House and wanted us to go as man and wife. I knew how much it meant to her, so I tried hard to please. Also, I'm not at all rich. My real estate business is just large enough to pay my way."

Early the next day in Bel Air, Zsa Zsa fumed when she read the disloyal statements from the husband who never was, and she gave some fiery interviews herself: "It's true that we aren't married. We were going to legalize our status in July, but I called it off. Truth was, he bored me. He was nothing but a playboy, whereas I'm a hard-working actress. It's over. Finis!"

The ball was back in Felipe's court, and he was ready with the backhand. Having read Zsa Zsa's personal insults, he responded angrily. "Zsa Zsa told me she's fifty-four. When I learned that she is actually nearly seventy,* I suddenly understood her inner tensions,

---

* The ages of the Gabor sisters are difficult, if not impossible, to gauge. But Zsa Zsa was certainly nowhere near seventy when she staged the mock wedding. She was probably born in 1922, meaning that she was sixty-one at the time. Magda was allegedly born in 1920 and Eva in 1924. Some reference works, such as the 1979 *Star Stats,* claim that Zsa Zsa was born in 1919 and Eva in 1921. On the other hand, Earl Blackwell's 1973 *Celebrity Register,* published by Simon and Schuster, officially lists Eva's birth date as February 11, 1926, meaning that she would have been thirteen when she married Dr. Drimmer and moved to Hollywood. That same reference guide hedges a bit on Zsa Zsa, stating that she was born on February 6 in "either 1921 or 1923."

her great frustration. She lives in a world of romantic fantasy. I told her, 'You will lose face by calling me a duke. I'm from Mexico, where we have no dukes.' But she ignored me." He concluded, "I wanted us to part as friends, but that was impossible. She made it impossible."

Some of Zsa Zsa's friends believe she staged the ceremony after Mike O'Hara reportedly yelled at her over the phone, "You're too old to find another husband." Perhaps this charade simply grew out of Zsa Zsa's unquenchable thirst to fashion a more beautiful world for herself instead of the cruel universe that middle age had brought.

Jack Ryan believes kindly that his ex-wife "dwells in a perpetual fairyland that never was." One of Jack's favorite anecdotes from his zany Gabor years illustrates his point. "I recall introducing her to a very famous German baron, a member of the old aristocracy. His roots stretched back to Charlemagne, making him one of the last true nobles in the world. We all went out to dinner. Zsa Zsa was talking about how life wasn't the same anymore, especially for aristocrats. The baron turned toward her. I could see by her face that she had the utmost respect for him. And I heard him say, 'Zsa Zsa, this is a fairy tale. Life never was that way for anyone, not even aristocrats.' "

Jack was grateful to the baron. "I hoped he would put some of Zsa Zsa's rampant uneasiness to rest. But she refused to believe it."

34

❊ New Faces

"*I* can't wait to see it, I really can't," gushed a young socialite nervously adjusting the folds of a Halston gown. Her escort, a bored tennis pro, swallowed a double scotch and stared straight ahead.

"Why the hell isn't this line moving?" said a matronly blueblood around whose neck was a waterfall of diamonds.

At the head of the receiving line, in the white-hot glare of fame, an actress said adoringly to the guest of honor, "My dear, it's perfectly breathtaking, the finest workmanship I have ever seen." Out of ear-shot, she whispered to an aging husband, "Do you see? Do you see what enough money can buy?"

The guests straggled backward through the desert sunset like a welfare line for the very rich and the superfamous.

There is nothing that Palm Springs society loves as much as an important unveiling. And this was one of the most spectacular in many years, more interesting than the bash for a recently acquired Picasso fountain or the dinner to show off the new wing of the Palm Springs Racquet Club. Even the receiving line was awesome. The ladies, many of them with famous faces, were gorgeously gowned. Their escorts were attired in white dinner jackets. The guests, a cross section of the desert's high rollers, waited in the seemingly endless line to catch a glimpse of the already legendary work of art.

As each guest reached the small rise of steps employed to make the showcase even more dramatic, Magda stepped forward to shake hands with each and to whisper softly, "If you must kiss Mama, please make it a Hollywood kiss on the forehead, darling. The stitches are just a bit tender."

Often the line became gnarled as some of the greedier partygoers couldn't take their eyes off the guest of honor—the ageless, lovely

Madame Edmund de Szigethy of Palm Springs, Manhattan, and West Palm Beach. Better known as Jolie Gabor, it was she who was unveiling the "brand-new me," refurbished at great cost by not just one but a team of renowned plastic surgeons.

Each privileged guest was allowed to take the dainty hand of Mama Gabor and gaze at the scalpel's ultimate wizardry for a few carefully allotted seconds and then was gently prodded along.

The formal invitations that had been mailed several weeks earlier referred to the affair as a "coming out party," as if the fresh countenance were that of a giddy debutante to be laid out publicly.

The face was certainly worth seeing; there was no denying that. Where dozens of tiny lines had been drawn about the eyes, there was now an adolescent freshness. Slightly puffy cheeks were now svelte, and a dowager's thick chin had vanished.

Lending authenticity to the emergence of this surgical ingenue was the respected society editor of the Palm Springs *Desert Sun,* who duly recorded it for posterity. Mingling with the crowd, she learned that the rampant whispers were not concerned with the incredible cheekiness of a reception for a face-lift but with the cost of the operation and *which* lift this was—number four, five, or six.

"Rumor had it," said a reporter, "that this was number five or, at the very least, number four."

Jolie wisely demurred from discussing her surgical scorecard, but she did reminisce about her first. "With my first windfall of profits from the jewelry business, $2,000, I did the only intelligent thing— I had my face lifted. But now I believe that all women must have the good face. If a person has not a good nose, if she has not a good chin, then she must make the chin and the nose. Even more than that— make everything!"

Shortly after this medical command performance, Magda, her classic cheekbones newly highlighted and her eyes cleared of wrinkles, hosted a similar party with equally triumphant results.

Then, several months after that, Eva journeyed to Palm Springs sporting a new, radiantly youthful facade. In May, when she was in the desert for a charity luncheon, friends pointed out that Eva looked fortyish. In July, at a gala for the Vincente Minnellis, Allene Arthur, society editor of the Palm Springs *Desert Sun,* sneaked a private conversation with her and was dazzled.

"I've always wanted to see you up close," she told Eva. Later Allene said, "I could hardly believe it. She now looked no more than thirty!"

Following this triple header, fresh gossip surfaced. First, back-fence legend in Palm Springs had it that the lifts had all been performed free by a famous plastic surgeon with the proviso that the trio recommend him to their closest friends. If this was the case, no name has ever

targeted Dr. John Williams, Eva's husband
surgeon. Despite the fact that Dr. Williams is
ous plastic surgeon, and that he has clinics in both
Palm Springs, there's no firm evidence that he was
cian in this case. Unlike her sisters, Zsa Zsa becomes
y mention of a face-lift. In fact, she has offered a standing
of $10,000 to anyone who can prove she has undergone
c surgery.

The face-lifts and the open manner with which three of the Gabors
treat them speak volumes about their eccentric tenure at Palm Springs,
now the matriarchal seat of power for the family. Not only does
Magda live there, but Eva and Zsa Zsa too, no matter how far away
their careers and social lives take them, gravitate to the desert regularly. "I insist that all my daughters call me at least once a day," Jolie
told Allene Arthur. "They do this no matter where they are or what
they are doing. This is the lifeline which keeps us together." (Jack
Ryan's remembrance that Zsa Zsa becomes hysterical if she skips a day
testifies to Jolie's relentless psychological control over her daughters.)

Palm Springs is also the base of the family's apparently endless but
secret source of wealth. The several homes they maintain there, the
lavish wardrobes they display, the jewels and furs, and the rich parties
they throw seem to be fed by an inexhaustible underground spring of
riches. Considerable folklore has grown up about the Gabor finances.

Magda's money is easiest to pin down, since it was inherited from
Tony Gallucci's estate. A New York *Post* reporter was told that Magda
"has a small handful of millions." Likewise, the sources of Eva's
wealth can be traced. The "very least" she earned from *Green Acres*
and its residuals was a million dollars, according to producers of the
show. And her wig company, which brought her at least $100,000
annually seven years ago, has undoubtedly grown in the 1980s. She
has also amassed a real estate empire that had its origins in the late
1940s.

More mysterious is Zsa Zsa's supposed fortune. When he married
her, Jack Ryan said she was quite "wealthy by an ordinary lady's
standards" and "slightly wealthy by her own standards." He claimed
that he helped her negotiate a series of department store appearances
that netted her "at least $250,000 a year." Although she accepted
alimony from only Conrad Hilton, persistent gossip has circulated that
she was endowed by some husbands with premarital stipends, perhaps
deposited in Swiss banks. Zsa Zsa has always angrily denied this.

As for Jolie, her swank jewelry emporium on Madison Avenue in
New York City has been coining money for three decades, and *her*
real estate investments, including a lavish four-story brownstone in
Manhattan, also began in the 1940s. Apparently her 1957 marriage

to De Szigethy, a war refugee, brought her no wealth. In *Jolie,* she wrote that "he escaped from Transylvania after all his properties had been confiscated and fled to the West with only two suits, wearing one on top of the other. When I first met him he had $27 left, of which he spent $25 on roses for me."

When Jolie and Edmund were first listed in Palm Springs's *Little Gold Book,* the society Who's Who of the desert, Jolie tried unsuccessfully to have him listed as a count. One socialite, long familiar with the Gabors, said, "Things like that go over very, very poorly in the desert."

Like minor royalty, Jolie and Edmund arrive annually for the Palm Springs formal season—November through April. They bring with them thirty-five suitcases and armloads of furs in airtight Vuitton bags. While members of old-line families, such as the Hearsts, dominate the traditional element there, Jolie, Edmund, and Magda are in many ways the leaders of the splashy celebrity set.

From the time they arrive until they leave, Jolie and Edmund are guests of honor at one party after another. "These parties are so frequent that no count is even possible," said Allene.

However, one big-city reporter at the Springs for the season calculated three years ago that he had recently attended either party number 274 or 278, depending on who did the counting. "It has now reached the point where it's laughable," he said off the record.

The same reporter (from New York) pointed out that Jolie initiates these events. "Darling, make me a party," she says. "She is far more intimidating than you can possibly imagine," the reporter said. "I know some women who are afraid *not* to give a party when Jolie waves her magic wand. And she often decides where a person will sit. Over the protests of some hosts, she actually gets up and rearranges the seating."

Jolie, unlike Eva and Zsa Zsa, openly courts the press. "I often find her so endearing and so touching," said Allene Arthur. "Often she will call up, tell me that the hostess of the moment forgot to invite me, and tell me to come. She always calls the shots."

There are other signs, however, that she coldly manipulates the press. One season, a woman journlist came to Palm Springs to write a series of stories. Jolie believed that the reporter had enormous national clout and made a big fuss over her, seeing to it that she was invited to an expensive gala function she was attending. Then several days later Jolie discovered that her power wasn't that great and cancelled the invitation.

Interviews with social leaders, magazine writers, and several organizers of charity balls off the record indicated that the entire family is "socially controversial," to quote one blueblood.

"They are written about and talked about so often that many members of the old guard are resentful, and perhaps jealous, because they are one of the few families who have made no real contribution to the community which gives them so much," said one matron, a past board member of the Palm Springs Chamber of Commerce.

A wealthy actress who moved to the Springs at the same time as the Gabors said, "I don't know what they get out of all this. I find them very, very selfish and not nice people at all."

Envy appears to be written all over these opinions. Other residents such as Lily Pons, the late Mamie Eisenhower, and the Hearsts have mixed freely with Jolie and Magda. The late Kay Spreckels Gable said she always found "the Gabors to be frank, refreshing, and more interesting than anyone in Palm Springs."

Perhaps these minority opinions may be the result of a quite American high society befuddled by the totally European habits of the Gabors, with their emphasis on charm, glamour, and splashy beauty. In any case, the sheer number of luncheons and receptions given for Jolie and Magda testifies to their enduring social power.

The profligacy of these affairs has become so immense that the *Desert Sun* has been forced to adopt an editorial policy about them. There was a mild protest from other socialites several seasons ago, resulting in a decision to cover the "Jolie luncheons" with several wrap-up stories once or twice a season.

When Allene was new as society editor and attending her first Gabor party, she gave it an enormous spread. Then there was inevitably another and another and another. Then one day she relegated the next one to an item in her regular column. The next morning Jolie telephoned her. "My dear, we're used to a lot more attention that that." Several parties later, Jolie drifted up to Allene and said to her, "Maybe you wonder why I go to so many parties. You're young, and you have many, many parties ahead of you. I'm old, and there are not so many parties ahead for me."

The command performance luncheons are all the same—only the dresses and seasonal flowers vary. With the woman formally dressed in splashy cocktail gowns and hats and the men in suits, they begin with wine or light cocktails in the early afternoon. Then a six-course lunch is served, often French cuisine, and lasting about three hours. Jolie is persuaded to sing the two songs in her repertoire, "Never on Sunday" and "Que Sera Sera." "She's really quite good," observed Allene, "and she is remarkably beautiful. Her eyes sparkle and her gestures accompany the music. The audiences are always captivated."

Jolie and Magda always come dressed to kill. At the 500 or so parties at which Allene has seen them, she has yet to ever notice the same dress twice. "Jolie is probably the most chic of the four," said the society editor. "She sweeps into the room like a cover from *Vogue.*"

The largest and most expensive party for Jolie and Edmund honored their twenty-fifth wedding anniversary in 1982. All three sisters made a rare appearance. But when a magazine featured a shot of Magda, Zsa Zsa, and Eva on the cover, with pictures of Jolie inside, the matriarch telephoned an editor. "The coverage was perfectly lovely, darling," she said. "But it would have been so much better if you had featured the *guest of honor.*"

Magda has a more traditional image in Palm Springs than her mother. Since she lives there full-time, there is none of the social carpetbagger about her. Her speech, though still impaired by the stroke, now consists of about a hundred words, which she uses adroitly. Two catch words, "believe me," are used in a variety of tones throughout her conversation. "She is the gutsiest woman I have ever known," said Allene. "At an age when most women fold up, Magda has become a social institution with her lovely home, marvelous parties, and progressions through health spas. She is very much in control."

35

✳ Just Two Working Girls

*A*n emotional storm crackled through the backstage murkiness like a frantic telegram, setting tempers on edge and signaling that something was very wrong out front. One assistant stage manager kept his eye glued on Zsa Zsa as she drifted under a baby spotlight lost in the dialogue that led to the first-act curtain. Suffering the first symptoms of a particularly virulent case of flu, the star appeared distracted.

Though this Philadelphia production of *Forty Carats* had been well advertised, the houses had been hard to fill. This night was no exception; applause was spotty and the laughter sporadic at best.

From the way she rushed offstage, the crew knew something had ignited Zsa Zsa's fury, and the hatches were battened down. She sailed a perilous course for her dressing room, snapping directions at no one in particular. It seems that there had been peculiar and allegedly annoying laughter from tables very near the front. And since the City Line Dinner Theater is arranged informally, many of the tables are only a few feet from the stage.

This fateful Tuesday evening in May 1983, most of the front-row tables were allotted to brain-handicapped patients from the nearby Wood's School. Just who knew about this special seating is still a matter of conjecture. But the crucial question that would be asked again and again during the scandal that followed was "Did Zsa Zsa Gabor know there were handicapped theatergoers at front row center?"

It seems undeniably certain that Zsa Zsa made some complaint or demand as she huffed toward her dressing room. Members of the cast and crew noticed the star talking angrily with several staff members; others claimed to hear a word or two before she forcefully shut the door of her dressing room.

About five minutes later, an embarrassed young man hesitantly approached the dinner theater's stageside tables. Progressing from one group to another, he elicited reactions of great alarm, followed by a shame that plainly played across the faces of wheelchair-bound patrons. One young girl burst into tears while another took the theater messenger's hand imploringly.

He was as stricken as they were and reacted by rushing backstage, where he was greeted by a strange calm. He talked to a superior, who disappeared into Zsa Zsa's dressing room and reappeared almost instantly shrugging his shoulders in helplessness.

When the young man walked back into the audience, there were several others with him, and all of them informed the handicapped members of the audience that they were to be banished to the back of the theater. They drew their wheelchairs together and held a caucus. Then, one by one, they rolled up the aisles and out the front entrance. Half a dozen of them were crying. A tidal wave of sympathy swept through an audience which perceived only that an unhappy charade was playing out before their eyes.

Backstage, Zsa Zsa's dressing-room door remained shut. The theater staff grouped around a desk in whispered conference. They all realized that they had violated a house rule that handicapped persons receive preferential treatment, but they stood by as the wheelchairs moved slowly through the audience and out the entrance.

When Zsa Zsa finally emerged for her second-act entrance there was an invisible curtain between herself and the management. But neither she nor the staff realized that a scandal had been set in motion that would close down their play and damage Zsa Zsa's career.

From that moment on, the star told one version and the management another. Neither bore the slightest resemblance to the other.

Bob Brandenburg, general manager of the City Line, said simply that Zsa Zsa walked offstage and told the staff to "get those wheelchairs out of here. I can't work with distractions like that." On Wednesday, three other staff members backed his claim.

Zsa Zsa, on the other hand, remembered that she "made some minor complaint but was *never* told that handicapped patrons were involved." She said, "It was their mistake entirely. Then they tried to blame it on me."

Hearing this, staff members told reporters two days later that Zsa Zsa indicated she was rattled by "grating laughter" from the wheelchair patrons. And this in turn fanned a fire of disaster. The sixteen patients involved, as it happened, suffered from a brain trauma that in some cases causes them to laugh a few seconds later than most people. If Zsa Zsa did indeed complain about this laughter, it seems certain that she was never informed as to its cause.

Zsa Zsa believes that the entire scandal can be attributed to a "vindictive staff who were already out to get" her. And this, she says, stemmed from a nasty casting battle that erupted during the first weeks of rehearsal. The young actor originally hired to play opposite her wasn't the right type, Zsa Zsa decided. So she replaced him. "He had a lot of friends in the company and at the theater," Zsa Zsa said. "When the scandal hit, all this bitterness poured out, and I got the blame. It was a conspiracy."

At first, it seemed that nothing would come of the unhappy incident. The Wednesday performance came and went with little trouble. A theater spokesman called Wood's School offering tickets for another production, and it seemed as if the peace offering worked.

On Thursday, Zsa Zsa awakened to a furor that seemed deliberately designed to hurt her and to make her a scapegoat in a battle for handicapped rights in Philadelphia, a battle that had been raging for more than a decade. The switchboard at Zsa Zsa's downtown hotel had received and refused to put through more than 500 calls from angry protestors. And shortly before noon a fistful of telegrams had been shoved under her door. Stunned by the ferment building around her, she sat in bed with a cup of coffee, opening the telegrams one by one. After reading one of them she gasped. Her hand flew to her mouth. "You'll pay for this, Zsa Zsa Gabor," it said. "You have less than twenty-four hours to live." She felt hysteria grip her as she pulled herself out of bed to face the day. She couldn't help but wonder, How did a backstage tiff become front page news?

In New York City, the emerging scandal was heralded by news bulletins on NBC's *Today* show and ABC's *Good Morning, America.* In Philadelphia the airwaves had virtually geen given over to the debacle, causing radio call-in lines to jam hopelessly. Unfortunately, a fellow cast member, no doubt meaning well, suggested to Zsa Zsa that she tell her story on Irv Homer's highly rated radio show. So, counting on complete objectivity, Zsa Zsa called the station, was told that Irv would take her call on the air, and then was put on hold.

There was an interminable silence. Finally, Irv's brisk voice came onto the line. "A pleasure to have you, Zsa Zsa," he said. After a few lines of pointless babble, he allowed her to explain: "I didn't know there were sick people out in that audience. I really didn't."

Irv immediately countered, "But Zsa Zsa, Bob Brandenburg said you *were* told." She reacted defensively: "Mr. Brandenburg is a real big liar." Irv, now annoyed himself, snapped, "Miss Gabor, exactly *who* is lying?"

Click! Zsa Zsa hung up on him, and a hundred thousand radio listeners heard the click. That simple gesture signaled a public and personal disaster for her. Within hours this impulsive action would be added to the growing list of her supposed crimes. Zsa Zsa probably aborted the call when she realized, finally and suddenly, how stacked the deck was against her. It was now apparent that the theater management had pushed their star out into the cold to face the charges alone.

When the sixteen wheelchair patrons were ordered to move, the anger was directed against the theater management primarily, and Zsa Zsa secondarily. Handicapped leaders had decided that, whether or not Zsa Zsa made the request, the theater management had willingly carried it out. For twenty-four hours, handicapped activists focused their anger on the City Line Dinner Theater. The media, however, had already tried and convicted the star. At a special press conference, Sig Shapiro, head of the Pennsylvania Coalition of Handicapped Agencies, told reporters, "Quite frankly, Zsa Zsa Gabor has done us a big favor by focusing attention on problems which have been hidden for years. All of a sudden people in this state are taking a good, hard look at the difficulties we face."

Insulated at her hotel, Zsa Zsa had no way to gauge the political tides that were swirling out of control around her. The nasty telegrams were followed by a particularly frightening caller who snarled at the switchboard operator, "You tell Zsa Zsa that she won't be alive tomorrow." This call did it! Zsa Zsa left by a rear entrance just after one P.M. Her hands were visibly shaking. Later, a third death threat was received at her agent's office in Beverly Hills.

As her Silver Cloud Rolls pulled up toward the theater doors, real battle lines had finally been drawn. Bob Brandenburg stepped outside to announce tersely that the theater union, Actors Equity, had sent a team to mediate between Zsa Zsa and a theater management that was now solidly aligned against her. "We will have no official statement until the negotiations are completed," Brandenburg told reporters.

Before she could dash into the theater, Zsa Zsa was cornered by a television reporter who asked, "Three people say they heard you specifically ask that the wheelchairs be moved. How do you respond to that?"

Zsa Zsa glared at her. "I can explain. Those people need the theater's money. Zsa Zsa Gabor doesn't. There is a conspiracy against me."

Zsa Zsa must have shuddered as she passed the angry crowd in front of the playhouse. Sixty protestors, including about a dozen in wheelchairs, moved in a circle, waving banners bearing such slogans as "Zsa Zsa! It Really Hurts!" "Think About It, Zsa Zsa!" and "Zsa Zsa, *Please* Say You're Sorry!"

Trying to freeze her mouth in a smile, Zsa Zsa swept past the crowd and through a door to the theater's murky interior. By that time, the media encamped on the lawn included reporters from ABC, CBS,

NBC, representatives from ten regional television stations, four newspaper reporters, and one Washington mini-cam team that was broadcasting live.

For two hours, however, there was virtually nothing to report. Both entrances to the theater remained locked, and the calm exterior gave no clue to the raging battle inside. Union representatives scurried back and forth between management and the star. Several times, Zsa Zsa had frantic telephone sessions with agents and attorneys in Hollywood. A secretary who was involved reflected that Zsa Zsa and her producers, who had put the show together as a team, split over the demand that the star be forced to publicly apologize. "The minute the apology was demanded, the negotiations broke off. Not even Actors Equity could get the two sides talking again."

It's important to note that Zsa Zsa had no ally in the face-to-face confrontation.

After the stalemate, John Kinnamon, the Washington producer of the *Forty Carats* road company, appeared on the theater's front steps and said briefly, "I'm shocked and appalled by Miss Gabor's attitude." Then, seeing that he had attracted a warm reaction from the handicapped protestors, he leaned toward a microphone. "Zsa Zsa Gabor will apologize or else!"

A few minutes after this, a secretary posted a notice on an outdoor bulletin board. "Zsa Zsa Gabor, as of six P.M. today, has been fired from the production of *Forty Carats*. The $20,000 to pay for the star's two weeks' notice has been placed in escrow until Actors Equity rules whether or not she broke her contract." (The Equity decision, whatever it was, was never announced.)

There had still been no word from the woman at the center of it all. She was shut inside her dressing room, agonizing over her predicament. "It boiled down to this: Either I apologized for something I didn't do or walked off with some of my pride left," Zsa Zsa said later. "I walked off." Less than an hour after this, she finally stood before the theater in a white gown she would have worn in the show. Her eyes were lined from strain.

She spoke hesitantly. "I won't apologize, because there's nothing to apologize for. I'm an actress who works for a living, and the easiest thing would be to say that I'm sorry." The words came hard, "You know, I've worked so hard for charities all my life. Whenever I know that there are handicapped persons in the audience I make certain that champagne and cake are sent to their tables and charged to me."

Zsa Zsa turned to go back into the theater but looked over her shoulder. "I wish I could apologize." She waved and then disappeared inside.

The pressure inside the theater had been intense all afternoon as the fruits of disastrous publicity crashed down on the ticket sellers. From one P.M. until five P.M., 5,000 ticket holders for the Zsa Zsa Gabor production cancelled. An in-person crisis was even more menacing. Eight senior citizens who had traveled from New Jersey for the show held a caucus in the theater lobby and voted to eat the dinner but to walk out if Zsa Zsa came on stage. And even worse, ticket orders for the play's remaining five weeks had virtually stopped. Economically, the producers had to shut down the house for a month.

Some patrons, only a handful, showed up that evening, read the closing notice, and then left, averting their eyes when they slipped past the wheelchaired protestors. Slowly the lights were dimmed and the marquee went dark.

At nine P.M. a uniformed chauffeur ran out the stage door, leaped into the Silver Cloud, and stopped at the private entrance. The door was opened, allowing Zsa Zsa to slip inside the car, cradling two small white dogs under her arms. She sat next to the driver and sadly waved goodbye to the protestors. Since she had checked herself out of the beleaguered downtown hotel, the actress booked a small room in a hotel near the theater. Telephone calls again sped from Zsa Zsa to her attorneys, to her mother and sister, Eva, and to several close friends.

Shortly after midnight, she called Philadelphia's Wood's School, from which the handicapped theatergoers had come. "I'm coming over. I want them to know that I wasn't responsible for what happened to them. And I want them to know that I care," she told the school's director, Dr. Harold Barbour. "How many chocolates should I bring?" she asked, leaving him speechless. Before he could answer she had hung up.

Ninety minutes later, Zsa Zsa's agent, Robert Hussong, called Dr. Barbour from Beverly Hills. "Miss Gabor has been harassed beyond belief," he said. "And her life has been threatened. She has been forced to leave Philadelphia and is sorry for any misunderstanding. She wanted me to tell you that she's unable to come to the school."

The next morning an exhausted Zsa Zsa checked into New York City's Waldorf Towers, where the press still dogged her steps. A Philadelphia reporter got through to her in time to hear her yell at him, "Philadelphia used to be one of my favorite cities. But now I will never perform in your theaters or your nightclubs again. If you guys don't like it, then that's too goddamned bad."

Forty Carats sat idle for almost a week until John Kinnamon hired Terry Moore to replace Zsa Zsa. No ticket-sale figures from the remaining engagements were released, but many reporters noted that the show often played to barren houses. Two weeks after that, Zsa Zsa, ill from the strain and a bout of flu, secretly checked into a West Los Angeles hospital, where her room was guarded around the clock by a private security force. "I've never seen her this run down," said a close friend. "How could all this have resulted from one simple incident?"

The Eastern press, with little regard for objectivity, unmercifully pilloried Zsa Zsa. Within five days after the disaster, newspaper columnists, TV journalists, and even radio talk-show hosts dredged up every scrap of derogatory innuendo about her stay in the City of Brotherly Love. She was tried, convicted, and executed under the harsh glare of publicity. Several big-name columnists, normally so objective, threw caution to the wind.

Frank Rossi, of the Philadelphia *Inquirer,* stated flatly that "Zsa Zsa Gabor, a former USO entertainer from the Civil War era, got rid of the six wheelchairs without thinking twice about it." Clark De Leon in the same newspaper said, "Zsa Zsa is *not* Philadelphia . . . Thank God!" With overkill, an *Inquirer* entertainment columnist, Dorothy Storch, wrote, "Zsa Zsa is a self-invented joke, a cartoon character made up of an increasingly blowsy assemblage of clichés."

All branches of the media congratulated themselves on building a body of circumstantial evidence against the evil witch from Beverly Hills. But what flimsy evidence it was. First, Zsa Zsa was accused of having a shrieking baby banished from one performance. Second, she had supposedly "forced" the producers to have her Rolls-Royce driven from her home in West Palm Beach to augment a limo already provided, and third, she had blown up at fellow actors during a rehearsal. None of these things, however, were the least bit out of the ordinary for a celebrity of Zsa Zsa's caliber.

But some real harm was done to Zsa Zsa's image by a temporary secretary, Debbie Robinson, who had been hired as part of the star's contract. Newspaper and television journalists zeroed in on her. "It was a nightmare," she told a reporter. "She has to have someone with her every second of the day—from seven A.M. until long after midnight."

The secretary, who quit after three days on the job, claimed that she couldn't even walk into another room without plunging the star into the depths of despair. "She would rush to find me, yelling, 'Where is my jewelry? Where are my dogs?' "

The secretary continued: "She bullied and abused everyone around her who was in the least subservient. She even shoved people around, even me, but only lightly, or I would have shoved her back. At rehearsals she flubbed lines and then screamed at everyone else, 'You people are only here to read lines back to me.' "

Much was made of the Debbie Robinson testimony, perhaps too much. The local writers sidestepped the fact that Zsa Zsa has done very little over the years to conceal her incendiary nature. Once when the *National Enquirer* ran a long item about one of the Gabor temper tantrums she called the tabloid's senior editor, Paul Levy, to complain not about the nasty words but because the gossip columnist referred to her as "slightly plump." Some of her milder diatribes have taken place on Merv Griffin's talk show or, during an earlier TV era, on Jack Paar's late-night shows.

Debbie Robinson summed up her personal feelings in a radio interview: "You know how she says on all the talk shows that she's spoiled. Well, you can't imagine how far she carries this. But you have to draw the line somewhere, or you cease being human. I wouldn't ever want to be her—not for the jewels, the furs, the money, or the glamour."

Interesting observation. But international fame is a one-way street. You can't suddenly wake up on a weary Monday morning and decide that being Zsa Zsa Gabor has become too tough a job, that having no secrets is too high a price to pay, that maintaining the expected gorgeous facade has become too enervating.

It seems certain that Zsa Zsa occasionally and Eva more often dream about stepping off the surrealistic roller coaster that goes higher and faster with each succeeding year. Despite her collision with hysteria in Philadelphia, Zsa Zsa had no choice but to rush off to another, even more taxing production of *Forty Carats* in Dallas, then another and another.

And despite the fresh heartbreak following the collapse of her fifth marriage, Eva marched off to a rigorous Broadway production of *You Can't Take It with You,* followed by four grueling spots on TV series like *Hart to Hart* and *Hotel.*

On the other hand, their dual careers have become a welcome, even comforting tradition, an anchor against the tides of old age.

For Zsa Zsa, the tradition started in Las Vegas. Over the decades, when the money has started to run low, Zsa Zsa has returned to the gambling capital to become a most enduringly popular attraction on the strip.

In 1970 when she returned to Vegas after a pause, she received a lavish welcome at the Las Vegas Flamingo. At ringside were Lana Turner, Rita Hayworth, Arlene Dahl, Margaret O'Brien, Jeanne Crain, and Jim Brown. And at a table just offstage Conrad Hilton hosted his daughter, Francesca, who was celebrating her nineteenth birthday. As she glided by, Zsa Zsa saw Connie and stopped in mid-song. "Darlings, please welcome my ex, Conrad Hilton. You know, for a divorce settlement I got 1,250,000 Bibles."

She glided over to Connie's table and let an ermine pelt slide across his shoulder. "We're still so friendly, darlings, I still have his name on all my towels."

In the mid-1960s, Zsa Zsa had first begun eyeing the stage with more and more curiosity, and she couldn't help notice what it had done for Eva's bank account. It could eventually become a money fountain for me, she thought. "You know they are starving out there for real glamour," she told columnist Dorothy Manners. "If I link up with the right play, or plays, I could probably tour forever."

This was easier said than done. She wanted to take out the first road company of *Hello Dolly,* and with this in mind she flew east and tried to interest producer David Merrick in taking a chance on her.

Before she got an official appointment with Merrick, however, a friend pointed him out to her at a theater reception. In true Gabor style, she bellowed at him across the room, "One day, I'll play Dolly Levi. You'll see."

The producer muttered to a friend, "It will be over my dead body."

Hello Dolly was to elude her, but another Merrick production, *Forty Carats,* was destined to become a trademark. "It all started when I came to New York from Chicago and wanted to take a friend to see the play. But tickets were impossible to get, even through scalpers."

Zsa Zsa called David on his unlisted line. "I need two tickets to *Forty Carats,*" she said.

"Fine," he answered. "There will be two house tickets for you at the door.

"We went and I adored the show," Zsa Zsa said. "I thought, This is a part I can play."

She called Merrick the next day. "Zsa Zsa, darling, you are persistent," he answered. "But this is an *American* play and calls for an *American* actress."

"But I *am* an American actress," she retorted. "I got my citizenship long ago."

Merrick laughed and hung up.

Since her nightclub act was playing to sold-out houses at the time, there was no need for her to worry about this rejection. Ironically, it was after one of her shows at the Las Vegas Flamingo that Merrick ate humble pie and called her. "Zsa Zsa, I was wrong. I think you would be perfect in *Forty Carats.* Could you replace Julie Harris when her contract is finished?"

There was no hesitation. "Yes," she answered.

Merrick pressed for her to sign for six months. She refused. She *did* sign for four months without thinking twice. Anyone who knows Zsa Zsa would realize that four months in one place would tie her down longer than her restless nature allowed.

But there were more practical problems. First, she had already agreed to tour during the time of the Broadway run for her cosmetics company, Zsa-Zsa Ltd. And second, she had been traveling with her own show for more than a year. She was, understandably, exhausted.

"Anyway, you cannot afford Broadway," one of her agents told her. "It costs a lot to live in New York, and all of your expenses on the Coast will continue."

Still she opened on schedule. But in the middle of the run, she balked at the contract, facing a $1,000 fine for each night she didn't show.

The dispute between Zsa Zsa and Merrick went to arbitration, and he won. He told her, "Someday, Zsa Zsa, you will come begging to me for a role on Broadway—*begging*—and I will turn you down flat."

Never, Zsa Zsa thought to herself. One season of Broadway was enough for her.

However, she resurrected *Forty Carats* and became one of the first superstars to put together her own tour package, taking it on the road at a salary several times larger than that paid by Broadway producers.

The transition from personality to actress didn't come easily to Zsa Zsa. "I have never seen anyone work so hard," said dancer Ann Miller. "It was frightening for her to go on the legitimate stage. Her triumph in *Forty Carats* was a tribute to her gutsy approach to life."

There have been, here and there, signs of temperament. At one opening in the Midwest, she staged a sit-down because a hairdresser wasn't available and sent an assistant in his place. She was eventually persuaded to go on. Later during the same production, Zsa Zsa's personal dresser was slow, and the curtain caught her still in her panty hose. "It was the most applause I ever got," she said. "That was my best entrance."

Zsa Zsa's success with *Forty Carats* has been duplicated and in some cases exceeded by Eva's tour with *Blithe Spirit*. In 1961, Eva was personally cast by Noel Coward to star in the play's New York revival. "Noel told me, 'Whenever you're broke do *Blithe Spirit*,' " Eva told columnist Earl Wilson. "And while I'm never broke, the play has been consistently good to me."

In 1976 a team of producers in Chicago decided that if one Gabor was an onstage triumph, two would be a gold mine. So Eva and Zsa Zsa were hired as a team to play the murderous sisters in *Arsenic and Old Lace* at Chicago's Arlington Heights Playhouse.

The comedy, about two spinsters who poison their lodgers, was given a more modern setting; the sisters were made quite a bit younger (about forty) and given chic, glitzy gowns. Naturally the sisterly rivals squared off early. The producers hired Nolan Davis to do the costumes, and he assembled a dazzling set of sketches. Nothing doing, said Eva. "My gowns will be designed by Luis Taylor, who creates most of my clothes." What she didn't say was that she and Luis were preparing a line of Eva Gabor gowns that would be aided greatly by *Arsenic and Old Lace* exposure. When Zsa Zsa heard this, she immediately insisted that the House of Elizabeth Courtney, a Beverly Hills firm, would design her costumes. "But Zsa Zsa at least allowed me to modify her dresses to blend with my costumes for the rest of the production," Nolan said. Eva's gowns remained off limits.

Eva took the production very, very seriously and approached the role as if it were a great satirical masterpiece. A month before the Chicago opening, she booked a conference room at the Bel Air Hotel, hired a drama coach, and began daily rehearsals. Line by line and inflection by inflection, she displayed a determination which would have outdone Sarah Bernhardt.

Jack Ryan was newly married to Zsa Zsa at the time and was amused at the offstage rivalry. "Eva put a lot of effort into preparing for the play. So every once in a while Zsa Zsa and I would drift over to the Bel Air Hotel to watch her. However, Zsa Zsa refused to become involved and participated only from the sidelines. She quite successfully relied on the humor of her own personality."

The war of nerves broke out into the open after the team flew to Chicago. "The company had hired a limousine to carry both Eva and Zsa Zsa from the hotel to the theater and back again, Jack recalled. "Zsa Zsa immediately commandeered it. It took her only a few seconds to engineer this feat of one-upmanship, but it threw Eva off completely." Significantly, Zsa Zsa retained use of the limo for the entire run.

Then it was apparently all smooth going during the rehearsals. But it was a deceptive calm before the real storm. On opening night the irrepressible Zsa Zsa ad-libbed two lines so humorous that the audience burst into spontaneous applause. This stopped Eva in her tracks while precious seconds slipped by. Finally, Eva made her own carefully rehearsed replies. Zsa Zsa repeated this practice during the following acts. Backstage, producers and directors huddled before agreeing to leave the Gabor and libs in the play. Naturally this was like waving a red flag in Zsa Zsa's face.

"She just made up things as the run progressed," Jack said. "She created so many good lines that her part far overshadowed Eva's." Eventually Eva's manager got into the act and filed an official complaint. The only solution was to give Eva some of her sister's inventive material, which, of course, only encouraged Zsa Zsa to make up more lines. Jack watched her in awe: "It was then that I began to respect the depth of her mind. She could probably portray Abraham Lincoln and get away with it."

After observing his wife onstage, Jack decided he wanted to put this natural vivacity to work. "I wanted to help her establish a regular, strong source of income, so I helped work out a deal for her with Montgomery Ward. She would make personal appearances with a rebuilt Rolls Royce. I also arranged for an aggressive young man to work out the deal. I even paid his fare from the East. Unfortunately, my interference was the straw which broke the back of the marriage." (Although she denies that the Rolls was ever put back together, Jack insisted, "People, including Zsa Zsa, deny the car's existence. She even said I never finished it publicly and had that claim written into the divorce proceeding. But none of this was true; I did complete it.") The deal made during the last days of the Ryan marriage apparently earned Zsa Zsa as much as $250,000 a year from these appearances alone.

Often personal tragedy results in a Gabor comeback. For instance, Eva's troubled divorce from Richard Brown after thirteen years of marriage careened her into a mad rush of stage and television work. This was repeated in 1983, when, after her ten-year marriage to Frank Gard Jameson sadly collapsed, she returned to Broadway in *You Can't Take It with You.*

The National Enquirer sounded the marital death knell, with the headline, "Eva Gives Millionaire Hubby the Heave Ho." It seemed, said the *Enquirer,* that Eva found evidence that Frank had been dallying with several younger women. Although this doesn't sound much like Jameson, a pillar of the Los Angeles community, no libel suit was initiated. Only one thing was certain, the marriage, which had begun ten years before at one of the splashiest weddings in Beverly Hills history, was over. It had been the sturdiest of all the Gabor alliances, carrying Eva to the heights of social power, privilege, and economic security.

"Did this happen suddenly?" asked one family friend.

"Of course not," Eva answered. "It fell apart bit-by-bit, day-by-day, until I found myself staring back into the mirror at unhappiness. I know both of us are feeling a little sad." But Eva quickly picked herself up, reactivated her career and set sail for the story book rainbow few ever reach.

The first hints of a comeback came when Eva was in New York City alone on February 21, 1983, the day that would have been the tenth anniversary of her marriage to Frank. She was asked by a New York *Post* reporter, "What about the rumor that you will take over from Colleen Dewhurst in *You Can't Take It with You?"*

"I heard that rumor also." She laughed. "I was watching TV when it was announced. It was news to me; nobody has asked me." Eva opened in the play about four months later. Ironically, the revival was at the Plymouth Theater, where she had had her first real success in *The Happy Time* more than three decades earlier.

"It's fun, but it's nerve-racking, since I have never played such a small part before, even when I was just getting started. But then I thought, If it's good enough for Colleen Dewhurst, whom I adore, I'm in wonderful company." Eva played a Russian grand duchess forced to flee from her homeland by the Communist revolution.

"But isn't your accent Hungarian?" a reporter asked. "No, darling, absolutely not. I was born a Hungarian, but I have traveled so much that my accent by now is cosmopolitan."

The actress told the New York *Times,* "It's an amazing psychological thing for me, going back to where my stage career started. I was here at the Plymouth for a year and a half. I love it, but I'm not crazy about the dressing rooms. They tell me that the front was entirely redone. That amazes me about Broadway. You see those glorious fronts, and then you go backstage and see the most awful holes and steps which are dangerous at best. But if I wanted to be comfortable I should have stayed home."

And she recalled a previous opening in Noel Coward's *Present Laughter,* which the playwright also directed. "He called me over after hearing that I was going to the Actors Studio. 'Going there is a no-no. The only thing you have to know are your words.' "

Back in Hollywood in February of 1984, Eva and Zsa Zsa signed to do a series called *Two Hungarian Maids* for their old friend Merv Griffin, a project that all the networks allegedly turned down. "But we'll syndicate it ourselves," said a Merv Griffin spokesman. "I don't know how well this will work out, darling," Zsa Zsa told a friend. "You know sisters! Particularly Gabor sisters!"

❊ Postscript

*T*he great crack of mallet against ball testified to the power and skill of the player, whose almost brutal wildness came from deep within. The magnificent Arabian horse beneath her seemed to stall in midair as she chased the ball down a grassed fairway. Zsa Zsa's hair worked itself loose from its tight chignon and was swept up in the rarefied breezes of Palm Beach.

The other players on the field paled in contrast to her high color that was like pastel stones surrounding an exquisitely cut diamond. While most of the world was buried in the snow of a ravaging 1984 winter Zsa Zsa haunted the perfumed polo fields of South Florida.

Her arm dove toward the ball as if to shatter it apart with the same reckless abandon that characterizes her life. Her eyes blazed as if to defy the march of time and to transform the hard glare of celebrity into the soft glow of personal romance.

And there is evidence that Eva, Zsa Zsa, and Magda have all learned to view their fame with candor and a sense of humor.

One afternoon recently, Eva was nude, sunning behind the protective walls of her secret garden. A large picture hat sat atop her head, and gloves shielded her hands and forearms from the sun. She was about to plunge into the pool for another lap when she felt the presence of someone watching her.

She locked eyes with the voyeur. Her thoughts tumbled over themselves. "I must say *something,* or else he will tell everybody in town." Just then the man smiled and waved, "Hi, Eva!"

She thought a fraction of a second before waving back, "Oh no, darling, not Eva, Zsa Zsa!" Then she laughed, her lusty voice echoing back at her.

With Zsa Zsa taking the lead, the Gabors have never experienced that self-pity which comes from lingering over unhappiness. "Only today exists for us," Jolie once said. "It's far too late to do anything about yesterday."

On October 6, 1983, Zsa Zsa held a dinner party to inaugurate a lavish ballroom Jack Ryan had built onto her mansion—an addition he paid for *after* the divorce. And, in addition to Fred Astaire, assorted millionaires, Barbara Carrera, and an Indian maharajah, there was Jack Ryan—the guest of honor.

"I thought—after all these years, after all we've been through—she made up for all the pain with one magical night," Jack mused. "Zsa Zsa really does improve with age, like the finest wine."

✳ Index